ICC Ethics and Compliance Training Handbook

Anti-corruption guidance by practitioners for practitioners

Edited by
François Vincke,
Julian Kassum

ICC Ethics and Compliance Training Handbook
Copyright © 2013

International Chamber of Commerce (ICC)
All rights reserved.

ICC holds all copyright and other intellectual property rights in this collective work. No part of this collective work may be reproduced, distributed, transmitted, translated or adapted in any form or by any means, except as permitted by law, without the written permission of ICC.

Permission can be requested from ICC through **publications@iccwbo.org**.

ICC Services
Publications Department
33-43 Avenue du Président Wilson
75116 Paris, France

ICC Publication No. 741E
ISBN: 978-92-842-0176-1

Contents

FOREWORD
by Jean-Guy Carrier 5

CHAPTERS

1. François Vincke
   A Daunting but Fascinating Task 8

   PART 1: The Fundamentals

2. Fritz Heimann
   The International Anti-corruption Conventions 18
3. Jean-Yves Trochon
   The Global Antitrust Landscape 32
4. Jean-Pierre Méan
   Glossary 42

   PART 2: How to Organize Compliance in Your Company

5. Jean-Daniel Lainé
   Risk Assessment 54
6. Pedro Montoya
   The Role of the Board of Directors 63
7. Dominique Lamoureux
   Codes of Conduct 71
8. Carlos Desmet
   The Ethics and Compliance Function and Its Interface with Management, Control, and Audit 82
9. Annette Kraus and Julia Sommer
   The Compliance Challenge for Smaller Companies 90

   PART 3: Appropriate Measures

10. Corinne Lagache
    Education and Training 100
11. Michael Davies, Q.C.
    Whistleblowing 109
12. Juan Jorge Gili
    Internal Investigations 115
13. Iohann Le Frapper
    Resisting Solicitation 124

PART 4: Managing Business Relationships

14. Richard Battaglia and Lucinda Low
    Agents, Intermediaries, and Other Third Parties 136
    APPENDIX – Due Diligence Sample Checklist 151
15. Massimo Mantovani
    Joint Ventures 152
    APPENDIX A – Due Diligence Guidelines 161
    APPENDIX B – Red Flags 163
16. François Vincke
    The ICC Anti-corruption Clause (2012) 165
17. Max Burger-Scheidlin
    Managing the Transition to a Clean Commercial Policy 171
    ANNEX I – ICC Rules on Combating Corruption 179
    ANNEX II – ICC Anti-corruption Clause 189
    ANNEX III – Key International Legal Instruments 202

Foreword

Jean-Guy Carrier

Secretary General, International Chamber of Commerce (ICC)

ICC and the market economy

The fight against corruption and anti-competitive practices is engrained in ICC's DNA. For ICC, the promotion of an open world economy, based on fair competition, has been a prime objective since its founding nearly 100 years ago. ICC today brings together millions of companies into the largest international business network and continues its leadership role in advocating high standards of corporate governance based on ethical business practices. In 1977, it became the first international organization to issue a set of Rules and Recommendations prohibiting all forms of corruption in business transactions.

A frontrunner on compliance

However, the mere condemnation of corruption is not enough. ICC has expanded its mission over the years to help companies generate a culture of integrity. This was done by the development of corporate Codes of Conduct, the establishment of ethics and compliance programmes, and the appointment of ethics and compliance officers. ICC's message about the need for business integrity and compliance was spelled out in the three editions of *Fighting Corruption*, ICC's International Corporate Integrity Handbook, which was first published in 1999 and re-edited in 2003 and 2008.

A need for practical education and training

Where do we stand today? High-quality international legal instruments to fight corruption have been adopted and integrated into the national laws of an increasing number of countries. There is now a strong awareness among business leaders about the need for integrity in commercial transactions. These corporate leaders have signalled their determination to accept nothing less than the highest standards. There is still, however, a perceived lack of practical implementation on the part of government and business.

Many companies have voiced their concern about a gap between the principles laid down in statutes and the realities they face in the field. They report being confronted with solicitation of bribes from politicians and public officials as well as unfair practices by competitors. Small and medium-sized companies continue to struggle with the implementation of new legal and ethical standards. Compliance officers and their teams are in need of solid and pragmatic support.

A World Economic Survey conducted by ICC and the Institute for Economic Research in Munich during the fourth quarter of 2012 shows that business experts worldwide strongly support the view that a greater emphasis on ethics and compliance training in their respective countries would improve productivity and attract foreign investment. Respondents from emerging markets overwhelmingly supported the statement.

What compliance officers want is effective guidance for their day-to-day work and not additional declarations of intent. A growing number of companies wish to benefit from down-to-earth integrity training provided by experienced practitioners. For example, installing a whistleblowing system, performing a risk assessment, exercising due diligence when selecting agents or intermediaries, and conducting internal investigations are all difficult and delicate policies to implement.

A train the trainers programme

In its recommendations to G20 heads of state and government, the global business community (as represented by the B20) identified the need to develop training materials and provide concrete practical training on anti-corruption compliance, including 'train the trainers' and other educational programmes, as one of the six top priorities to advance G20 and B20 work in the field of anti-corruption.

This Ethics and Compliance Training Handbook is a direct response to this call. The following pages address, independently from theoretical considerations, the challenges which companies of all sizes must overcome in order to build and implement their corporate compliance programmes. It is a guide designed by and for compliance practitioners.

This Training Handbook will serve as the cornerstone of a Global Training Programme which ICC will develop and deliver with its network of national committees and chambers of commerce around the world. Each chapter of this Handbook is conceived as a module for a training session on a key compliance topic. Through this Handbook and the training sessions based on its successive chapters, the compliance officers of today and tomorrow will benefit from the hands-on expertise of distinguished fellow practitioners in the field of corporate integrity.

It is our hope that the compliance officers who will enrol in this ICC Global Training Programme will in turn train their colleagues and successors, and thus contribute to fostering a culture of ethics and compliance across today's global markets.

NOTE FROM THE EDITORS

This Ethics and Compliance Training Handbook has been written by experts from the business community for members of the business community. It is the result of a collaboration involving some of the leading practitioners in the field of ethics and compliance. Most of its authors are active members of the ICC Commission on Corporate Responsibility and Anti-corruption.

The 17 chapters of this Training Handbook explore the wide range of policy tools and measures that ethics and compliance officers can draw upon, with the support of management, to create a robust culture of integrity in their organizations. They propose straightforward answers to the question of how to best organize the prevention of corrupt and anti-competitive practices in different business contexts.

It should be noted that the authors are writing as individual experts. Their views do not necessarily represent the position of ICC or other organizations with which they are affiliated. Neither ICC nor the authors will accept any liability for any errors, omissions, or misleading statements caused by negligence or otherwise.

We take this opportunity to express our appreciation for the numerous contributions to the preparation of this Handbook made by Philip Kucharski, Viviane Schiavi, Laetitia de Montalivet, Jeff Dombrowski, Aisling Achoun, Marie-Dominique Fraiderik, Brigitte Horn, Taylor Holland, and Anouk Leibig van Huffel of the ICC International Secretariat in Paris.

ABOUT THE EDITORS

François Vincke is a Member of the Brussels Bar. He worked 26 years for PetroFina, a European oil, gas and petrochemicals company, including 11 years as Secretary General and General Counsel. Since 1994, he is the Head of Anti-corruption at ICC, first as Chairman of the Commission on Anti-corruption and later as Vice-Chair of the Commission on Corporate Responsibility and Anti-corruption. He has written a number of articles and led several conferences on matters related to ethics and compliance.

Julian Kassum is an independent consultant working for a number of international organizations, including ICC and the World Economic Forum. Between 2004 and 2010, he was successively Policy Manager for the ICC Commission on Anti-corruption and for the ICC Commission on Business in Society, two working bodies which later merged to form the ICC Commission on Corporate Responsibility and Anti-corruption. In 2009, he worked as Legal Counsel for the Compliance and Corporate Social Responsibility Department of the oil and gas company Total.

ABOUT THE INTERNATIONAL CHAMBER OF COMMERCE (ICC)

ICC is the largest, most representative business organization in the world. Its global network comprises over 6 million companies, chambers of commerce and business associations in more than 130 countries, with interests spanning every sector of private enterprise.

A world network of national committees keeps the ICC International Secretariat in Paris informed about national and regional business priorities. More than 2,000 experts drawn from ICC's member companies feed their knowledge and experience into crafting the ICC stance on specific business issues.

The United Nations, the World Trade Organization, the G20 and many other intergovernmental bodies, both international and regional, are kept in touch with the views of international business through ICC.

For more information please visit: www.iccwbo.org

Chapter 1
A Daunting but Fascinating Task

François Vincke

Member of the Brussels Bar,
Former Secretary General and General Counsel of PetroFina

There are a plethora of documents and guidelines on ethics and compliance but only a few are designed for those responsible for making sure that integrity standards trickle down to all parts of the 'body corporate'. The tone set by upper management is important, but it is equally essential that the ethics and compliance message reach the bottom of the company without distortion. It will be the ethics and compliance officer's task to ensure that this message becomes part and parcel of the company's daily life. In the first chapter of this Ethics and Compliance Training Handbook, written by one of its editors, we shed light on the educational purpose of the Handbook and offer some insights on the ethics and compliance officer's role and place in the corporate organization.

A TRAINING HANDBOOK ESPECIALLY FOR YOU

This Ethics and Compliance Training Handbook is especially dedicated to you who are involved in compliance or will be in the near future.

You may be working part time on compliance in a small structure or full time in a larger organization. Your company is headquartered in an OECD country (where compliance is becoming embedded in corporate practice) or in an emerging economy (where compliance is still only beginning). You may be the only person tasked with compliance in your company or you are part of a larger team. You are a member of your company's legal department or you belong to a newly created compliance department. You are directly involved in compliance or you are closely associated with it, for instance through a control function in internal or external audit.

To all of you, this Handbook offers practical guidance and useful suggestions based on the expertise and experience of some of your most respected colleagues. Many of them are long serving (and particularly active) members of the ICC Commission on Corporate Responsibility and Anti-corruption. We have called upon these recognized compliance practitioners to review, item per item, the challenges and pitfalls that you will encounter in your daily practice.

FRANÇOIS VINCKE

A TRAINING TOOL

This Handbook is essentially a training tool, not another treatise on anti-corruption and fair competition. We will not dwell on theoretical considerations regarding the need for companies to be compliant with legal and ethical rules.

ICC and other prominent voices have devoted significant effort to making company executives more aware of the need to implement both Codes of Conduct and corporate compliance programmes. Chief Executive Officers and Boards of Directors of leading companies have issued bold statements condemning corruption and other illicit business practices. But the time has come to delve deeper into the corporate organization and reach the 'working level', where you, in the ethics and compliance function, have to overcome concrete dilemmas and make difficult judgment calls.

What is expected from you is to translate the directive from the top of your company into day-to-day reality regarding its business activities. Ultimately, your company's success in reaching high ethical standards will depend (largely but not exclusively) on your sustained efforts to help foster an effective culture of integrity. Your role is to instil in the organization a new set of reflexes, allowing your colleagues to act spontaneously in the right way. In the end, companies are judged on their deeds, not on their words. As always, what counts in business is the result.

The guidance provided in this Handbook is not only destined for large multinational companies (many of which have already established robust anti-corruption and antitrust systems) but also to the vast universe of smaller enterprises which often find themselves at the beginning of the journey. These companies are frequently exposed to fraud and corruption, but only scant efforts have been made to address their specific circumstances.

Yours is a daunting task. But, once you will have used this Training Handbook, we hope that you will also find it fascinating. Helping your colleagues adopt new integrity practices is one of the biggest and most exciting challenges for businesses today.

TRAIN THE TRAINERS

New compliance attitudes should permeate throughout the whole 'body corporate'. Those who have been trained should in turn train their (present and future) colleagues and assistants. This Training Handbook is conceived in such a way that today's trainees can become the trainers of tomorrow.

With this in mind, ICC has embarked on the development of a Global Training Programme, based on this Ethics and Compliance Training Handbook. This Global Training Programme, which will count on the support of ICC national committees around the world, will be designed to help you build your own compliance and training activities in your company. A team of specialists in corporate compliance will stand ready to assist you in planning your own corporate training programme.

KNOW YOUR COMPANY

As a person entrusted with a compliance function, you should have an adequate knowledge of your company's products, services, processes, and procedures. You may retort that anybody working in a company is expected to have a fair knowledge of its functioning. However, in your compliance capacity, you should be able to speak with the highest degree of credibility to everyone in the company, from top to bottom. To be in a position to advise, encourage, warn, admonish, forbid, or even blame or sanction, you should be recognized by your colleagues as being 'one of them', and not viewed as somebody parachuted in from the outside.

Colleagues will come find you with the following sorts of questions: "Should I approve this payment?", "Should I go along with the appointment of this intermediary?", "Should I report this circumstance?" To be fully credible in your answers, you must be able to demonstrate that you have a full grasp of the situation at hand, in both its ethical and business aspects.

It will therefore be crucial that you keep abreast of your company's industrial, commercial and financial developments. Don't lock yourself up in your new function. Keep an eye on the company's new products and services, and be aware of its expansion into new countries. Stay informed about its new marketing channels, and watch out for changes to the company's governance model.

YOUR PLACE IN THE ORGANIZATION

There is no uniform or even preferred pattern for plotting the compliance function on the organizational chart. Compliance may be located within the legal department or it can be established as a new department, standing on its own – thereby emphasizing its specific and often novel mission. Compliance can also be integrated as part of the internal audit function or attached to the finance department. In reality, the place of the compliance function in the organization will often be pragmatically dictated by the size of company, its management style (which can be centralized or decentralized), and the nature of its activities.

While the localization of the compliance function may not be of overwhelming importance, its operational autonomy and its right to access the top of the company will be decisive factors for the ultimate success of your mission.

YOUR OPERATIONAL AUTONOMY

To deploy its activities and implement company-wide initiatives, the compliance function will require an adequate degree of operational autonomy.

Note that we speak here of 'autonomy' and not 'independence'. Aiming for full independence of the ethics and compliance function would lead to delusion. It is clear that individuals outside the ethics and compliance group will define the human resource parameters for ethics and compliance officers, such as their performance evaluation, their remuneration, their benefits and their career development. Other individuals, also outside the ethics and compliance group, will approve, reject, or amend the budget requests proposed by the ethics and compliance function.

What really matters, however, is that ethics and compliance officers and their teams enjoy a genuine freedom of action and a freedom of speech. They should be able to define their priorities (based on a risk assessment), to draft and amend the company's Code of Conduct and compliance programme, to establish corporate policies on specific subjects, to communicate their messages efficiently throughout the organization, to control activities everywhere in the company, and to take action every time the company's ethical standing is at stake.

AN UNHAMPERED ACCESS TO THE TOP OF YOUR COMPANY

These freedoms are epitomized by what can be described as an unfettered access to the top of the company: in no way should the ethics and compliance function be denied free and preferably regular access to the company's highest authorities. Whenever a serious matter is raised, which can endanger the ethical reputation of the company, the ethics and compliance function should have the right and the duty to bring such concern to the top. If access to the top is conditioned, hampered, obstructed, or denied, compliance cannot properly function.

What do we mean by 'access to the top'? Again, there is no uniform answer. In many cases, this will mean access to the Chief Executive Officer or to another high-level corporate executive, such as the Chief Financial Officer or General Counsel. Alternatively, this could also mean access to the Chairman of the Board of Directors, the Supervisory Board, or the Audit Committee. From a governance viewpoint, the latter option may seem preferable, as the Chairman of the Audit Committee will generally be an independent director, placing him above possible conflicts of interest. Moreover, the Audit Committee has a duty to mitigate financial, operational and compliance risks. However, not all companies have an Audit Committee and Audit Committees usually meet only a limited number of times per year.

Whatever the body chosen, ethics and compliance officers have to be in a position to give warnings at the highest corporate level, to stop or help stop misconduct, to warn against existing or potential malpractice, and to propose changes to the company's policies and practices. Ideally, such a dialogue should take place at regular intervals by following a calendar of sessions scheduled in advance with the company's upper management. By scheduling regular meetings, ethics and compliance officers will be able to continuously review the company's full compliance situation. If such meetings cannot be arranged, the ethics and compliance officer will have to schedule meetings each time it is deemed necessary. The latter solution is only a second-best solution, since the ethics and compliance officer will only meet with top management in crisis situations, which is not optimal for building a long-term dialogue.

COMPLIANCE: A SHARED RESPONSIBILITY

By appointing an ethics and compliance officer or creating a compliance function, the top executives of the company make a necessary and intelligent move. They want to fend off corruption and anti-competitive practices and install a new ethical culture in the organization. By going the route of organized and systematic compliance, they choose the best path to reach these objectives.

However, it would be a mistake to believe that the mere appointing of ethics and compliance officers relieves middle and top management of their duty to care about ethics and compliance. Compliance, even when administered by specialists, should be of continual concern to everyone. Though compliance professionals will make their best efforts to bring about new attitudes and embed new corporate practices in the company, everybody in the organization has to contribute, in his or her proportionate part, to the genuine and thorough implementation of the compliance message.

To illustrate this point, let's make a simple comparison: a company designates a health, safety, environment and quality manager. It would be wrong to think that – from that moment on – the management of the company can turn a blind eye to environmental risks. The Board will have to vote budgets to install adequate environmental technology. Management must put in place efficient air, water, sound, ground, and raw materials controls and the workforce should learn to use the tools made available to them. Clearly, appointing a health, safety, environment, and quality specialist does not relieve anybody of their own environmental and safety duties. The same is true for ethics and compliance.

YOUR MISSION STATEMENT

The novelty of your task, the difficulty of your mission, and the specificity of your function will require that you define – together with your company management – the terms of reference for your work. These terms of reference may differ from one organization to the other, but they usually contain explicit elements on the following three subjects:

(i) Your basic assignments (what you are supposed to do for the company);

(ii) The practical means you use to reach your objectives (the tools and budgets you receive to realize your tasks); and

(iii) The authority which will be vested in you to achieve what is expected (the power you will enjoy to realize your tasks).

A company will generally expect an ethics and compliance officer to accomplish the following:

- Define the company's ethical values and corporate rules and policies;
- Improve and regularly update the company's ethics and compliance documents in order to keep them in line with legal and societal expectations;
- Establish procedures to ensure the implementation of the company's values and ethical rules;
- Advise, encourage, and motivate the colleagues in favour of compliance;
- Answer their concerns and help them take the right decisions while facing difficult dilemmas;

- Educate and train company personnel in all the company's divisions, and possibly agents, intermediaries, and other third parties who have a long-term relationship with the company; and
- Create a culture such that behaving ethically becomes a second nature for all who work in and with the company.

The budget you will be allocated will evidently depend on the size, structure, and ethical determination of your company. To try to figure out what kind of budgetary resources would be adequate to your company's needs, you will have to ask your management the following questions:

- Are your ethics and compliance duties a full-time job or will you have other assignments in addition to your ethics and compliance duties?
- In the latter case, how does management expect you to allocate your working time between your different assignments? Will you stand alone as compliance officer coping with all the company's compliance challenges or will you be joined by one or more qualified assistants?
- How will the company subsidiaries, affiliates, and other entities in which the company has an interest (as for instance joint ventures or consortiums) cooperate in the company's overall compliance effort? Will the company's subsidiaries and affiliates appoint personnel in charge of compliance, who will report to you in addition to their direct superiors?
- Will you have the means to organize regular training sessions for the company's executives, managers, and employees?

YOUR AUTHORITY

Your mission statement now lists the assignments to accomplish, and you know the means you will receive to realize them. The next task is to ensure that you enjoy sufficient authority to make your voice effectively heard in the organization. This may be the most sensitive issue to address in the process of establishing your mission statement. Giving authority to a new department or function in the organization will always be a delicate issue.

To measure the authority vested in you, receive clear answers to the following questions:

- Are you allowed to cross hierarchical lines to give recommendations or instructions on corporate practices to managers in the company's divisions, subsidiaries, affiliates, and other entities connected with the company?
- Will you have a (decisive) say in the selection, appointment, and remuneration of third parties working for the company, for instance a veto right?
- In which manner will you be able to interact with contractors, subcontractors, suppliers, customers, or others with whom the company has a significant relationship?
- Will you be consulted (in advance) on the agreements the company is going to conclude with third parties, and in particular on their provisions relating to business practices?

- And in general, what authority will you have to review the faithful implementation of the company's Code of Conduct and compliance programme?

The answers to these questions may be verbally given to you. This does not make them less valuable, but a written statement, which can be shared with others and made known throughout the company, will add significant strength to your authority.

Compliance work is not supposed to yield positive results overnight. Having strongly worded terms of reference, firmly delineating the 'ground lines' of the company's ethics and compliance work, will help you achieve your mid-term and long-term objectives in a confident matter.

WHAT IF AN INCIDENT OCCURS?

You have now taken full command of the company's ethics and compliance function. Your mission is well defined. You know which resources are available and your level of authority. Everybody in the organization, from top to bottom, wants to preserve the company's reputation and supports its ethics and compliance efforts.

All of a sudden, a scandal erupts. Contrary to all expectations, a rogue employee or a business partner indulged in fraudulent activities which everybody thought belonged to the past. A commercial manager, hard pressed by a diminishing order book, felt he should protect the company's market shares and exchanged sensitive information with competitors. An intermediary, contrary to all instructions, paid to obtain illicit advantages in a heavily contested procurement contract.

All look in your direction. Were you not supposed to make such things impossible? Should you not have done everything possible to precisely avoid this? The question is asked: *have you, as ethics and compliance officer, been vigilant and active enough?*

This questioning brings us back to two realities.

First: no compliance system, however sophisticated, will ever guarantee a total absence of failure. There always will be a risk of a human or administrative flaw. Companies have spent years building elaborate ethics and compliance systems before being confronted with incidents of incredible misconduct. All ethics and compliance work is 'in progress' and nobody as manager or ethics and compliance officer should expect or guarantee that the ethics and compliance system established by the company be flawless.

Second: there is a substantive difference between being responsible for not properly fulfilling a professional duty and being liable for an offence. An ethics and compliance officer has to make his or her best efforts to prevent an offence from being committed. If he or she fails to make sufficient efforts in this endeavour, such a failure can be held as professional negligence against him or her, but (with the rare exception of gross negligence) the offence itself should not be blamed on the ethics and compliance officer.

THERE WILL BE RESISTANCE

As for all changes in an organization, many will cooperate and welcome new practices, but there will also be resistance. For some in the company, compliance will rhyme with administrative paralysis, fussy controls and rigid reporting. New procedures will mean for them less flexibility, reduced commercial aggressiveness and protracted decision-making processes. Ambitious commercial managers will be inclined to blame their difficulties on the hurdles that you, as ethics and compliance officer, have placed on their way to success. They may see you as the one responsible for making them lose business deals, and the bonuses that come with them.

Don't simply brush away these complaints. Instead, take the time to review and experiment with your colleagues using the control mechanisms you propose to put in place. Test every new administrative procedure and examine its compliance and commercial efficiency. In doing so, you will be able to distinguish undeserved criticism, possibly meant to cover up professional negligence on the part of your interlocutor, from more legitimate objections. If a procedure is creating unnecessary obstacles, try to find a way to make it more commercially neutral, without opening the gate for abuse. In short, try to find an adequate answer which satisfies both the commercial needs of the company and its rigorous ethics and compliance objectives. In some instances, you may have to eliminate or adapt overly cumbersome procedures. But always remind your interlocutors that it is their duty to rigorously comply with the law and the company's ethical rules.

YOU ARE NOT A COP

In your job, your first goal is not to control and punish, but to create a climate that is favourable to complying with legal and ethical standards. Such a task requires persuasion and an ability to encourage and foster progress. This will only be possible in an environment of confidence and trust, not in an atmosphere of systematic suspicion. Be more an educator than a prosecutor. Be more an advisor than a cop.

An ethics and compliance officer should take the time to explain that ethics and compliance – despite its unavoidable downsides in terms of commercial effectiveness – will be beneficial to all in the company. Some short-term business opportunities may be lost due to strict ethical constraints, but how does this compare to the huge and sometimes irreparable harm a single ethics scandal can inflict on the company?

START BY EVALUATING RISKS

You are now almost set for your new assignment, but bear in mind that no genuine ethics and compliance policy can be set in motion without beginning with a risk assessment of your company, as explained in Chapter 5 of this Training Handbook. Mapping your company's exposure to ethics and compliance risk will enable you to evaluate your company's strengths and weaknesses and to set your priorities. As an ethics and compliance officer, you need to identify the most sensitive areas in your company, which countries or business units present the highest risk exposure, and which instances or activities have led to the highest number of incidents.

A thorough risk assessment, which is generally conducted under the authority of the Board of Directors or at the instruction of the company's top management, will have to be regularly updated. This precious tool will enable you to direct your time and energy on your company's most pressing needs.

It would be impossible to draw conclusions at the beginning of this Training Handbook. But it can be said with certainty that your new job as an ethics and compliance officer is a challenging one, in which you may, if you are systematic and organized, make a decisive contribution to your company's societal position.

About the author

François Vincke is a Member of the Brussels Bar. He worked 26 years for PetroFina, a European oil, gas and petrochemicals company, including 11 years as Secretary General and General Counsel. Since 1994, he is the Head of Anti-corruption at ICC, first as Chairman of the Anti-corruption Commission and later as Vice-Chair of the Commission on Corporate Responsibility and Anti-corruption. He has written a number of articles and led several conferences on matters related to ethics and compliance.

PART I

THE FUNDAMENTALS

Chapter 2
The International Anti-corruption Conventions

Fritz Heimann

Former Associate General Counsel of the General Electric Company

Over the last decades, a number of international anti-corruption instruments have been adopted, but two international conventions are usually regarded as the milestones in the fight against corruption: the *Convention on Combating Bribery of Foreign Public Officials in International Business Transactions* adopted by the OECD in 1997 (referred in this Handbook as the *OECD Convention*) and the *Convention Against Corruption* adopted by the United Nations in 2003 (referred in this Handbook as the *United Nations Convention*). Ethics and compliance officers should be familiar with the provisions of these conventions and understand the dynamics of their implementation. This Chapter describes the relevance of both conventions for business and stresses the complementarities and differences between their respective provisions.

INTERNATIONAL CONVENTIONS, AN ESSENTIAL TOOL

International conventions are essential to combating corruption because corruption in a global economy operates on a global scale and cannot be dealt with effectively by national governments or corporations acting on their own.

The legal structure for combating corruption consists of three interdependent levels:

(i) **International conventions** that impose requirements and standards for action by national governments;

(ii) **Laws and regulations** enacted by national governments to implement convention requirements; and

(iii) **Corporate compliance programmes** meeting national laws and regulations.

International conventions are collective commitments undertaken by their states parties. Follow-up monitoring is crucial for their success. An effective monitoring process is necessary to ensure that governments implement the provisions of conventions, and that corporations adopt and carry out compliance programmes in accordance with national laws. Because consistent action is necessary to achieve a level playing field, the monitoring process must be conducted by the international body sponsoring the international convention. Companies, business and professional organizations, as well as governments, have to play an active role to make this monitoring process work.

This Chapter deals with the *OECD Convention* and the *United Nations Convention*. These two Conventions are very different. The *OECD Convention* is a narrow instrument of great strategic importance to multinational enterprises. It requires its states parties to prohibit foreign bribery. Because its states parties, currently numbering 40, include most of the world's leading exporters, the *OECD Convention* represents a major step toward creating a level playing field in global trade.

The *United Nations Convention* has worldwide membership, now numbering 167 countries. It has a very broad scope covering a wide range of preventive measures, criminal law enforcement, international cooperation, and asset recovery provisions. It has great potential, but it will require considerable time to attain its full potential. Conditions for doing business without being hampered by corruption will improve as its provisions are increasingly implemented around the world.

Other (regional) conventions against corruption are listed in Annex III of this Training Handbook.

I. THE OECD CONVENTION

The *OECD Convention* was signed in 1997 and became effective in 1999. It has been ratified by all 34 OECD members, as well as by six other states. The parties comprise over 75% of world exports and an even larger share of world investment. Accession discussions with other importing trading countries including China, India, and Indonesia are under way.

IMPORTANCE OF THE OECD CONVENTION

The *OECD Convention* is of great strategic importance in the fight against international corruption because the OECD member states are the home states of most major international corporations. This makes the OECD the ideal forum for curbing the supply side of international corruption.

The Convention was a major breakthrough because it overcame a previously insurmountable obstacle. After the United States passed its *Foreign Corrupt Practices Act* in 1977, the first law making foreign bribery a crime, there was a two-decade stalemate. Other countries were unwilling to prohibit foreign bribery without assurance that their major competitors would do so at the same time. Agreement at the OECD cut the Gordian knot.

The Convention provides a solid framework and an effective system to prohibit bribery of foreign officials:

- "Bribery" is broadly defined to include both direct and indirect bribery, which means bribery conducted by agents and intermediaries. "Foreign official" is broadly defined to include both government officials and officials from state-owned corporations.

- Penalties must be "effective, proportionate and dissuasive". They must be comparable to those for the bribery of domestic officials, including provisions for prison terms.
- Bribes and the proceeds of the bribery are subject to seizure and confiscation. Proceeds are defined as "the profits or other benefits derived by the briber".
- Accounting and auditing standards are required to prohibit the establishment of off-the-books accounts and other techniques for hiding bribery.
- Mutual legal assistance must be provided to other governments in connection with criminal investigations and other proceedings. Bank secrecy may not be asserted, and extradition is provided for.

THE OECD MONITORING PROGRAMME

The Convention requires the parties to cooperate in carrying out "a programme of systematic follow-up to monitor and promote the full implementation of th[e] Convention". This is of critical importance to assure that all parties are held to high standards in carrying out the Convention's requirements.

The monitoring programme is conducted by the OECD Working Group on Bribery, which consists of delegates from all the parties and meets four times a year. The Working Group conducts about half a dozen country reviews each year. These include country visits by 'lead reviewers' from two member states accompanied by experts from the OECD Secretariat.

The monitoring programme is conducted in three phases. Phase 1 evaluates the adequacy of national laws implementing the requirements of the Convention. Phase 2 reviews the structures in place to enforce the national laws. Phase 3 focuses on progress made in enforcement and progress made in correcting deficiencies identified in prior reviews.

Country visits include meetings with government officials, as well as with representatives of the private sector and civil society. The review team prepares a detailed report, often more than 50 pages long, which is first submitted in draft form to the government under review and then presented for discussion and approval at a meeting of the full Working Group on Bribery. Governments are expected to report back to the Working Group on the actions taken to correct deficiencies, orally after one year and in writing after two years. When the Working Group on Bribery is dissatisfied with the adequacy of corrective action, it can order a second country visit. This has been done several times, including for the United Kingdom and Japan.

The OECD monitoring programme has received excellent marks. Its reports are particularly thorough and of high professional quality. They are published and are available on the OECD website. The Working Group on Bribery consults regularly, not only with ICC, but also with the OECD's business and trade union advisory groups and with Transparency International.

The progress of foreign bribery enforcement by parties to the *OECD Convention* is uneven, but is continuing to improve. According to an annual progress report published by Transparency International in September 2012, there was active enforcement in seven countries with 28% of world exports; moderate enforcement in twelve countries with 25% of world exports, and little or no enforcement in 18 countries with 10% of world exports. There has been substantial increase in the number of cases brought in countries with active enforcement. The United States leads with 275 cases, an increase of 48 since the last year; Germany has 176 cases, an increase of 41 since last year; Switzerland has 52 cases, an increase of 17 since last year; Italy has 32, an increase of 14 since last year; and the United Kingdom has 23 cases, an increase of six since last year.

THE FUTURE SCOPE OF THE OECD WORKING GROUP ON BRIBERY

- Continuation of rigorous monitoring by the Working Group on Bribery, including country visits, is essential because the goal of the Convention – to establish a corruption-free, level playing field for international trade and investment – has not yet been achieved. The continued OECD monitoring programme in its Phase 3 has two key objectives:
    - To assure that governments which have taken little or no enforcement action against foreign bribery undertake significant enforcement without further delays; and
    - To assure that governments correct deficiencies identified in prior reviews.
- Because self-regulation by companies is essential for the success of the Convention, the Working Group should promote corporate integrity programmes at the international, national, and industry sector level. Governments should encourage the adoption of effective integrity programmes by taking them into account in sentencing guidelines and in decisions on bringing lawsuits as well as in settlements.
- While the prime focus of the Convention is on the supply side of corruption, international business continues to be exposed to widespread solicitation and extortion by foreign officials. The Working Group on Bribery should address this issue by promoting cooperative action by member governments to assist their companies in overcoming extortion threats, including joint intervention with governments where such threats are common. The High-Level Reporting Mechanism sponsored by OECD, which is further discussed in Chapter 13 of this Training Handbook (*'Resisting Solicitation'*), is an initiative to overcome solicitation and extortion. The government of Colombia has launched a pilot programme.
- Two long-recognized inadequacies in the coverage of the *OECD Convention* need to be addressed:
    - bribe payments to foreign political parties, party officials, and candidates for office; and
    - bribe payments by foreign subsidiaries of companies based in OECD countries.
- On bribery in the private sector, ICC proposed that OECD introduce provisions in its anti-corruption instruments prohibiting private-to-private corruption.

- Facilitation payments, which are defined in Chapter 4 ('*Glossary*'), were not covered when the Convention was adopted. The thinking of the business community about facilitation payments has changed substantially in recent years, reflecting greater recognition of the damage such payments cause. Multinational companies, confronted with divergent practices in different countries, increasingly opt for zero tolerance policies. The OECD has now introduced a recommendation restricting the use of facilitation payments.

- Whistleblower protection: corporations recognize that readily accessible complaint procedures can contribute substantially to uncovering corruption and other economic fraud and make it possible to solve problems at an early stage. Effective protection of whistleblowers against retaliation is essential. ICC published *Guidelines on Whistleblowing (2008)* and the OECD recommends that member governments provide whistleblower protection.

- There should be more cooperation between the OECD and the monitoring programmes of other anti-corruption conventions including the United Nations Convention, the monitoring programme of the Council of Europe, the *Inter-American Convention Against Corruption (1996)* and the *African Union Convention on Preventing and Combating Corruption (2003)*. Such enhanced cooperation is important to avoid duplicative monitoring and to build on the experience of these different programmes.

- In recent years South Africa, Israel and Russia have joined the *OECD Convention* and are being monitored by the Working Group on Bribery. Accession to the Convention by other major trading countries, including China, India, Indonesia, and Saudi Arabia, as recommended by the G20, is important for the achievement of a corruption-free level playing field.

- The OECD has surmounted the political difficulty of amending the Convention – which would require securing approval by the legislatures of all the parties – by adopting 'recommendations' specifying changes and providing that implementation of these recommendations will be reviewed by the follow-up monitoring process. This provides an innovative technique to update and strengthen the Convention.

    - The *Recommendation of the Council for Further Combating Bribery of Foreign Public Officials* adopted on 26 November 2009 changes the provision on facilitation payments and also makes corporations liable for failure to implement adequate internal controls, ethics, and compliance programmes or measures.

    - The 2009 Recommendation includes an Annex II entitled *Good Practice Guidance on Internal Controls, Ethics, and Compliance*. This document spells out in considerable detail the elements of effective corporate compliance programmes.

II. THE UNITED NATIONS CONVENTION

The *United Nations Convention* is of compelling interest for international business because it provides a global framework for combating corruption. This Convention has been ratified by 167 parties, including key players in international trade such as China, India, and Indonesia in addition to almost all OECD countries. With a much broader scope than the *OECD Convention,* the *United Nations Convention* is capable of tackling many issues that cannot be effectively dealt with by the OECD or regional anti-corruption conventions.

OVERVIEW OF THE UNITED NATIONS CONVENTION AGAINST CORRUPTION

The *United Nations Convention* was adopted in 2003 and became effective in December 2005. The Convention's parties include industrialized, emerging, developing, and least-developed economies. By comparison, the *OECD Convention* includes only 40 industrialized nations, while the regional conventions only cover countries in their regions.

The scope of the *United Nations Convention* is particularly ambitious. There are 28 articles covering criminalization and law enforcement, including foreign and domestic corruption, extortion as well as bribery, corruption in the public and private sector, embezzlement, illicit enrichment of public officials, abuse of functions, and trading in influence.

In addition, the *United Nations Convention* contains important preventive measures designed to strengthen the capability of states to fight corruption, provisions on international cooperation, including mutual legal assistance, extradition and joint investigations, ground-breaking provisions on asset recovery, as well as provisions on technical assistance and information exchanges.

Several examples can be used to illustrate the provisions of the *United Nations Convention* which are of particular relevance to multinational enterprises:

- The provisions for international cooperation should substantially improve cooperation among national enforcement officials. There are detailed articles dealing with mutual legal assistance and extradition. These should expedite prosecutors' ability to obtain evidence and witnesses located in other countries, thereby overcoming one of the biggest obstacles obstructing foreign bribery cases.
- The criminalization provisions break important new ground. Particularly noteworthy is the article on "Compensation for damages" which provides for private rights of action to enable those damaged by acts of corruption to obtain compensation from those responsible for the damage. Also of interest is the article requiring governments to "address consequences of corruption", including annulling contracts and withdrawing concessions.

- The *United Nations Convention* includes innovative provisions on asset recovery designed to enable governments, most commonly in the South, to recover funds deposited abroad by corrupt officials, often in the North, but increasingly elsewhere. In the past, asset recovery has been very difficult to pursue. The World Bank and the United Nations Office on Drugs and Crime have launched a Stolen Assets Recovery initiative to increase and accelerate this process. Companies dealing with corrupt officials must exercise high levels of diligence to ensure that any assets that they may obtain as a result of dealings with corrupt officials, or other politically exposed persons, cannot be frozen and confiscated in asset recovery proceedings.

The *United Nations Convention's* broad scope and worldwide participation provide unique potential for global progress against corruption. However, these same factors present difficulties and complexities in their implementation that will take time to overcome. The parties are at different levels of political, legal and economic development. The provisions of the Convention are not self-executing and require governments to pass new legislation, to build and strengthen organizations and provide them with adequate funding and staffing. Some of the *United Nations Convention's* provisions are mandatory ("Governments shall adopt laws"), others are discretionary ("Governments shall consider adopting laws"). Some are spelled out in great detail: the article on mutual legal assistance includes 30 sections; others are expressed only in broad generalities.

The rate at which the implementation of the *United Nations Convention* will progress will be uneven. That almost all the parties which have signed the Convention have also ratified it is a positive sign and means that governments recognize the need for comprehensive international action in the fight against corruption.

There is widespread recognition of two fundamental points: (a) globalization of economic life will continue to expand, and (b) corruption operates on a global scale and is continuing to grow. Therefore, there is a compelling need for the *United Nations Convention* to evolve into effective action programmes.

PROVISIONS DIRECTLY AFFECTING INTERNATIONAL BUSINESS

The provisions of most direct impact on international business are primarily in the Convention's Chapter on Criminalization and Law Enforcement.

The provision on "Bribery of national public officials" is mandatory and requires that governments criminalize domestic bribery (active corruption) and solicitation (passive corruption). The *OECD Convention* only deals with bribery of foreign public officials. Bribery of national officials is prohibited by the criminal laws of most countries.

The provision on "Bribery of foreign public officials and officials of public international organizations" is also mandatory and requires that governments criminalize foreign bribery. However, the criminalization of solicitation by foreign public officials is left discretionary. The prohibition of solicitation applies whether the company solicited is domestic or foreign. The *OECD Convention* covers bribery of foreign public officials, but does not deal with solicitation.

United Nations Convention, article 16
BRIBERY OF FOREIGN PUBLIC OFFICIALS AND OFFICIALS OF PUBLIC INTERNATIONAL ORGANIZATIONS

"1. Each State Party shall adopt such legislative and other measures as may be necessary to establish as a criminal offence, when committed intentionally, the promise, offering or giving to a foreign public official or an official of a public international organization, directly or indirectly, of an undue advantage, for the official himself or herself or another person or entity, in order that the official act or refrain from acting in the exercise of his or her official duties, in order to obtain or retain business or other undue advantage in relation to the conduct of international business.

2. Each State Party shall consider adopting such legislative and other measures as may be necessary to establish as a criminal offence, when committed intentionally, the solicitation or acceptance by a foreign public official or an official of a public international organization, directly or indirectly, of an undue advantage, for the official himself or herself or another person or entity, in order that the official act or refrain from acting in the exercise of his or her official duties".

The provisions on "Trading in influence", "Abuse of functions", and "Illicit Enrichment" are discretionary and have considerable potential for broadening the reach of criminal law beyond the traditional prohibitions of bribery and extortion. The provision on "Illicit Enrichment" is particularly important because it shifts the burden of proof on to public officials who get rich in office. All these provisions go beyond the *OECD Convention*. Companies need to consider whether to cover "Trading in influence" under their anti-bribery policies; this can raise the difficult issue of distinguishing between legitimate lobbying activities and improper trading in influence.

United Nations Convention, articles 20 and 21
ILLICIT ENRICHMENT

"Subject to its constitution and the fundamental principles of its legal system, each State Party shall consider adopting such legislative and other measures as may be necessary to establish as a criminal offence, when committed intentionally, illicit enrichment, that is, a significant increase in the assets of a public official that he or she cannot reasonably explain in relation to his or her lawful income".

BRIBERY IN THE PRIVATE SECTOR

"Each State Party shall consider adopting such legislative and other measures as may be necessary to establish as criminal offences, when committed intentionally in the course of economic, financial or commercial activities: (a) The promise, offering or giving, directly or indirectly, of an undue advantage to any person who directs or works, in any capacity, for a private sector entity, for the person himself or herself or for another person, in order that he or she, in breach of his or her duties, act or refrain from acting; (b) The solicitation or acceptance, directly or indirectly, of an undue advantage by any person who directs or works, in any capacity, for a private sector entity, for the person himself or for another person in order that he or she, in breach of his or her duties, act or refrain from acting".

The provisions on "Bribery in the private sector" and on "Embezzlement of property in the private sector" are both discretionary. Their implementation is important because the line of division between the private sector and the public sector has become blurred with the private sector taking on traditional public functions. These provisions go beyond the *OECD Convention*.

The provision on "Laundering of proceeds of crime" is mandatory. It provides that the corruption offences covered by the *United Nations Convention* shall be predicate offences triggering the anti-money laundering prohibitions. This provision goes beyond the *OECD Convention*, which makes foreign bribery a predicate offence only in countries where bribery of domestic officials is a predicate offence.

The article on "Liability of legal persons" is mandatory and calls for corporate liability for the offences covered by the *United Nations Convention*. This is an important step because it should accelerate the abandonment of the antiquated concept that only individuals and not corporations shall be criminally liable for offences. This article provides that the liability of corporations may be criminal, civil or administrative; thus, it does not require that corporations shall be criminally liable. Governments must provide that corporations are "subject to effective, proportionate and dissuasive criminal or non-criminal sanctions, including monetary sanctions". The treatment of corporate liability under the *United Nations Convention* is similar to that of the *OECD Convention*.

> **United Nations Convention, article 26**
> LIABILITY OF LEGAL PERSONS
> "1. Each State Party shall adopt such measures as may be necessary, consistent with its legal principles, to establish the liability of legal persons for participation in the offences established in accordance with [the] Convention.
> 2. Subject to the legal principles of the State Party, the liability of legal persons may be criminal, civil or administrative.
> 3. Such liability shall be without prejudice to the criminal liability of the natural persons who have committed the offences.
> 4. Each State Party shall, in particular, ensure that legal persons held liable in accordance with this article are subject to effective, proportionate, and dissuasive criminal or non-criminal sanctions, including monetary sanctions".

The provision on "Statute of limitations" is mandatory and calls for long statutes of limitations for corruption offences. It also provides for a longer limitations period or a suspension of the statute where there is evasion by the offender. This provision is stronger than the *OECD Convention*.

The article on "Freezing, seizure and confiscation" is mandatory and calls for the confiscation of the proceeds of corruption and of property used in or destined for use in corruption. Bank and other financial records shall be made available and bank secrecy may not be asserted. The *OECD Convention* also provides that bribes and the proceeds of bribery are subject to seizure and confiscation.

The provision on "Protection of reporting persons" is a discretionary one and aims at ensuring the protection of persons who report offences under the Convention to the competent authorities (whistleblowers). This subject matter is not covered in the *OECD Convention*.

As already mentioned above, the *United Nations Convention* contains a provision on the "Consequences of acts of corruption". This provides for annulling or rescinding contracts or withdrawing concessions in case of corruption. This matter is not covered in the *OECD Convention*.

Another important innovation is Article 35 on "Compensation for damages", which contains a mandatory provision calling for measures to enable persons damaged by acts of corruption to obtain compensation from those responsible for such damages. This provision for private rights of action has far-reaching implications. It enables companies to take action to obtain compensation even when public prosecutors fail to do so. The *OECD Convention* does not provide for private rights of action.

This provision is broadly worded. Its scope and effect will depend on implementing legislation and court decisions. Presumably lawsuits could be brought by unsuccessful competitors and by various other damaged parties. It will be interesting to see how broadly courts will construe the category of potential plaintiffs: "entities and persons who have suffered damage as a result of an act of corruption." Similar questions are raised regarding the category of potential defendants: "those responsible for that damage." Presumably lawsuits could be brought against corrupt companies and against corrupt officials. It is possible that lawsuits could also be brought against governments that maintain corrupt procurement systems.

The article on "Cooperation with law enforcement authorities" provides that governments may mitigate punishment or grant immunity to persons cooperating in investigations and prosecutions of corruption. This is not covered by the *OECD Convention*. Several OECD countries, including the United Kingdom and the United States, take account of self-reporting or other actions by companies.

The Convention's Chapter IV on "International Cooperation" includes provisions on mutual legal assistance, law enforcement cooperation, joint investigations and special investigative techniques. These are important to international business because they should speed up the traditionally cumbersome and time-consuming procedures for dealing with international corruption.

As already mentioned above, Chapter V on "'Asset Recovery" is of principal benefit to countries whose corrupt officials have deposited stolen assets in foreign countries. Companies making foreign acquisitions need to assess, as part of their due diligence reviews, whether properties to be acquired could be subject to seizure and confiscation because of corruption by prior owners.

The successful implementation of the asset recovery chapter of the *United Nations Convention* will be of far-reaching importance, because the attractiveness of corruption will be sharply reduced if corrupt leaders can no longer count on safely depositing the proceeds of corruption in foreign banks. In addition, recovery of stolen assets would contribute greatly to international development because a large share of the estimated billions of dollars of such assets originated from the poorest countries in the world.

STRENGTHENING NATIONAL INTEGRITY SYSTEMS

The Convention's provisions on "Preventive Measures" are important to companies because they will strengthen integrity and accountability, thereby curtailing corruption and improving conditions for doing business more broadly. The *OECD Convention* does not include preventive measures.

The article on "Preventive anti-corruption policies and practices" requires governments to develop anti-corruption policies that reflect the rule of law, integrity, transparency, and accountability. Periodic evaluations are called for to determine the adequacy of anti-corruption measures. This article should provide a useful advocacy tool for private sector and civil society groups.

The provision on "Preventive anti-corruption bodies" requires governments to establish organizations to implement the policies referred to in the preceding paragraph. Such bodies shall be granted the necessary independence to enable them to carry out their functions, as well as the necessary material resources and specialized staff.

The article on "Codes of conduct for public officials" requires governments to promote integrity, honesty, and responsibility among its public officials by means of codes of conduct. Such codes should encourage reporting of violations. Also called for are declarations by public officials of outside activities, investments, assets, and substantial gifts from which conflict of interest may result.

The provision on "Public procurement and management of public finances" addresses two areas of government activity long subject to widespread corruption. Governments are required to establish public procurement systems based on transparency, competition and objective criteria in decision-making, including effective systems of appeal. They shall also promote transparency and accountability in the management of public finances, encompassing procedures for the adoption of the national budget, timely reporting on revenue and expenditure, accounting and auditing standards and risk management and internal control. Improvements in these areas would be of great benefit to business.

An article on "Public reporting" provides for public access to decision-making authorities and periodic reports on the risks of corruption in public administration.

United Nations Convention, articles 9 (excerpted) and 10

ARTICLE 9 - PUBLIC PROCUREMENT AND MANAGEMENT OF PUBLIC FINANCES

"Each State Party shall, in accordance with the fundamental principles of its legal system, take the necessary steps to establish appropriate systems of procurement, based on transparency, competition and objective criteria in decision-making that are effective, inter alia, in preventing corruption […]"

ARTICLE 10 - PUBLIC REPORTING

"Taking into account the need to combat corruption, each State Party shall, in accordance with the fundamental principles of its domestic law, take such measures as may be necessary to enhance transparency in its public administration, including with regard to its organization, functioning and decision-making processes, where appropriate. Such measures may include, inter alia:

(a) Adopting procedures or regulations allowing members of the general public to obtain, where appropriate, information on the organization, functioning and decision-making processes of its public administration and, with due regard for the protection of privacy and personal data, on decisions and legal acts that concern members of the public;

(b) Simplifying administrative procedures, where appropriate, in order to facilitate public access to the competent decision-making authorities; and

(c) Publishing information, which may include periodic reports on the risks of corruption in its public administration"

A provision on the "Private sector" calls for governments to take measures to prevent corruption in the private sector, including enhanced accounting and auditing standards, codes of conduct, prevention of conflicts of interest, restrictions on employment of former public officials, internal controls, prohibitions of off-the-books transactions and disallowance of tax deductibility of bribes.

United Nations Convention, article 12 (excerpted)
PRIVATE SECTOR

"Each State Party shall take measures, in accordance with the fundamental principles of its domestic law, to prevent corruption involving the private sector, enhance accounting and auditing standards in the private sector and, where appropriate, provide effective, proportionate and dissuasive civil, administrative or criminal penalties for failure to comply with such measures. [...]

In order to prevent corruption, each State Party shall take such measures as may be necessary, in accordance with its domestic laws and regulations regarding the maintenance of books and records, financial statement disclosures and accounting and auditing standards, to prohibit the following acts carried out for the purpose of committing any of the offences established in accordance with [the] Convention:

(a) The establishment of off-the-books accounts;
(b) The making of off-the-books or inadequately identified transactions;
(c) The recording of non-existent expenditure;
(d) The entry of liabilities with incorrect identification of their objects;
(e) The use of false documents; and
(f) The intentional destruction of bookkeeping documents earlier than foreseen by the law.

Each State Party shall disallow the tax deductibility of expenses that constitute bribes, and where appropriate, of other expenses incurred in furtherance of corrupt conduct.

The provision on "Participation of society" requires governments to promote active participation of individuals and groups outside the public sector in the fight against corruption. This includes business as well as non-governmental organizations. Another article calls for ensuring that the public has effective access to information and protects the freedom to publish and disseminate information concerning corruption. Anti-corruption bodies are required to provide access for reporting, including anonymously, of corruption offences.

The provision on "Measures to prevent money laundering" calls for a comprehensive regulatory and supervisory regime for banks and other financial institutions to deter and detect all forms of money laundering.

The foregoing preventive measures provide an invaluable foundation for strengthening government capability to combat corruption, strengthening private participation, and enhancing corporate integrity programmes.

THE IMPLEMENTATION REVIEW MECHANISM

Experience has shown that follow-up monitoring is essential to make anti-corruption conventions work. It is particularly important for a convention as complex and with as many parties as the *United Nations Convention*.

The need for monitoring was debated during the 2002-03 Vienna negotiations that led to the adoption of the Convention. When it proved impossible to reach agreement on monitoring, the Convention was adopted with a decision on monitoring deferred for future action. It took six years, until the Third Conference of States Parties in 2009 in Doha, Qatar, before an agreement on an 'Implementation Review Mechanism' could be reached. ICC, as well as the World Economic Forum, the United Nations Global Compact and Transparency International, played an active role in advocating for an effective monitoring mechanism.

The Review Mechanism started in July 2010. The initial five-year cycle of country reviews covers the Convention's chapters on criminalization and international cooperation. The second five-year cycle will cover preventive measures and asset recovery. Each year about 40 countries will be reviewed, an extremely ambitious undertaking.

Policy direction for the Implementation Review Mechanism is provided by the Conference of States Parties which meets every two years. An Implementation Review Group has been established which meets (at least) annually and provides oversight between the Conference of States Parties meetings. Country reviews are conducted by two peer review states, one from the same region and one from a different region than the country being reviewed. The United Nations Office on Drugs and Crime acts as the Secretariat for the *United Nations Convention* and helps to manage the review process.

The experience of the first three years indicates that completing country reviews on schedule is difficult. Most governments have agreed to have country visits by the review teams, an important element for effective reviews. Most country reviews have permitted participation by private sector and civil society organizations, another important element. An executive summary, prepared by the United Nations Office on Drugs and Crime, is published after each country review. Some but not all governments have permitted the publication of the full text of the country review.

Keeping a review process involving 167 countries on schedule is a formidable challenge. However, the quality of the reviews must not be compromised. The private sector can play an important role in the conduct of individual country reviews and in pressing for adequate funding for the review process.

A rigorous review process is crucial for the success of the *United Nations Convention*. Implementation must be consistent between countries and for the different Convention provisions. Unless there is consistent global implementation, the *United Nations Convention* cannot achieve its objectives. For example, asset recovery can be circumvented as long as some banking centres fail to implement the Convention's asset recovery provisions. Stolen funds will flow to countries with little or no implementation, particularly those that retain banking secrecy laws.

About the author

Fritz Heimann is an American corporate lawyer and is one of the founders of Transparency International. He was formerly Associate General Counsel of the General Electric Company. He is a member of the ICC Commission on Corporate Responsibility and Anti-corruption and leads its work on international anti-corruption conventions. He is the co-editor of 'Fighting Corruption: International Corporate Integrity Handbook' published by ICC in 2009.

Chapter 3
The Global Antitrust Landscape

Jean-Yves Trochon*

Deputy General Counsel of Lafarge

Until recently, the field of ethics and compliance focused almost exclusively on the fight against corruption, and was seen as separate and distinct from other matters of compliance. In the last few years, however, there has been a growing awareness that the areas of antitrust and anti-corruption, while facing different challenges, share similar features and are often brought together under the common denominator of "corporate compliance". This Chapter introduces the global antitrust landscape and describes the main legal instruments governing antitrust in the United States and the European Union. We, as compliance practitioners, learn about the tenets of competition rules and the key features of antitrust compliance programmes.

INTRODUCTION

The management of antitrust risk has become a real challenge, especially for companies operating in numerous countries across several continents. Yet, this challenge arises not only in countries where competition legislation has been on the statute books for a long time but also in countries where competition law has only been recently adopted and is being implemented pursuant to standards 'imported' from so-called mature jurisdictions.

Assessing the competition risk for your company and defining the proper compliance standards to be followed by its business units will not be an easy task. You may be confronted with at least three categories of countries when making such assessment:

(i) Jurisdictions where sophisticated legal instruments and clear guidelines exist (for example, the United States and the European Union);

(ii) Jurisdictions which have enacted competition legislation but which have weak enforcement authorities and have provided little guidance as to the interpretation of their legislation; and

(iii) A small number of jurisdictions where no competition law is yet in place.

As a result, it is difficult to come up with uniform compliance standards that are applicable worldwide. However, as a matter of consistency, a global corporate approach is required despite existing discrepancies

---

* The author wishes to thank Alexandra Badea for her valuable contribution to the preparation of this Chapter.

JEAN-YVES TROCHON

between legal frameworks. Whatever jurisdiction is at stake, the challenge is to protect the global reputation of the company by mitigating exposure to potentially significant financial penalties, civil suits as well as criminal sanctions. As it is often rightly said, reputation is the main asset of a company and global compliance is critical in this respect.

THE ORIGINS OF COMPETITION LAW – AND MOST RECENT DEVELOPMENTS WORLDWIDE

Competition law was 'invented' in the 19th century in the United States. The European Union came long after the United States and more precisely in the 20th century, calling it competition law rather than antitrust law. Thereafter, and especially under the influence of the International Monetary Fund, the World Bank and the OECD, a vast majority of countries around the world decided to implement competition legislation which broadly mirrored European and United States standards. The best symbol of this 'globalization of competition legislation' is the adoption in 2008 by the People's Republic of China of competition rules largely inspired by European standards. It is fair to say that competition rules, along with anti-corruption rules, are now quite similar in the vast majority of countries. There are only a handful of countries without competition law, making the challenge of global compliance even more complex.

THE NEED FOR A WORLDWIDE COMPETITION COMPLIANCE PROGRAMME

Establishing a worldwide competition compliance programme is now a 'must-do' for multinational companies and other businesses with international operations. Such antitrust compliance programme should clearly define which behaviour is acceptable and which is not. Defining the company's 'do's and don'ts' will only be possible after having done a thorough and complex risk management analysis, which should involve business people as well as competition lawyers.

How do you shape and enforce your company's compliance commitments in less mature jurisdictions? This is a serious task for companies operating in countries where there are still significant discrepancies in the way competition laws are construed and enforced. And the challenge of interpreting different competition laws will become even more important. For instance, the use of economics to bring evidence of possible collusion among competitors differs from one jurisdiction to another. The structure of some markets and certain pricing trends are increasingly challenged by competition authorities, even though they may be the natural result of the evolution of supply and demand. Assessing the potential infringement of competition rules is sometimes far from being clear cut. As a result, there is a significant 'risk management' element in any global antitrust compliance programme, and your company will need to provide sufficient expertise and resources to help employees face complex dilemmas.

A compliance programme should not be purely 'process-driven', but rather designed to foster a sustainable culture of antitrust integrity in all entities and countries where the company operates. In that sense, it should also be 'value-based'. A training programme focusing solely on rules and processes may prove ineffective if it falls short of creating a culture of compliance through senior management buy-in and commitment.

Smaller companies are also required to establish and communicate on internal compliance rules, especially when operating in multiple jurisdictions. However, this should be done in a way to minimize the associated cost and additional organizational complexity.

ANTITRUST LEGAL INSTRUMENTS IN THE UNITED STATES AND IN THE EUROPEAN UNION

The past decade has witnessed a greater convergence between the United States and the European Union with regard to law enforcement by their respective competition authorities. While there still are a number of technical (and sometimes not insignificant) discrepancies between both legal systems, it can be said that there are now more similarities than differences between both jurisdictions.

Why are these two jurisdictions setting global antitrust standards? Among the various reasons are (i) the existence of mature and long-standing antitrust systems and instruments; (ii) the presence of influential antitrust policy-making bodies (such as the OECD and the International Competition Network); (iii) the existence of large databases of case law; and (iv) the substantial policy-making activity on both sides of the Atlantic. Last but not least, the vast majority of antitrust lawyers, policy-makers and economists still originate from European and North American universities. However, it is fair to say that law enforcement in Asia is such that, in few years time, Asian countries will most likely play a key role in global standard-setting.

The United States antitrust model

THE UNITED STATES ANTITRUST LAWS

The United States has a complex and sophisticated antitrust legal system derived from the very nature of its federal political system. In a nutshell, the following acts are in force:

- The **Sherman Act** is the original, principal and foremost antitrust statute in the United States. It provides both civil remedies and criminal penalties for the principal antitrust violations: conspiracy to restrain trade, monopolization, attempted monopolization, and conspiracy to monopolize.

- The **Clayton Act** is a federal statute that imposes restrictions on proposed mergers and acquisitions to control the formation of trusts and monopolization.

- The **Robinson-Patman Act** prohibits specific business practices such as price-discrimination.

- The **Federal Trade Commission Act** establishes the Federal Trade Commission, which has regulatory authority to enforce the antitrust acts.

- The **Hart-Scott-Rodino Antitrust Improvement Act** imposes premerger notification requirements for certain kinds of mergers, acquisitions, and other concentrations of two or more business operations.

- The **state statutes**: in addition to the federal statutes, each state in the United Stated has its own antitrust statutes, often similar to, but in some instances significantly different from, the federal acts.

THE UNITED STATES ENFORCEMENT AGENCIES

The **Antitrust Division of the Department of Justice** and the **Federal Trade Commission** generally have concurrent jurisdiction for civil enforcement actions for violations of the federal antitrust laws. Only the Department of Justice can bring criminal actions for violations of the Sherman Act, and it is the sole jurisdiction for certain industries.

At state level, **state attorneys general** may bring federal antitrust lawsuits on behalf of individuals with residence in their respective states.

Private parties can also bring lawsuits to enforce antitrust laws, especially through "class actions". In fact, most antitrust lawsuits are private actions brought by legal entities and individuals seeking damages for violations of either the Sherman Act or the Clayton Act. This is one of the main differences with the European Union system, where private parties are limited in their ability to introduce class or civil actions to obtain compensation for competition law violations by businesses. However, as we will see hereafter, this situation may soon evolve.

The United States may cooperate in **cross-border investigations** with foreign competition authorities on matters having an impact on United States consumers.

CARTEL ENFORCEMENT IN THE UNITED STATES

In the United States, federal law and state statutes provide for both criminal and civil sanctions. Criminal sanctions are mostly applied to 'hard core' antitrust violations (as for instance price-fixing, market allocation and bid rigging).

The Department of Justice is the principal government enforcer of the criminal aspects of the law. Exemptions or immunities may be available in very limited circumstances, based either on the protection of constitutional rights (for instance certain government petitioning activities) or on a legislative exemption created by Congress to protect certain industries or activities (for instance a regulated activity/industry under pricing approval regime by a regulatory agency).

SANCTIONS

The Sherman Act provides for a maximum fine of up to US$ 100 million for a legal entity or a fine of up to twice the gain derived from the criminal conduct or twice the loss suffered by the victims. For individuals, the same Act provides for fines of up to US$1 million and prison sentences of up to 10 years or alternatively, fines of up to twice the gain to the individual or twice the loss suffered by the victims. However, when it comes to individuals participating in a cartel, the sanctions have focused on jail time rather than large fines.

LENIENCY

The United States was the first jurisdiction to introduce a leniency policy in 1978. In order to encourage cartel members to self-report, immunity from criminal sanctions is granted under certain conditions (including voluntary disclosure and timely reporting). This policy was substantially developed in 1993, and in 2008, additional clarifications and detailed public guidance were provided in order to make the leniency programme more transparent and easier to apply.

SETTLEMENT UNDER THE UNITED STATES ANTITRUST PROCEDURE

A settlement is a system of individual plea negotiations between the Department of Justice and the participants in a cartel. The Department of Justice is allowed to 'settle' criminal cartel charges bilaterally and consecutively with different parties, applying its sentencing guidelines with a large discretion to offer rebates and to cut the scope of the alleged cartel in order to reach an agreement.

For the Department of Justice, the settlement procedure is a dynamic investigation tool, with a 'generous' discount for the first company to plead guilty and with progressively smaller discounts for the latecomers.

The European Union competition law model

THE EUROPEAN UNION LEGAL PROVISIONS

The main European Union legal provisions on cartels derive from the Treaty on the Functioning of the European Union, which regulates horizontal and vertical agreements and also provides for possible exemptions.

Article 101 of the Treaty on the Functioning of the European Union refers to agreements and practices that have the effect or the object of distorting competition (such as price fixing, market sharing, and more generally any type of agreement, in whatever form, restricting competition to the detriment of consumers).

Article 102 of the Treaty on the Functioning of the European Union prohibits any abuse by one or more undertakings of a dominant position. A dominant position may be held either independently or collectively. Dominance is not a problem in itself, only the abuse of a dominant position is prohibited (through 'exploitive' or 'exclusionary' practices).

Besides the basic provisions contained in the Treaty on the Functioning of the European Union, a number of regulations adopted either by the Council of the European Union or the European Commission as well as non-regulatory documents adopted by the European Commission (such as notices and guidelines) also form part of the European Union's legal framework.

THE EUROPEAN UNION ENFORCEMENT AGENCIES

The **European Commission's Competition Directorate General** is the main actor in the fight against cartels at European Union level. The European Commission has extensive investigative powers. For instance, it has the power to conduct investigations not only at a company's premises but also, with a specific search warrant, at the homes and vehicles of employees of a company suspected of having participated in a law infringement. The European Commission decisions may be ultimately challenged before the Court of Justice of the European Union.

The **National Competition Authorities** are national agencies in charge of fighting cartels in the member states of the European Union. European law has primacy over national law and takes precedence in case of conflict.

Article 101.3 of the Treaty on the Functioning of the European Union provides for exemptions from the prohibition of restrictive practices when certain conditions are met. This will be the case, if the agreement (i) improves the production or distribution of goods or services or the promotion of technical or economic progress; (ii) allows consumers a fair share of the benefit; (iii) does not contain any unnecessary restriction; and (iv) does not eliminate competition in the relevant market. However, it will be up to the companies to conduct, at their own risk, a self-assessment as to the legality of the agreement they intend to conclude.

Certain agreements, which are called 'hard core' cartels (such as price fixing and market allocation agreements) are considered restrictive of competition 'as such' and cannot be redeemed.

CARTEL ENFORCEMENT AND COOPERATION OUTSIDE THE EUROPEAN UNION TERRITORY

Bilateral cooperation agreements between the European Union and certain non-European Union countries may allow the European Commission to obtain information and evidence from outside the European Union. Any agreement concluded outside the Union, but affecting competition within its territory, can be tested against the European Union competition rules.

SANCTIONS

Unlike the United States, the European Union competition law does not provide for criminal sanctions against individuals who infringe competition rules.

In addition, no fine can be imposed against individuals, but only against legal entities. However, in some member states of the European Union, such as the United Kingdom and France, criminal penalties can be imposed on individuals.

FINES

Fines cannot exceed 10% of the sanctioned company's turnover. These are imposed based on the seriousness and the duration of the infringement.

In 2006, the European Commission published new guidelines for the determination of fines. As we will see below, these guidelines have led to a considerable increase of their monetary amount.

LENIENCY

A leniency policy was first introduced in the European Union in 1996 and was further developed in 2002. This policy is inspired from the United States model but with some minor changes, such as the amount of the reduction and the rules to be followed by the company to which leniency is granted.

Total or partial immunity from fines is granted to companies collaborating with competition authorities and bringing evidence against cartels (for instance, a complete immunity from fines will be given to the first company reporting a cartel and bringing evidence about it, provided however that the same company did not coerce other companies to participate in the cartel). This leniency policy proved to be successful in practice. In the last few years, the vast majority of cartels were discovered thanks to this leniency technique.

SETTLEMENTS

A settlement procedure was introduced in 2008. It starts when the European Commission has finalized its review and its legal assessment of the evidence on file, including the voluntary submissions by the companies involved in a leniency notice and the companies' responses to information requests.

The settlement procedure in the European Union is quite different from the one existing in the United States. A specificity of the European settlement procedure is that no discrimination is allowed between members of the same cartel. It applies to cartels only, such as agreements on prices, outputs, and on market sharing or customer allocation.

Unlike the United States, a settlement procedure in the European Union is not an investigative tool but a case closure mechanism. Once settlement discussions have started, the European Commission will show its charges and will give access to key evidence; the parties will have the right to respond and to present their positions. If they agree on paying a fine, in exchange of renouncing their right to appeal, they will be granted a 10% fine reduction.

Similar mechanisms exist in most of the European Union member states.

THE DIRECT IMPACT OF REGULATORY ENFORCEMENT: AN INCREASING NUMBER OF HEAVY FINES

Fines imposed on companies breaching competition rules can be very severe. In the European Union, the largest fine imposed on a single company (namely Saint-Gobain in 2008) for a cartel prohibition infringement amounted to €896 million.

In December 2012, European competition Commissioner Joaquín Almunia announced a record €1.47 billion fine on companies for running during nearly a decade a price fixing cartel for TV and monitor cathode-ray tubes. This is the highest fine imposed on members of a single cartel by the European Commission to date. Philips (the Netherlands) was imposed the highest penalty (€700 million), followed by Panasonic (Japan), Samsung (South Korea), Technicolor (France), and Toshiba (Japan). The Taiwanese company Chunghwa Picture Tubes had blown the whistle on the cartel and escaped a fine. Until this announcement, the largest monetary penalty for a cartel was imposed on car glass industry companies for a total of €1.3 billion.

Between 2005 and 2009, the overall amount of fines reached over €9 billion, whereas during the period from 2000 to 2004 it totalled about €3.5 billion (and €850 million between 1990 and 2000). This considerable increase is mainly due to the adoption of the 2006 fining guidelines, which aimed at enhancing deterrence against cartels. Between 2008 and 2012, the overall amount of fines already reached €9 billion, notwithstanding the deep economic crisis experienced by Europe.

The fines imposed by the United States Department of Justice are relatively lower: they totalled €1.5 billion between 2005 and 2008 and €2 billion between 2009 and October 2012. However, the amounts of penalties imposed on companies in the European Union and the United States tend to be in balance when adding the total damages resulting from class actions in the United States – not to mention the criminal sanctions imposed against individuals, which are perceived as the most efficient tools to deter cartel infringements. In many other jurisdictions (such as India and Brazil), the authorities are following the trend set by

the European Union, where the only limit is 10% of the turnover of the sanctioned company (sometimes of the global turnover, like in Malaysia).

KEY FEATURES OF A COMPETITION/ANTITRUST COMPLIANCE PROGRAMME

A global competition compliance programme should be a key component of the company's broader corporate ethics and compliance programme. Antitrust compliance should go hand in hand with the other compliance policies and initiatives, such as anti-corruption, fraud prevention and the like.

In 2013, the ICC Commission on Competition, and its specialized Task Force on Antitrust Compliance and Advocacy, published an *ICC Antitrust Compliance Toolkit*, which provides practical tips, guidance and advice to assist companies in building and reinforcing credible antitrust compliance programmes, taking into account both the risks these companies face and the resources available to them.

This global Toolkit, which benefited from contributions from antitrust specialists closely associated with in-house efforts around the world, is available on ICC's website[1]. Its introductory 'Starter Kit' (for smaller enterprises and others starting to introduce a compliance programme) is reproduced below.

Starter Kit

Excerpt from the ICC Antitrust Compliance Toolkit *(2013)*

FOUNDATION ELEMENTS OF THE PROGRAMME

1. Embedding an antitrust compliance culture and policy
   - Recognize that your company faces antitrust risks associated with its activities and objectives;
   - Consider how your company can set out antitrust standards all employees must meet when doing business;
   - Get business leaders to show personal support actively for ethical business practices.

2. Compliance organization and resources
   - Nominate a suitably senior individual to oversee the implementation of the antitrust compliance programme;
   - Make sure that they can and will report to highest levels of management;
   - Decide how to involve subject matter experts (including antitrust lawyers) to develop policies and/or guidance.

3. Risk identification and assessment
   - Decide how to identify antitrust risks and trends, ideally as part of your general risk management process;
   - Consider what controls are needed to manage, minimize or eliminate the risks identified;

---

[1] http://www.iccwbo.org/Advocacy-Codes-and-Rules/Areas-of-work Competition/ICC-Antitrust-Compliance-Toolkit/

- Share insights on the assurance process and scope for improvements with senior management.

4. Antitrust compliance know-how

- Tailor antitrust know-how guidance to the risk profile and needs of the company;
- Decide on the best way to deploy interactive training and updates.

REINFORCEMENT OF AN EXISTING PROGRAMME

5. Antitrust concerns-handling systems and investigations

- Embed a successful reporting culture that supports timely reactions and fair outcomes;
- Consider the merits of appointing an external provider to act as a 'hotline'.

6. Internal investigations/due diligence and disciplinary action

- Consider the most efficient way of investigating potential concerns (time may be of the essence);
- Devise a simple but effective way of dealing with individuals who violate company policy.

7. Antitrust certification or incentives

- Think about asking employees to certify their understanding and commitment to compliance requirements;
- Consider compliance incentives (in reward structures or promotion processes) to reinforce engagement.

8. Monitoring and continuous improvement

- Decide how you will monitor the effectiveness of your controls (e.g. periodically run targeted in-depth reviews);
- Introduce a compliance improvement plan if necessary (e.g. if concerns arise or the company risk profile changes).

DO COMPETITION COMPLIANCE PROGRAMMES HAVE A MITIGATING EFFECT?

As stated by the European Commission in its brochure on Compliance Programmes, "the mere existence of a compliance programme will not be considered as a mitigating circumstance, nor an aggravating circumstance", "the purpose of a compliance programme is to avoid infringement in the first place", and "the mere existence of a compliance programme is not enough to counter the finding of an infringement of competition rules".

The same may not be said about certain member states of the European Union. In the United Kingdom, the Office of Fair Trade may reduce the financial penalty by 5 to 10% in the presence of an effective compliance programme. In France, the competition authority ('Autorité de la Concurrence') issued guidelines intended to encourage and possibly reward (through reductions of fines for infringement of competition rules) companies having established an effective compliance programme.

In the United States, compliance programmes do not seem to be taken into consideration when determining issues of corporate liability according to the Attorneys' Manual of the United States Department of Justice. The same principle is applied when it comes to prosecuting companies. However, under the *Federal Sentencing Guidelines*, compliance programmes are taken into account when determining sentences for corporations.

All in all, when seeing the scant effect, in certain jurisdictions, of competition compliance programmes in terms of fine reduction, companies may ask themselves whether it is still worthwhile establishing one. There are, nonetheless, many good reasons for companies to develop their own competition compliance programme:

- First, a compliance programme helps creating and maintaining a global ethics and compliance culture through continuous awareness-raising and training initiatives.
- Second, a compliance programme helps improving the company's governance by introducing appropriate checks and balances. Transparency and segregation of duties are necessary to make sure that rules are set, applied and controlled in the best interest of the company.
- Last but not least, competition authorities are expected to become increasingly sympathetic to the idea that corporate compliance programmes yield positive effects on the economy at large and for the benefit of consumers in particular. One may equally hope that the authorities will consider, when determining a sanction for an unintentional breach of competition rules, whether and how a compliance programme was implemented. There is no reason for the authorities not to at least consider the effective implementation of a compliance programme as a potential attenuating circumstance, likely to decrease the amount of the fine – as is the case in corruption and other criminal law matters.

About the author

Jean-Yves Trochon is an international in-house lawyer who held successive positions in the legal and international departments of various companies operating worldwide, including Lagardère, Bouygues, EADS, and Lafarge. He is currently Deputy General Counsel of Lafarge and Vice-Chair of ICC France's Competition Commission.

Chapter 4
Glossary

Jean-Pierre Méan

Of Counsel at MCE Legal,
Former General Counsel and Chief Compliance Officer of SGS

Ethics and compliance practitioners need to develop a precise and concrete understanding of the fundamental concepts which form the foundations of anti-corruption and antitrust. In this Chapter, you will find a glossary of the most important terms in these two fields. For each of them, a short definition is included as well as the relevant provisions of the *ICC Rules on Combating Corruption* (2011), developed by the ICC Commission on Corporate Responsibility and Anti-corruption. A full version of the *ICC Rules on Combating Corruption* is available in Annex I of this Training Handbook.

Bribery is the offering, promising, authorizing or accepting of an undue advantage, a bribe, in order to obtain or retain an improper advantage, for instance in connection with public or private procurement contract awards, regulatory permits, taxation, customs, judicial and legislative proceedings. A bribe can consist of money or of any other advantage such as expensive gifts, a discount, a waived fee, an inflated fee for a consultancy contract, an inflated price for an item, a position for the bribed person or a person close to him or her, a medical treatment, or a vacation. Although bribery and corruption are often used indifferently, bribery has a narrower meaning than corruption, which is sometimes used to include practically any perversion of integrity.

Business partners is a term used to refer to any party associated with another party in the pursuit of business. Preventive anti-corruption measures are increasingly focusing on business partners since they are often used to perform high-risk activities on an enterprise's behalf.

> According to the *ICC Rules on Combating Corruption* (2011), enterprises should conduct appropriate due diligence on the reputation and capacity of their business partners, which include, for this purpose: third parties (as defined hereafter), joint venture and consortium partners, as well as contractors and suppliers. Enterprises should also have the possibility to suspend or terminate a relationship if they have a unilateral good faith concern that a business partner has engaged into corrupt practices.

- Third parties (when used in the context of anti-corruption) are parties subject to the control or determining influence of an enterprise; they include agents, business development consultants, sales representatives, customs agents, general consultants, resellers, subcontractors, franchisees, lawyers, accountants, or any kind of intermediaries; they act on an enterprise's behalf, often in connection with marketing or sales, the negotiation of contracts, the obtaining of licenses, permits or other authorizations, or other activities which benefit the enterprise.

    According to the *ICC Rules on Combating Corruption* (2011) enterprises have a responsibility to instruct third parties not to engage in corruption, not to use them as a channel for bribes, to hire them only to the extent appropriate for the regular conduct of the enterprise's business and not to pay them more than an appropriate remuneration for legitimate services. Enterprises should also obtain a commitment from third parties that they will not engage in any corrupt practice and should have the possibility to audit the third parties' books and accounting records. Payments to third parties should not be made in cash and should only be made in the country of their incorporation or residence, where their headquarters are located, or where the mission is executed. Enterprises should also ensure that their central management has adequate control over third parties and maintains a record of their names, terms of engagement and payments made to them.

    The *ICC Guidelines on Agents, Intermediaries and Other Third Parties* (2010)[2] and Chapter 14 of this Training Handbook provide further guidance on how to choose, monitor, and pay third parties.

- Joint venture or consortium partners are partners of an enterprise for a specific project or activity. Joint venture or consortium arrangements can take the form of a partnership or a joint subsidiary company. They may, however, be used as a subterfuge for corruption, especially when they involve a local partner in a country with a high corruption risk.

    The *ICC Rules on Combating Corruption* (2011) provide that enterprises should take measures within their powers to ensure that their anti-corruption policy is accepted by their joint venture or consortium partners with respect to the joint venture or consortium.

    Chapter 15 of this Training Handbook provides further guidance on how to manage corruption risks arising from joint ventures.

- Contractors and suppliers are parts of an enterprise's supply chain, linking together a supplier of materials or components, a manufacturer, a distributor or retailer, and ending with the consumer. A supply chain typically aims at rationalizing the distribution of work. However, outsourcing by an enterprise of certain functions to, for instance, local partners can be used by this enterprise as a way to avoid a direct involvement in areas particularly exposed to corruption.

---

[2] http://www.iccwbo.org/advocacy-codes-and-rules/document-centre/2010/icc-guidelines-on-agents,-intermediaries-and-other-third-parties/

> The *ICC Rules on Combating Corruption* (2011) provide that enterprises should take measures within their power and, as far as legally possible, ensure that their contractors and suppliers comply with the *ICC Rules on Combating Corruption* (2011) in their dealings with the enterprise or on behalf of the enterprise. Enterprises should also avoid dealing with contractors and suppliers known or reasonably suspected to be paying bribes.

Charitable contributions are donations made to support an organization dedicated to philanthropic goals such as educational, religious, social, or other activities serving the common good. However, charitable contributions can also be used to disguise a bribe when they benefit only a very limited group of individuals. This would be the case, for instance, of a foundation for heart diseases headed by the wife of a high ranking public official, which uses its funds to cover the costs of a heart operation for a child of this official.

> The *ICC Rules on Combating Corruption* (2011) provide that charitable contributions should be transparent and that enterprises should establish reasonable controls and procedures to ensure that no improper charitable contributions are made and that special care should be exercised in reviewing contributions to organizations in which prominent political figures, or their close relatives, friends, and business partners are involved.

Conflicts of interest arise when the private interests of an individual or of individuals close to him or her diverge from those of the organization to which the individual belongs. Conflicts of interest are a particular form of corruption where an individual grants himself or herself an improper advantage by exercising his or her decision-making power to his or her advantage (or to that of a person close to him or her). Typical conflicts of interest include hiring relatives or favouring relatives as suppliers of goods or services.

> The *ICC Rules on Combating Corruption* (2011) provide that enterprises should closely monitor and regulate actual or potential conflicts of interest, or the appearance thereof, of their directors, officers, employees, and agents and should not take advantage of conflicts of interest of others.

A **corporate compliance programme** is a programme which contains adequate procedures and is adopted by an enterprise to reduce the risk of corruption (and of other misconduct as specified in a corporate Code of Conduct). Under the *United Kingdom Bribery Act* (2010), unless a corporation can demonstrate the existence of such adequate procedures, it will be liable for any bribe paid by any person associated with it in relation to the conduct of its business. Although such strict liability does not exist under the law of other countries, the implementation of a compliance programme will be considered when determining the corporation's liability. Where no programme or only an insufficient programme exists, enforcement authorities may require the introduction or reinforcement of one and may impose a compliance 'monitor' during a certain period of time in order to ensure that it is properly implemented.

The *ICC Rules on Combating Corruption* (2011) include a list of elements to be included in a corporate compliance programme. This list, which is reproduced in Chapter 8 of this Training Handbook, reflects best practices featured in leading legal and guidance instruments.

Criminal liability is the liability, defined in a criminal code, which attaches to offences committed by either a physical person or a corporation and which are sanctioned by penalties (such as imprisonment, fines, debarment, or suspension of political or civic rights). The most usual form of criminal liability is the criminal liability of a physical person. Corporate criminal liability was introduced in relatively recent conventions and legislations.

Corporate criminal liability is the liability of a corporation that attaches to offences, such as corruption, committed in the conduct of the corporation's business. All countries having signed the *OECD Convention* (1997) had to introduce in their national law some form of corporate liability. The severest form of corporate criminal liability is that introduced by the *United Kingdom Bribery Act* (2010): it provides that corporations are criminally liable for corruptive acts unless they prove that they had adequate procedures in place to prevent corruption. Corporate criminal liability can extend to parent companies for acts of their subsidiaries if they knew or should have known that acts of corruption were taking place or if they did not have adequate preventive procedures in place.

Corruption is sometimes used restrictively as a synonym for bribery and sometimes extensively to connote any perversion of integrity. According to the *ICC Rules on Combating Corruption* (2011), corruption includes bribery, extortion or solicitation, and trading in influence, whether the intended recipient, extorter or solicitor of a bribe is a public official, a politician or a private individual. It also includes laundering the proceeds of corruption.

This definition is in line with the *United Nations Convention* (2003) and its provisions concerning the private sector; however, it goes further than the *OECD Convention* (1997), which deals with active bribery of foreign public officials (offering a bribe, for instance). The *OECD Convention* (1997) does not cover:

- the corruption of national officials;
- passive bribery, which includes accepting, extorting or soliciting a bribe;
- the bribing of politicians, unless they hold a public mandate (in which case they qualify as public officials); and
- private bribery (also called commercial bribery).

Furthermore, the *OECD Convention* (1997) only deals with bribery occurring in the conduct of international business.

In general, national laws implementing the *OECD Convention* (1997) cover both active and passive bribery of national and foreign public officials as well as bribery in the private sector. Some national laws also cover corruption of politicians, while only a few cover trading in influence.

- **Direct corruption** takes place when a bribe is passed on without intermediary from the briber (the giver of the bribe) to the recipient from whom an undue advantage is expected.
- **Indirect corruption** takes place when an intermediary, such as an agent, subcontractor, consultant or other third party, is used to channel a bribe.
- **Grand corruption** is the corruption that takes place in relation with the award of contracts for large orders or projects; it usually involves high-ranking officials, such as heads of government, ministers or their close relatives; the amount of bribes involved is large; they are often expressed as a percentage of the order or project and are typically transferred through intermediaries and letter box companies in tax havens.
- **Petty corruption** is the 'corruption of the poor'; it involves for instance a customs, harbour or immigration official, the police or an individual in charge of delivering permits, licenses, or other official documents; the amounts of the bribes are modest. The bribe can serve to accelerate an administrative procedure without breaching the law (in which case it will be considered a facilitation payment - see below for the definition of 'Facilitation Payments') or to obtain a preferential treatment in breach of the law.
- **Political corruption** is the corruption of politicians and political parties. It can involve amounts close to those of grand corruption. Its purpose is to create goodwill with a party in anticipation of its accession to power. Political corruption can also be organized by politicians in power in order to secure the financing of their party in anticipation of future elections. Both Helmut Kohl, the former Chancellor of Germany, and Jacques Chirac, the former President of France, have been convicted of participating in the organization of illegal financing for their parties. The United Kingdom has experienced a scandal revolving around loans granted to a party in exchange for life peerages. Such abuses in the area of the financing of political activities have led countries to regulate this domain. **Graft** is a form of political corruption in which a public official helps himself or herself to an improper advantage by abusing his or her position, or his or her political influence, for instance by buying land earmarked for government development knowing that its value will increase. **Clientelism** or **patronage** is the rewarding of political support with, for instance, the appointment to an office or the award of business or subsidies.
- **Private sector or private corruption** is any form of corruption where the purpose of the bribe is to entice a private person, such as a director, officer, or employee of a private sector enterprise to breach his or her duties towards that enterprise.
- **Public sector or public corruption** is any form of corruption where the purpose of the bribe is to obtain an undue advantage from an act or omission of a public official in relation with his or her public duties.

Extortion or solicitation is the demanding of a bribe, whether or not coupled with a threat if the demand is refused. In certain countries, police may for instance stop drivers to obtain a payment for a purported infringement. Extortion is generally not recognized as a justification against allegations of corruption. While the defenses of necessity and duress are available, they only apply in extreme situations, for instance when the health, security, or safety of individuals is involved.

> The *ICC Rules on Combating Corruption* (2011) provide that enterprises will oppose any attempt of extortion or solicitation; enterprises are further encouraged to report such attempts through available formal or informal reporting mechanisms, unless such reporting is deemed to be counterproductive under the circumstances.

> Chapter 13 of this Training Handbook and the RESIST scenarios[3] provide practical guidance on how to prevent and respond to inappropriate demands.

Facilitation payments are unofficial, improper small payments made to a low-level official to secure or expedite the performance of a routine or necessary action to which the payer of the facilitation payment is legally entitled, such as for instance obtaining official documents; processing papers, like visas and work orders; providing police protection, mail pick-up and delivery; obtaining a telephone line or power and water supply; loading and unloading cargo; or protecting perishable foodstuffs; scheduling inspections associated with contract performance or transit of goods across country. Facilitation payments do not fall within the ambit of the *OECD Convention* (1997) because they are not considered to constitute payments to obtain or retain business or other advantage. In its 2009 Recommendation, however, the OECD changed its position and encouraged "companies to prohibit or discourage the use of small facilitation payments in internal company controls, ethics and compliance programmes". Under the *United States Foreign Corrupt Practices Act* (1977), they are allowed but only if paid abroad. However, they are prohibited (but not always prosecuted) in several jurisdictions.

> According to the *ICC Rules on Combating Corruption* (2011), enterprises should not make facilitation payments, but it is recognized that they may be confronted with exigent circumstances, in which the making of a facilitation payment can hardly be avoided, such as duress or when the health, security or safety of the enterprise's employees are at risk. If a facilitation payment is made under such circumstances, it must be accurately accounted for in the enterprise's books and accounting records.

Favouritism or **nepotism** consists of favouring friends (favouritism or cronyism) or family members (nepotism, from the Italian word for nephew: nipote) without objective justification, for instance when hiring people or adjudicating orders. Favouritism or nepotism are forms of corruption or of conflicts of interest, which consist of granting an improper advantage to a close individual and so benefiting indirectly from that improper advantage.

---

[3] The RESIST toolkit was developed by ICC and three other international organizations involved in the fight against corruption. It is available at: http://www.iccwbo.org/products-and-services/fighting-commercial-crime/resist/

Gifts and hospitality are ways of expressing feelings of friendship or of welcoming guests and form part of the nexus of social customs. However, they can be, and in fact sometimes are, used as a subterfuge for corruption.

- **Gifts** are donations of an item or in some cases of money. Gifts are made at special occasions such as the New Year, a birth or a birthday, a wedding, a successful examination, a religious feast such as Christmas, or to express gratitude or friendship. In the business world, gifts are made to clients or business partners to reinforce a business relationship.

  Excessive gifts, beyond what is socially usual and acceptable, may be a subterfuge for corruption by creating a moral necessity to reciprocate with a favour; especially frequent and generous gifts may create a climate leading to a favourable treatment when the recipient will have to make a decision affecting the giver.

- **Hospitality** consists of expenses made to entertain guests, for instance by inviting them to a restaurant or to a sports or cultural event or by covering a guest's travel and accommodation expenses. Excessive hospitality may be a subterfuge for corruption.

Public officials in many countries are subject to precise rules with respect to gifts or hospitality which they may accept or not.

> According to the *ICC Rules on Combating Corruption* (2011), enterprises should establish procedures on the offer or receipt of gifts and hospitality in order to ensure that (i) they comply with national law and international instruments, (ii) are limited to reasonable and good faith expenditures, (iii) do not improperly affect, or be perceived as improperly affecting the recipient's independence of judgment towards the giver, (iv) are not contrary to the known provisions of the recipient's Code of Conduct, and (v) are neither offered nor received too frequently nor at an inappropriate time.

Intermediaries – see the definition for 'Third parties' above.

Kickbacks are a form of bribery which consists of returning, or sending back, a portion of a contract payment or of a bribe to government or political party officials or to employees of a contracting party, their close relatives, friends, or business partners. Kickbacks are often paid through an intermediary and on an account in an offshore financial centre.

Laundering the proceeds of corruption is a form of corruption consisting of concealing or disguising the illicit origin, source, location, disposition, movement, or ownership of property, knowing that such property is the proceeds of corrupt practices.

Political contributions are an acceptable way to support the democratic process. However, they can also be used for the purpose of political corruption (see above under 'Corruption – Political Corruption').

> The *ICC Rules on Combating Corruption* (2011) provide that enterprises should only make contributions to political parties, party officials, and candidates in accordance with applicable law and public disclosure requirements and that the amount and timing of political contributions should be reviewed to ensure that they are not used as a subterfuge for corruption. Enterprises should also establish reasonable controls and procedures to ensure that improper political contributions are not made.

Procurement is the process by which governments or enterprises manage their purchases of goods and services. Procurement is an area particularly exposed to corruption and procurement procedures are therefore key in the prevention of corrupt practices. They should aim at establishing a transparent process and at eliminating discretionary decisions in procurement processes in excess of defined figures.

> The *ICC Rules on Combating Corruption* (2011) provide that enterprises should conduct their own procurement in accordance with accepted business standards and in a transparent manner to the extent possible.

A **Public official** is any person holding a legislative, administrative, or judicial office at any level of government, national, or local. International civil servants are also public officials. Employees of public enterprises (enterprises over which a government exercises a dominant influence) are public officials unless the enterprise operates on a commercial basis on its market like a private enterprise. Employees of a private enterprise performing an activity in the public interest such as customs inspections or tasks delegated in connection with public procurement are also considered as public officials in that respect.

Restrictive practices are practices restricting competition in violation of competition law. Competition law was one of the initial focuses of the European integration process, since restrictive practices tend to prevent the integration of national markets. Now the focus of European Union competition law is more and more on the protection of customers. In the United States, antitrust law focused initially, as its name indicates, on the prevention of the formation of trusts or monopolies in a number of industries, such as railways, steel, oil, sugar, or aluminium.

Restrictive practices fall into the following categories:

- **Abuse of a dominant position**: there is a dominant position when an enterprise occupies most or all of a market, be it that it has absorbed or eliminated all or most of its competitors or that the market is too small to accommodate enough competitors for a workable competition; competition law does not prohibit the creation of a dominant position as such but does repress its abuses; these include refusing to deal, discriminatory pricing, dumping, imposing leonine conditions, or tying the purchase of products not naturally related. Competition law also attempts to keep the creation of dominant positions in check by imposing control procedures for mergers and acquisitions potentially leading to an uncompetitive market.

- **Horizontal agreements**: horizontal agreements take place between enterprises at the same level of the supply chain, for instance between suppliers, manufacturers or distributors of the same or similar products, and include among others price-fixing or the carving up of the market by allocating territories. A **cartel** is a horizontal agreement which includes all or most enterprises in an industry.
- **Vertical agreements**: vertical agreements take place between enterprises at different levels of the supply chain, for instance between a supplier or manufacturer and a distributor or retailer; they include among others exclusive dealing, territorial protection or resale price maintenance.
- **Exchange of information between competitors**: this is a sensitive practice in competition law, because the mere exchange of information between competitors can precede a restrictive practice; this will be the case of exchange of price (or other sensitive) information which can lead to concerted pricing behaviour in a market with a limited number of actors.

Revolving doors refer to the practice of offering an activity or employment to a public official after he or she leaves public office. A **cooling-off period** is the period recommended by good practices or imposed by law before a former public official can be offered an activity or employment relating directly to the functions held or supervised during his or her tenure.

> The *ICC Rules on Combating Corruption* (2011) provide that former public officials shall not be hired or engaged in any capacity before a reasonable period has elapsed after their leaving office, if their contemplated activity or employment relates directly to the functions held or supervised during their tenure. In any case, restrictions imposed by national legislation shall be observed.
>
> In OECD countries, the length of the cooling off period for public official varies from six months to five years. Most countries have, however, opted for a cooling off period in the order of one to two years.

Sponsorships are a special kind of donation whereby the sponsor supports typically a sports or arts event or a specific cause in return for exposure of its name and brand. Sponsorships are necessary to finance certain activities. However, they can also be used as a subterfuge for corruption.

> The *ICC Rules on Combating Corruption* (2011) provide that sponsorships should be transparent and in accordance with applicable law.

Trading in influence is a form of corruption consisting in the offering or soliciting of an undue advantage to a public official or any other person in order for the latter to exert an improper advantage, real, or supposed influence with a view to obtaining from a public official an undue advantage for the payer of the bribe or for any other person.

Whistleblowing refers to the reporting of misconduct, including any form of corruption, especially by individuals employed by the organization where this misconduct is taking place.

The *ICC Rules on Combating Corruption* (2011) provide that no employee shall suffer retaliation or discriminatory or disciplinary action for reporting in good faith violations or soundly suspected violations of the enterprise's anti-corruption policy or for refusing to engage in corruption, even if such refusal may result in the enterprise losing business. Enterprises are further expected to offer channels to raise, in full confidentiality, concerns, seek advice or report violations.

The *ICC Guidelines on Whistleblowing* (2008)[4] and Chapter 11 of this Training Handbook provide further guidance on how to establish internal whistleblowing systems.

About the author

Jean-Pierre Méan was General Counsel and Chief Compliance Officer for SGS, the world's leading verification, inspection, and certification company, from 1996 to 2008. In 2002 and 2003, he was Chief Compliance Officer for the European Bank for Development and Reconstruction in London before returning to his position at SGS. He is now Of Counsel at MCE Legal, a law firm based in Lausanne, Switzerland. Jean-Pierre Méan holds a doctor of laws degree from the University of Basle and an LL.M. from Harvard Law School, and is admitted to the bar in Switzerland and Canada. He is President of the Swiss Chapter of Transparency International and a member of the ICC Commission on Corporate Responsibility and Anti-corruption. He chaired the Task Force which drafted the *ICC Rules on Combating Corruption* (2011).

---

[4] http://www.iccwbo.org/advocacy-codes-and-rules/document-centre/2008/icc-guidelines-on-whistleblowing/

PART 2

HOW TO ORGANIZE COMPLIANCE
IN YOUR COMPANY

Chapter 5
Risk Assessment

Jean-Daniel Lainé*

Former Senior Vice-President, Ethics & Compliance, Alstom

In this Chapter, we move closer to the field and start with one of the most essential tasks you as ethics and compliance officer have to undertake: understanding and measuring your company's exposure to corruption and antitrust risks. This is usually done at the behest of the Board of Directors by performing a comprehensive and methodical review of these risks, an exercise otherwise known as an ethics and compliance risk assessment. This Chapter explains the basic steps for performing a risk assessment. The author then draws on his company's experience to illustrate some key practical aspects you should take into account as you plan and implement your company's own risk policy.

INTRODUCTION

Every company needs to identify, measure, and manage the most significant risks that may affect its business operations and jeopardize its social license to operate. Among these risks, corruption and antitrust require special attention. A single act of corruption or a single antitrust breach may indeed cause devastating legal, financial, and reputational damage for a company, its employees, and its shareholders.

Because illicit practices can appear in virtually any part of an enterprise, an important first step for a company and its Board of Directors is to understand the company's vulnerability to corruption and antitrust risks. This can be done by conducting a comprehensive and thorough ethics and compliance risk assessment (or risk evaluation), as described in the following pages. This management tool helps identify what could go wrong, the probability of occurrence, and the potential consequences should an incident occur.

---

* The author wishes to thank Tiphaine de Sachy, Compliance Officer, Alstom Integrity Programme Development, for her valuable contribution to the preparation of this Chapter.

THE ROLE OF THE BOARD OF DIRECTORS

Performing systematic reviews of your company's risks is not a 'nice to have' policy but rather an essential part of any proper governance approach. The OECD, in the *Principles of Corporate Governance* (2004)[5], states that reviewing and guiding the company's risk policy is one of the key functions of the Board of Directors. This allows Board members to act on a fully informed basis, in good faith, and with due diligence and care, as required by their fiduciary duties.

> **DO ALL COMPANIES PERFORM AN ANTI-BRIBERY AND CORRUPTION RISK ASSESSMENT?**
>
> The answer is: no, not every company does.
>
> The Global Anti-Bribery and Corruption Survey 2011, commissioned by KPMG and conducted with 214 executives of large companies in the United States and the United Kingdom tells us that a third of the respondents to the survey do not perform an anti-bribery and corruption risk assessment.
>
> Another survey conducted by PricewaterhouseCoopers with 144 members of the PwC Fraud Academy in April 2010 leads to a similar conclusion: 70% of respondents stated that ethical risks were identified (in a risk assessment exercise) but only 34% of respondents said that ethical risks were adequately measured and evaluated.

It is therefore a primary responsibility of the Board of Directors to give the initial impetus to the definition of the company's risk policy. It will do so by requesting the company's management to plan and implement a systematic ethics and compliance risk assessment. Once this has been done, and the results of the assessment have been presented to the Board, it is, again according to the OECD *Principles of Corporate Governance* (2004), the Board's duty to define the company's desired risk profile, specifying the types and degree of risk that the company is willing or not to accept in pursuit of its goals.

By defining the company's risk profile, the Board of Directors outlines the limits of the company's risk appetite. It establishes the rules and procedures for evaluating whether any particular industrial, commercial, or financial project (such as moving into a new country, embarking on a new product line, or using a new financial instrument) involves acceptable or unacceptable risks. In a number of companies, the Board of Directors will create a Risk Committee to cover the implementation of the company's risk policy.

AN ANALOGY

To explain the rationale behind conducting risk assessments, let's start with an analogy. For a dam project, engineers will focus on the main design to frame its structure and use calculations linked to resistance factors to test its robustness under all conditions. Their purpose is to anticipate and address all issues and risks which could arise during the dam's life. For these kinds of projects, risks are so huge that no stone should be left unturned in pursuit of safety. Every detail is critical.

---

[5] http://www.oecd.org/daf/ca/corporategovernanceprinciples/31557724.pdf

The assessment of bribery and corruption risks should be conducted in a comparable way. Risk assessment is a practical tool that enables a company to detect all risks and issues that can occur in business transactions. More detailed risk reviews may sometimes be necessary to fully embrace risks linked to specific activities or to certain types of business partners with whom the company may be engaged or that it may plan to engage.

> **AN ETHICS AND COMPLIANCE RISK ASSESSMENT IS A COMPREHENSIVE AND CONTINUOUS PROCESS FOR:**
> - Understanding a company's exposure to ethics and compliance risks;
> - Identifying the most significant business process risks;
> - Evaluating the extent and adequacy of existing controls or mitigation factors;
> - Modifying control or mitigation factors to address gaps, areas for improvement and implement adequate procedures; and
> - Monitoring controls to ensure that the procedures are effectively performing.

METHODOLOGY FOR CONDUCTING AN ETHICS AND COMPLIANCE RISK ASSESSMENT

There is no 'one size fits all' solution for conducting ethics and compliance risk assessments. Each company's risk assessment approach should be designed in a way that is proportionate to its size, the nature of its business, its organizational structure, and the geographical diversity of its operations.

The ethics and compliance risk assessment of a company can be performed on a stand-alone basis. It is, however, increasingly common to integrate such specific exercise in a broader assessment of all risks the company faces, as is done in Enterprise Risk Management. By using an integrated approach, an enterprise can avoid inconsistencies between separate risk assessments and ensure that the risk assessment is updated regularly and receives appropriate attention from senior management.

There are three basic steps to conducting an ethics and compliance risk assessment, as illustrated in the diagram below:

It is essential to identify key risk factors through an overall analysis of the enterprise's business operations and the key drivers of its commercial successes: its products, its services, its customers, its marketing channels, and its geographical markets.

A whole range of external and internal factors can have a direct impact on the corruption and antitrust risks that a company may face. For example:

EXTERNAL FACTORS

Country risk Some countries (or regions) have a higher perceived corruption risk stemming from a lack of anti-corruption legislation, a low level of enforcement, weak institutions, or an overall lack of transparency.

Sectoral risk Some industry sectors are said to be more prone to corruption than others, such as extractive industries. Special attention should also be devoted to large-scale infrastructure projects.

Transaction risk Special attention should be given to business transactions concluded between companies and governments, government agencies, or government-affiliated enterprises (for example through public tenders); this will also be the case for projects that involve high value transactions and for business activities which are subject to licenses or permits delivered by public officials.

Business partnership risk The use of business partnerships, such as joint ventures, consortiums, or agents, intermediaries, contractors, and other third parties, may constitute an additional risk factor.

INTERNAL FACTORS

Size of the organization Affiliates and other group entities not totally under the control of the company or in shared control should be given special attention.

Organizational structure Is the organization centralized or decentralized? Group entities in remote locations or subject to limited reporting obligations may form another risk factor.

Leadership and governance Entities with non-conventional governance models require special care.

History of claims, litigation, and external inquiries In the presence of existing or past legal issues, an analysis of their impact and recurrence will be required (with the help of internal and external lawyers).

The method a company decides to adopt to address all its identified risks and to implement mitigation action will also depend on the way it is structured and organized. Based on the assessment for each specific risk, a centralized or decentralized approach may be preferred. Note, in this context, that the *ICC Rules on Combating Corruption* (2011) recommend that enterprises ensure that their central management has adequate control over third parties and maintains a record of their names, terms of engagement, and payments to them.

ALSTOM'S RISK ASSESSMENT PROCESS

The Alstom Integrity Programme

Like all companies involved in infrastructure projects, Alstom is exposed to numerous risks. These risks may be of a technical, financial, political, or legal nature. They may relate to health, safety, and environmental issues. The company may also face risks relating to fraud, corruption, and infringements of competition law. To help face these risks, Alstom has put integrity at the top of its corporate agenda and seeks to promote a visible culture of ethics and compliance.

To implement such policy in a global group of nearly 100,000 employees, Alstom has set up the Alstom Integrity Programme, which is built on a Code of Ethics, detailed corporate rules and instructions, as well as on training and communication activities. The Alstom Integrity Programme covers a large scope of ethics and compliance issues and areas relating to business transactions and personal integrity, such as:

- Prevention of corruption;
- Competition law;
- Business advisors, representatives, and resellers;
- Joint ventures and consortiums;
- Suppliers and sub-contractors;
- Engineering and project management;
- Conflicts of interest;
- Charitable and political contributions;
- Gifts and hospitality; and
- Sponsorships

The Alstom Integrity Programme, which is supported by a dedicated professional team, is continuously enhanced through meetings and exchanges of good practices with industry peers, anti-corruption experts, and specialized law firms. To achieve a best-in-class programme, a regular certification process has been put in place in 2009.

The Programme is based on a careful assessment of the specific ethics and compliance risks to which the company is exposed. The Alstom ethics and compliance risk assessment is part of the group's risk management policy and constitutes a section of the company's yearly risk assessment review and risk mapping exercise.

Ethics and compliance in the context of Alstom's Risk Mapping exercise

Since 2006, Alstom conducts a yearly risk assessment review as a part of the preparation of its annual budget and of its three-year planning process. The objective is to update the group's risk mapping exercise by identifying, analysing, and anticipating significant risks facing the company. The risk assessment review is prepared with the input of the company's four industrial sectors (Thermal Power, Renewable Power, Grid, and Transport) and of the main corporate functions, including internal control; internal audit; finance; tenders and projects; information systems; human resources; legal; ethics and compliance; and environment, health and safety.

At the Board of Directors level, the Ethics, Compliance, and Sustainable Development Committee is responsible for reviewing the mapping of ethics, compliance, sustainable development, and social responsibility risks and for advising the Board of Directors about identified risks and existing risk prevention procedures. The updated risk mapping and the main elements of the risk management system are presented every year to the company's Audit Committee and to the Board of Directors.

Through this exercise, Alstom is able to take into account the effect potential events may have on the achievement of its corporate business objectives. Such events are considered from two perspectives, namely 'likelihood' and 'impact'. The 'likelihood' element represents the possibility that a given event occurs, while the 'impact' element represents the potential operational, financial, and legal consequences such event may have on the company. A combination of qualitative and quantitative criteria is used in making these assessments.

Data from past events are incorporated into risk assessments, as they provide a more objective basis than subjective assessments. Detailed information on the potential impact and likelihood of occurrences is checked and assessed. Potential events are assessed both individually and as part of a sequence or of a combination of events.

A time horizon of three years is used to assess the impact of risk. Accordingly, a proposed mitigation action is also included in the annual budget and the three-year plan. Any major risk assessed outside a three-year period is continuously kept under review. The risk mapping exercise also allows confirming that the appropriate insurance cover has been obtained for insurable risk.

Because it is advisable and useful to document every risk assessment, the Ethics and Compliance Department of Alstom produces a risk sheet every year. This risk sheet contains the following elements:

- A description of ethics and compliance risks and their causes;
- An evaluation of potential consequences;
- An analysis of the (long-term) evolution of risks;
- Actions already implemented to mitigate identified risks;
- Actions still to be implemented to mitigate risks; and
- Indicators for monitoring risks and the effectiveness of the mitigation action.

Alstom's Ethics and Compliance Risk Assessment

To gather more detailed information on corruption risks and to ensure that all potential risks have been taken into account, the Ethics and Compliance Department of Alstom also conducts its own Ethics and Compliance Risk Assessment.

The Ethics and Compliance Risk Assessment is designed to:

- Help set key priorities;
- Share findings with key internal stakeholders;
- Create the most appropriate ethics and compliance programme for the company;
- Assess the effectiveness of current tools;
- Develop new actions to mitigate risks; and
- Ensure the continuous improvement of the Alstom Integrity Programme.

The Ethics and Compliance Risk Assessment is based on an in-depth analysis of the group's activities with a focus on the following aspects:

- **Its business model**: industry; markets; countries; customers;
- **Its operational processes**: tendering (including through the use of intermediaries); sales; engineering; sourcing; procurement; supply chain; project execution (including partnerships and consortiums);
- **Its support functions**: strategy (mergers and acquisitions, joint-ventures); legal; human resources; finance;
- **Cross-cutting topics**: gifts and hospitality; charitable and political contributions; conflicts of interest; facilitation payments.

A total of 40 items form part of the Ethics and Compliance Risk Assessment. Each item is ranked on a scale of four steps from 'low' to 'very high' risk. For each item, the company identifies mitigation factors, which are either currently in place or which remain to be implemented.

The analysis of ethics and compliance risks is complemented by external sources of information, including the following documents:

- The *United States Federal Sentencing Guidelines*[6];
- The *United Kingdom Bribery Act* (2010)[7] and its Guidance[8];
- The *OECD Guidelines for Multinational Enterprises* (2011)[9];
- The *ICC Rules on Combating Corruption* (2011);
- The *Transparency International Business Principles for Countering Bribery* (2009); and
- The *Transparency International Corruption Perceptions Index (CPI)*.

In particular, the company conducts every year a 'country risk analysis', which is prepared on the basis of the CPI and which takes into account the company's geographical footprint in terms of sales. Countries are ranked according to their risk level in the following way:

- CPI value between 7.5 to 10 = Moderate risk countries;
- CPI value between 5 to 7.5 = Medium risk countries;
- CPI value between 2.5 to 5 = High risk countries; and
- CPI value between 0 to 2.5 = Very high risk countries

Specific risk reviews of business partners: the example of business advisors

As a further step in the Alstom risk assessment process, the company conducts more detailed risk reviews for certain categories of business partners.

The matrix below combines two criteria: (i) the level of exposure to corruption risk and (ii) the required level of control for each category of business partners the company is dealing with.

---

[6] http://www.ussc.gov/Guidelines/2011_guidelines/Manual_HTML/8b2_1.htm
[7] http://www.legislation.gov.uk/ukpga/2010/23/contents
[8] http://www.justice.gov.uk/downloads/legislation/bribery-act-2010-guidance.pdf
[9] http://www.oecd.org/daf/inv/mne/oecdguidelinesformultinationalenterprises.htm

Corruption Risk exposure level high	Tenders Consortiums Joint Ventures Acquisitions *Ongoing and ad hoc reviews*	Business Advisors *Strict control and management*
low	Minority Shareholding/Participation Partnerships *No specific concern*	Suppliers and Sub-Contractors *Periodic reviews*
	low **Control level** high	

At a glance, we see that business advisors, also called agents or sales intermediaries, constitute a type of business partner that represents a high risk. Therefore, the company puts a high level of control for business advisors.

Alstom has put in place a system designed to ensure it only engages or does business with reputable and qualified business advisors who have an appropriate level of skills, expertise and resources, and who (i) act with integrity, (ii) are compliant with applicable laws and regulations, (iii) enjoy an untarnished reputation, and, (iv) do not create conflicts of interest with Alstom employees, its customers, or any public official.

Before any business advisor is appointed, a thorough due diligence is undertaken to assess the suitability of such appointment. As part of the due diligence process, Alstom checks and compiles information on the business advisor's company status, financial background, reputation, media exposure, and legal records (for instance by examining any past criminal investigations or fines). In addition, Alstom orders a business intelligence report from an independent firm.

In addition, risks are mitigated through the introduction of strict anti-corruption clauses in contracts with business advisors, and by running a comprehensive check before any payment is made.

Business advisors working for Alstom are asked to submit an updated 'business advisor profile' at least every second year after their initial appointment, but also whenever there is a significant change in circumstances, or at any other time at the request of the company. The company also orders an update of the original business intelligence report.

Due diligence is fully updated on a regular basis, and fully reviewed every second year.

CONCLUSION

Risk assessment generally follows the well-known trilogy: identifying, measuring, and managing risks. This exercise is the cornerstone of any robust ethics and compliance programme. It is a powerful management tool which helps detect the most sensitive areas in a company and allows allocating resources where they are most needed. It is accurately documented in regularly produced reports. It also provides a basis for designing appropriate mitigation action and defining the key priorities of a company's compliance programme.

About the author

Jean-Daniel Lainé was Senior Vice-President for Ethics & Compliance at Alstom from January 2006 to June 2013. Jean-Daniel is a mechanical and electrical engineer and graduated in Finance at Sorbonne University. He started his career at Compagnie Electro-Mécanique in France. He joined Alstom in 1983 and held different operational positions in power generation and transportation activities, followed by various functional positions in Strategic Development, International Network, Finance and Human Resources. He was appointed Vice President at the Chairman's Office in 1999 and then Vice-President, Compliance, for Power sectors in 2004.

Chapter 6
The Role of the Board of Directors

Pedro Montoya*

Group Chief Compliance Officer of EADS

The success of any corporate ethics and compliance policy will critically depend on the 'Tone at the Top' set by the company's leadership. In this respect, your company's Board of Directors has a crucial role to play in providing explicit support for the company's ethics and compliance programme and in designing a governance system in which the ethics and compliance function can operate. In this Chapter, we explore some of the key duties and responsibilities of your company's Board of Directors in these areas. In particular, we look at some of the concrete steps your Board of Directors can take to empower the ethics and compliance function and to create a genuine culture of integrity within the company.

THE BUSINESS OF BUSINESS IS BUSINESS?

Not so long ago, it was widely accepted that the only objective of any business was to reach adequate levels of profitability: the business of business was business. As long as a company was making money, and that it was doing it legally, everything was fine.

Things have changed dramatically in recent years. Your company is still expected to be profitable, but in addition it will have to take into account the broader expectations of society and the possible impact of its activities on the communities in which it operates. In other words, your company's behaviour should meet the expectations of its stakeholders, while its corporate structure should ensure an appropriate degree of transparency and accountability.

This entails two basic consequences: first, the highest governance body in your company (for the sake of simplicity, the Board of Directors) and particularly its Audit Committee has a duty to define how the company will discharge its social responsibilities, and second, it has to set the standard for the company's ethical behaviour.

---

* The author was assisted by François Vincke, co-editor of the Handbook, for the preparation of this Chapter.

> **Pressure on the Board**
>
> "The board, and in particular the audit committee, has a key role to play in assisting the company to mitigate the risk of bribery and corruption. Regulators have made it clear that a top-level commitment to an anti-bribery and anti-corruption culture is required from the board. Key elements of an effective anti-bribery and anti-corruption compliance program require significant board input and sponsorship. The audit committee is, among other things, responsible for overseeing fraud, bribery and corruption risk assessments and the related controls and compliance programs".
>
> Source: *Growing Beyond: a place for integrity*, Ernst & Young, 12th Global Fraud Survey, 2012, p. 14.

WHY BOARDS NEED TO ACT

New corporate governance theories, while redefining the distribution of roles and powers within companies, have imposed high standards of accountability on Board members and corporate executives in the discharge of their duties. Directors and executives have to attend to company business by adequately and efficiently performing their fiduciary duties with loyalty and care, and in the best interests of their company and its shareholders and stakeholders. They have to provide – in a spirit of transparency – timely, accurate, and relevant information on material matters concerning the company.

According to the *OECD Principles of Corporate Governance* (2004)[10], "The Board has a key role in setting the ethical tone of a company, not only by its own actions, but also in appointing and overseeing key executives and consequently the management in general. High ethical standards are in the long-term interests of the company as a means to make it credible and trustworthy, not only in the day-to-day operations but also with respect to longer-term commitments".

TONE AT THE TOP

To start with, there should be a clear message from the Board of Directors and the Chief Executive Officer that fraudulent, corrupt, and anti-competitive practices are prohibited, and that preventive measures will be put in place to shield the company and its business partners from such practices. Such a clear and unequivocal message from the highest level in the corporation will be essential to lay the basis for a genuine ethics and compliance policy.

Boards of smaller companies should not shy away from their ethical responsibility as they are, even to a larger extent than their more sizeable counterparts, exposed to severe compliance risks. As suppliers or subcontractors of larger groups, smaller companies will sometimes receive the support of their lead contractors and corporate customers. However, to take ownership of their compliance efforts, smaller companies should also have a proactive attitude and decide for themselves how best to articulate their own set of values and ethical practices.

---

[10] http://www.oecd.org/daf/ca/corporategovernanceprinciples/31557724.pdf

'Tone at the Top' is critical for setting the ethical culture of a company

The survey commissioned by PricewaterhouseCoopers in April 2010 and mentioned earlier in Chapter 5 has shown "a resounding agreement from respondents that Tone from the Top is vital in developing and maintaining the ethical integrity of the business. Without it, the ability to mitigate the risk of something going wrong is significantly impaired".

Source: *Tone from the Top: Transforming words into action*, PricewaterhouseCoopers, April 2010, p.4.

... AND VOICE FROM THE BOTTOM

The affirmation of a basic set of values by the Board of Directors and the Chief Executive Officer will have a greater impact if it seeks to integrate the input and experience of the company's managers and employees. In other words, the 'Voice from the Bottom' should also be heard. Hearing the 'Voice from the Bottom' will give additional credibility and reliability to the Board's message as it will also be based on the positive and forward-looking contributions brought by the company's employees, and in particular the younger ones.

Many leading companies have launched their ethics and compliance policy only after having extensively tested its principles and implementation in the various business segments and geographical areas where they operate. Ultimately, the Board of Directors will have to take responsibility for formulating the company's policy, but the 'Tone at the Top' will have a stronger repercussion if all in the company, or as many as possible, are given an opportunity to shape its content.

A practical example: how to deal with gifts, hospitality, and entertainment

A major French company wanted to set rules on the offering and receiving of gifts, hospitality, and entertainment. The top management started by establishing a general framework, which was made compulsory for the whole organization, but refrained from imposing uniform conditions on certain specific issues, such as the value of gifts, hospitality and entertainment under which it would not be required to have the prior approval of a principal. The company then asked its subsidiaries and affiliates 'to fill in the blanks' with what they considered the most compliant and appropriate practices in the light of their respective regulatory and business environments. By not imposing worldwide uniform standards, and by associating various parts of the group to the elaboration of the rules, the company was able to create a feeling of ownership and obtain the buy-in of employees for the implementation of these rules.

EXEMPLARITY

The duty of Boards of Directors and Chief Executive Officer will be to provide, in words and deeds, an example of preferred ethical behaviour and to indicate what should be done at all levels of the company to address ethical lapses. In corporate messages from top management to co-workers, it will be important to set forth the values of the company, the prohibitions on unethical behaviour, and the recommended best practices.

In doing so, the Board and the company executives should not only express a normative view of what the company's ethical model should be. They should also perform their day-to-day professional duties in an exemplary way, without seeking to benefit from elusive privileges, to enjoy far-fetched exemptions from corporate rules, or to grant themselves immunity for their mistakes.

Their behaviour, right or wrong, will be scrutinized and commented upon by everyone in the company. Co-workers will take the top management's attitudes as a yardstick for determining what is permissible and what is prohibited. Why indeed would anyone care for the rules if they are bluntly ignored by those who issued them? On the contrary, if top management demonstrates that it intends to go by the book, corporate rules will permeate much more smoothly and permanently throughout the company.

CREATING AN ETHICS AND COMPLIANCE PROGRAMME

The next step will be for your company's Board of Directors to establish a system for prohibiting misbehaviour, preventing illegal and unethical conduct, and imposing sanctions in case of infringement of corporate standards. This prevention system should be incorporated into an efficient corporate ethics and compliance programme. Such programme should be fully endorsed by the Board of Directors and the Chief Executive Officer. Article 10 of the *ICC Rules on Combating Corruption* (2011) (reproduced in Chapter 8) provides an extensive list of processes and instruments which they may opt to include as part of the programme, based on what is most adapted to the company's size and resources. The Board of smaller companies will probably select a limited number of such measures.

'All hands on deck'

Nobody should remain idle when ethics and compliance are at stake. Corporate policies should indicate that all those working for your company – executives, officers, and employees alike – will have to act in compliance with the ethics and compliance programme. It should be made clear that compliance with corporate policies is the responsibility of all individuals at all levels of your company and that there is no place for exceptions or privileges.

Control measures

Ethics and compliance cannot be decreed, it has to be organized. The mere promulgation of one or more documents full of good intentions will not suffice. Your company's Board of Directors should select and endorse the proper control and compliance methods to make the rules a living part of your company's daily activities.

In doing so, the Board will have to make a number of important choices. Your Board may either opt for a centralized and uniform compliance organization or it may prefer, based on the nature of the company's business, to entrust the compliance function to its subsidiaries and affiliates. The Board can go for a full blown whistleblowing system or, on the contrary, it may rely on the company's traditional means of communication. The Board may give priority to internal controls rather than to external controls. Furthermore, in case the Board would like to ensure that its compliance measures are in line with internationally recognized best practices, it may ask a specialized certification, verification, or assurance body for advice on how to possibly upgrade the company's programme.

The company's governing body has to demonstrate its commitment to the programme: it cannot establish a number of rules, and then appear uninterested in their effective application. If it were to do so, it could be criticized for using a corporate Code of Conduct and an ethics and compliance programme as mere public relations or marketing tools, or worse, as devices primarily designed to shield senior management from responsibility for the actions of subordinates.

THE CORPORATE GOVERNANCE OF COMPLIANCE

In particular, a key responsibility of the Board of Directors will be to establish an ethics and compliance function and to design a governance system in which it can operate:

- **Appointment of a Chief Ethics and Compliance Officer**

The appointment of the Chief Ethics and Compliance Officer (or any suitably senior individual in the organization with another title but a similar function) should be made by the Board of Directors, probably after having been debated in the Audit Committee (or, in certain companies, the Ethics Committee). The Chief Ethics and Compliance Officer should have a deep knowledge of the company's business and governance structure, as well as an impeccable professional and ethical record. This person should enjoy the trust of all his or her co-workers.

- **Empowerment of the ethics and compliance function**

As explained in Chapter 1 of the Handbook, the newly appointed holder of the compliance function should be given a clear mandate and mission statement. The mandate given by the Board of Directors will be the cornerstone of the Chief Ethics and Compliance Officer's empowerment. It should be followed up by a roadmap to be approved by the Board. The Chief Ethics and Compliance Officer's position on the organizational chart should enable him or her to report directly either to the Board of Directors (or to its Chairman) or to the Audit Committee (or to its Chairman) or alternatively to the Chief Executive Officer.

- **Setting objectives and defining responsibilities**

The mission of the ethics and compliance function will take the form of an operational programme contained in a roadmap. The roadmap should start with a risk assessment, which will be constantly updated and adapted to the company's changing circumstances. The mission of the new ethics and compliance function should be easily traceable with a set of quantitative and qualitative objectives that can be measured through performance indicators. The ethics and compliance function will be accountable for these objectives.

- **Resources allocated to ethics and compliance**

To fulfil these objectives, the Board of Directors should ensure that the ethics and compliance function enjoys the necessary support from the company's management. In particular, the Chief Ethics and Compliance Officer should receive assurance that the ethics and compliance function will receive the financial and human means required to fulfil its task. This starts with a team of skilful and trained professionals with access to company resources, such as corporate training facilities and internal communication tools.

- **Monitoring the ethics and compliance programme**

The Chief Ethics and Compliance officer will have to report to the Board of Directors or the Audit Committee on a regular basis (and possibly every time the need arises). Such reporting should include a presentation and discussion of a dashboard describing the objectives of the ethics and compliance programme and highlighting the most significant developments relating to the implementation of different compliance policies and the management of misconduct (enquiries, investigations, and sanctions). Thanks to these periodic reviews, top management and the compliance function will be able to share views about the evolution of the programme and propose improvements when needed.

CONTINUOUS MONITORING AND INTERNAL CONTROLS

When designating the departments or individuals who can best ensure effective day-to-day control of the implementation of the ethics and monitoring programme, the Board of Directors should take into consideration the nature and structure of the organization.

No two companies are alike. Some may have stronger controlling bodies than others, for instance external and internal auditors, corporate or outside lawyers, and human resources departments, which in each company have their strengths and weaknesses. On this basis, the Board will have to determine whom to entrust with which control function. In general, control over accounting and financial recording will be entrusted to financial managers and auditors, while behaviour, as it relates to compliance with ethical standards, is more likely to be the province of management or corporate lawyers.

Having designated the specific departments and individuals, the Board will have to determine – and its Audit Committee will have to oversee – the systems or procedures for control and decide how, and with what frequency, the controls will be exercised. Such procedures should be devised with the aim of preventing violations of the company's Code of Conduct and of its ethics and compliance programme. The greater the risk of violation, the more stringent the procedures should be. As always in business, the means to be used should be adjusted to the specific circumstances the company is facing.

MAKING MAJOR COMPLIANCE DECISIONS

Beyond its function of conducting periodic reviews of the ethics and compliance programme, the Board of Directors will be called upon to make major decisions which will define the contours of the programme and its practical implementation. In particular, it may be involved in making the following determinations:

- Tolerating facilitation payments (under certain conditions) or fully prohibiting them;
- Establishing a gifts, hospitality, and entertainment policy (with or without a monetary ceiling);
- Defining reasonable, proportionate, and dissuasive disciplinary sanctions for verified violations of the ethics and compliance programme;
- Installing a whistleblowing system in the company and under which conditions;
- Supporting the participation of the company in collective action initiatives, such as proposing or joining anti-corruption pacts regarding specific projects or anti-corruption long-term initiatives with the public sector and with peers in the company's respective business segments; and
- Supporting the company's participation in programmes conducted by business or professional associations in the field of ethics and compliance.

GROUP-WIDE COMPLIANCE

The Board of Directors should not devote attention only to what happens within the parent corporation. The ethical policies put in place by the parent company's Board should be applied in the economic group in its entirety, at home as well as abroad, in all of the group's divisions, branches, wholly-owned subsidiaries, and majority-held joint ventures, as well as in affiliates in which the group exercises de facto control or a large influence. Moreover, as far as feasible, they should be applied in all non-controlled entities working closely with the corporation. A special effort will be required to make subcontractors, outsourcing partners, and intermediaries aware of, and compliant with, company standards. Worldwide policies will be applied uniformly but some room should be left for differences between national jurisdictions, whenever the laws and regulations of certain countries require a specific approach (as for instance on private data protection).

About the author

Pedro Montoya was appointed Group Chief Compliance Officer by the Board of Directors of EADS in October 2008. Under the authority of the Board's Audit Committee, he designed and set up the newly created Corporate Compliance Office. Reporting to the Group CEO, he leads the EADS Ethics and Compliance Programme with 190 full time employees. Mr. Montoya graduated from the Universidad Complutense of Madrid and obtained his Master in Laws by the Instituto de Empresa. He started his career in 1986 in Procter & Gamble and four years later joined the Spanish Aerospace Group CASA where he became General Counsel and Company Secretary. Before his appointment as Group Chief Compliance Officer of EADS, he served three years as General Counsel of EADS International.

Chapter 7
Codes of Conduct
Dominique Lamoureux
Vice-President, Ethics and Corporate Responsibility, Thales

Introducing a Code of Conduct into a company requires preparation and should be the result of a process involving all stakeholders. To create ownership of your company's Code of Conduct, every effort must be made to bring to the table all those involved in integrity matters. In this Chapter, we learn about the key steps in producing a Code of Conduct. We discuss the purpose of a Code and its content (with a focus on provisions and guidelines relating to anti-corruption and antitrust), how to promote it, and dealing with possible violations. What is essential is that your company's Code of Conduct be genuinely credible, so that all employees can accept it as a guide to their daily business behaviour.

INTRODUCTION

To be a 'responsible company' means behaving ethically, caring for the environment, and setting an example as a business and as an employer. By developing a Code of Conduct, your company creates an agreed and shared way of behaving and operating that all employees can understand and comply with.

The Code of Conduct of your company will be the stepping stone on the way to a new integrity model. As we have seen in Chapter 5 of this Training Handbook, an organization starts by conducting a full risk assessment. Once it has mapped its strengths and weaknesses on the ethics and compliance front, it defines the basic rules which will underlie its ethical approach. Many stakeholders will provide input into the drafting of the Code, but it will be up to the Board of Directors (or the highest body of the company) to give the document its ultimate sanction, thereby expressing the 'Tone from the Top'.

Some companies prefer speaking about their Ethical Charter, others will be more inclined to refer to their Company's Values, and others will use yet another name. Our recommendation is simple: do not stumble over terminology, concentrate on the content.

ICC does not believe that all Codes should be the same or even that they have to look alike. On the contrary, a Code should reflect the specific culture and spirit of each individual company or of a sector of activity. The diversity of corporate Codes is proof of their authenticity. Clearly, the basic principles will always be the same, but the approach taken by every individual company will be different from one company to the other.

What is essential is that a Code of Conduct be genuinely credible, so that all parts of the organization can accept it as a guide to their daily business behaviour. Compliance with it should be natural in all circumstances. In short, all members of the organization should become owners of 'their' Code.

Beyond that, the Code of Conduct should incite all employees to be fully responsible for their behaviour: we are not talking here about simple, servile respect for the rules, based on compliance. This process implies trusting and respecting the judgment of employees. The famous French economist Jean-Baptiste Say was saying the same thing way back in the 19th century: "If you want to be obeyed, the last thing to do is to order people to obey you. It is not enough to want people to do something; you must entice them to do it."

Codes of Conduct are important to employees

In March 2007, Ernst & Young surveyed a large number of multinationals in 13 European countries and found that: *"Employees are not hostile to corporate anti-fraud measures and would welcome clarity and encouragement to act positively in the best interests of the company."*

Ernst & Young further noted that: *"Most people would prefer to work in an environment which has a code of conduct. Most respondents [to the survey] believe that people in their companies need a unified and agreed set of guidelines on what is right and wrong in the company [...]. Without a code of conduct, employees are left to work it out for themselves, and there is no clear set of standards other than their own personal ethics against which behavior can be measured.*

Source: *A Survey Into Fraud Risk Mitigation in 13 European Countries*, Ernst & Young, 2007

WHAT IS A CODE OF CONDUCT?

The purpose of a Code

A Code of Conduct is a summary of the principles and standards of business conduct that all employees, wherever they operate, are expected to follow. The phrase 'all employees' means in this context: all persons on the payroll at the parent company, but also at all its divisions, subsidiaries and affiliates and, as much as possible, in the entities over which the company has a significant influence. In addition, all agents, intermediaries and other third parties with whom the company has a contractual relationship should be requested to adhere to the Code. All these persons should find in the Code, and its accompanying material, practical guidance on how to deal with important ethical issues. The Code should offer general guidance on situations that may arise in the day-to-day activities conducted on behalf of the company.

A CODE OF CONDUCT SERVES TO AFFIRM THE FOLLOWING PRINCIPLES OF CONDUCT:
- Comply with the law at all times;
- Conduct business with honesty and integrity; and
- Have zero tolerance for corruption.

All employees should be familiar with the Code of Conduct and live up to the standards set by it. No Code of Conduct will ever answer all questions, nor will it offer ready-made solutions to all ethical dilemmas which may arise when conducting business. It is only the beginning, not the end, of a process. A Code of Conduct should continue to evolve as the company does. New regulations may apply and new risks may arise. The guidelines contained in the Code may vary according to local laws.

How to write a Code of Conduct?

In view of the foregoing, it would be wise not to delegate the responsibility for drafting your company's Code of Conduct to outside consultants or experts unaware of your company's culture. On the contrary, every effort should be made to bring together around the drafting table all those segments of your company which can bring a distinctive contribution to the development of this important document. While the final responsibility for adopting the text will lie with the Board of Directors, all divisions of your company should be involved and consulted during the drafting process. Those in charge of human resources and legal matters should have a decisive role, but this should not inhibit contributions from managers of local affiliates, marketing operatives, internal auditors, accountants, treasury staff, and all parts of your organization that deal with matters concerning integrity on a daily basis.

If, at the outset, people of various professional, cultural, and educational horizons are brought together during the drafting phase, the final Code will have an enhanced legitimacy and gain greater acceptance. The drafting process will take time and may involve difficult discussions. Some drafters may opt for a hard line. They may want to impose stringent rules and impose a zero tolerance standard, while others may prefer a more lenient course. There could also be a confrontation between those who want to cover as many details as possible (to avoid future problems of interpretation) and others who prefer broader, more open principles.

A Code of Conduct should be written in a way that is easy to read and to understand for everyone. Avoid legalese and other sophisticated expressions. Translate the Code into the main languages used within your company and in the countries where it operates. If the Code of Conduct is opaque and uses overly complicated terminology, some employees may misinterpret it or simply not understand its content.

Depending on the diverse regulatory provisions or local customs or practices, it may be required, convenient, or simply desirable to associate trade union representatives with the common effort, for instance in matters concerning disciplinary sanctions in case of non-compliance, or on the introduction of a whistleblower hotline or an ethical alert system. A discussion with the unions and their acceptance of the agreed rules will increase the credibility of the texts, around which everyone will be inclined to unite.

How to make your Code of Conduct known?

The Code of Conduct is a charter for the company: it should be launched and rolled out with some fanfare. It should be easy to find copies of the document, and 'all employees', as defined above, should be provided with printed copies. To make the Code fully accessible, upload it on your company's intranet. In some companies, all newly hired employees are asked to sign an acknowledgement form confirming that they have read the Code of Conduct and that they agree to abide by its provisions. If possible, all employees should be required to make or repeat similar acknowledgements on a periodic basis.

Who should comply with the Code?

A Code of Conduct should be applicable without discrimination or privilege to all echelons of the company from the Board of Directors to the workers on the shop floor. This is true for all persons working on behalf of the company, be they full or part time, permanent or temporary, executive or subordinate, white collar or blue collar.

WHAT TO FIND IN A CODE OF CONDUCT

Complying with the law

As a general principle, employees should comply with the law. They should act with integrity and honesty in all matters, and be accountable for their activities. They need to use good judgment in fulfilling their job and avoid even the appearance of improper behaviour.

Integrity means doing what is right. There should be compliance with laws and regulations applicable in the countries where the company operates, pursuant to the provisions established by the United Nations, the OECD and the International Labour Organization, and the European Union, especially on matters relating to anti-corruption, competition, and employment.

Violations of the law should be avoided under all circumstances. In particular, it is expected from employees that they avoid indulging in activities and behaviour that could involve them, other employees or the company in unlawful activity. Breaking the law can have serious consequences both for the company and for the individuals involved. As a consequence, companies and their employees need to acquire sufficient knowledge of the rules applicable to their activities.

WHEN IN DOUBT ABOUT DO'S AND DON'TS, EMPLOYEES SHOULD ASK THEMSELVES:

- Is it legal?
- Is it ethical?
- Is it consistent with the Code of Conduct?
- Am I setting the right example?
- Would I want people to read about it in the newspapers?
- Is there someone else I should consult?
- How would the person(s) I respect the most view this course of action?
- How would this affect our shareholders?

When in doubt, the golden rule is to speak up and to discuss the matter openly.

Don't cut corners: antitrust is public order law

As we have seen in Chapter 3, antitrust law forbids a company to enter into agreements that would restrain competition in the marketplace. In addition, all companies should endeavour to promote fair competition among market participants and ensure equitable treatment of their partners and customers.

Competition law may vary from one country to another, making it difficult for employees to evaluate the different situations they may encounter. When in doubt, employees are expected to seek guidance and consult with their legal department. Violating antitrust laws can have very severe consequences not only for the company but also for individual employees, as antitrust infringements are sanctioned not only civilly but also criminally in certain jurisdictions.

EXAMPLES OF BEHAVIOUR THAT THE CODE SHOULD PROHIBIT

- Obtaining sensitive information about a competitor, through theft, bribery, or communication of false or truncated information, for instance in a public or private procurement process. In general, engaging in illegal or illicit activity with a view to obtaining a competitive advantage.
- Exchanging data about prices and other sales conditions, production costs, sales quantities, market shares, or other sensitive parameters which may determine or influence companies' competitive behaviour.
- Asking a former employee of a competitor about information which this person is legally obliged not to reveal (such as for instance a competitor's trade secrets).
- Agreeing with competitors to exclude other (potential) competitors from the market or agreeing with competitors to boycott or refuse to deal with certain suppliers or customers.

Exclude all forms of corrupt practices

The Code of Conduct should make it clear that employees are required at all times not to engage in any form of corrupt practices, whether directly or indirectly, or to be complicit in any form of corruption or trading in influence. Chapter 4 of this Training Handbook ('*Glossary*') provides further detail about the terminology applicable to corrupt practices.

In addition, you should pay particular attention to the following matters when drafting your company's Code of Conduct:

a. Dealing with government officials

Sometimes, the global nature of your business will require your company to interact with officials of governments around the world. Turn to Chapter 4 to find the precise definition of 'public official' in the context of anti-corruption. In addition, keep in mind that transactions with governmental representatives are covered by special legal provisions and are not identical to those covering business between private parties.

b. Dealing with customers and suppliers

The company should value its relationships with customers and suppliers. Employees should treat these partners in the same manner they expect to be treated themselves. The company should expect its suppliers not to act against the principles of the corporate Code of Conduct. The owner of each supplier relationship should ensure adherence to the Code of Conduct as a condition to the conclusion of any supply agreement.

c. Gifts and hospitality

Here again, turn to Chapter 4 to find a definition of 'Gifts and Hospitality' and ICC's recommendations in this respect. Accordingly, your Code should reflect the following basic principles:

- Employees and third parties should avoid giving or receiving gifts if such gifts may improperly influence the recipient's judgment or may be perceived to do so.
- Employees may only offer or accept reasonable meals and gifts of symbolical value and which are appropriate under the circumstances, and they shall not accept or offer gifts, meals, or entertainment if such behaviour could create the impression of improperly influencing the business relationship.
- When assessing a particular circumstance, employees should seek guidance before accepting or giving any gift.

> **EXAMPLE: THALES'S GIFTS AND HOSPITALITY POLICY**
>
> "Thales formally prohibits the offering or receiving of payments in the form of cash. The choice of a gift or hospitality for a customer must be made in accordance with the '4Rs rule' – Regulations, Reasonable, Responsible, and Record – as the basis on which the Group, or where applicable a legal authority, will rule in the event of disputes or legal proceedings.
>
> - **Comply with the REGULATIONS**
>
>   Comply with limits set by local laws and regulations.
>
> - **Be REASONABLE**
>
>   Respect the local culture and customs of each country, company, and organization. Do the 'newspaper test'.
>
> - **Be RESPONSIBLE**
>
>   Act within the limits of your authority and use common sense.
>
> - **Keep RECORDS**
>
>   Transparently record expenses, and keep specific registers when local legal requirements or management decisions require this".

d. Conflicts of interest

Conflicts of interest arise more often than you think. They are so diverse in nature and appear in so many different circumstances that they are difficult to legislate on. They are, however, more and more the object of general public reprobation. To test the presence of a potential or actual conflict of interest, use the criteria contained in the definition of 'Conflicts of Interest' in Chapter 4. More generally, in the presence of a potential conflict of interest, employees should ask themselves: could my personal interests interfere with those of the company? May it appear so to others, either inside or outside the company?

Employees are expected to adhere to the highest integrity standards and to avoid any conflict of interest. Nonetheless, a corporate Code cannot address every potential conflict of interest, so employees will need not only to comply with the corporate rules but also to use good common sense and act according to their conscience.

e. Financial and accounting records

Accuracy is an essential part of running a business legally, honestly, and efficiently. Companies have a duty to make sure that their records are accurate and comprehensive and that they are in accordance with applicable regulations and with internal procedures. Ensuring accurate and complete accounting and financial records is everyone's responsibility, not just that of accounting and finance personnel. Accurate recordkeeping and reporting and respect for the securities legislation reflects on the company's reputation and credibility, and ensures that the company meets its legal and regulatory obligations.

Employees should never engage in fraudulent or other dishonest conduct involving the property or assets or the financial accounting and reporting of the company or of any third party. Employees should strive to be accurate when preparing or transmitting information for the company. Admittedly, honest mistakes occasionally happen. Only intentional efforts to misrepresent or improperly record transactions, or otherwise to falsify a company business record, should constitute a violation under the Code of Conduct.

DEALING WITH VIOLATIONS OF THE CODE OF CONDUCT

Raising concern and whistleblowing processes

As further developed in Chapter 11 ('*Whistleblowing*'), if you as an executive or an employee are aware of or suspect unethical or illegal conduct, you have a duty to report the issue or to seek guidance; you should speak first to your superior, to a manager with whom you feel comfortable, or to a human resources or legal department representative. Raising a concern in good faith means that you have make a genuine attempt to provide honest and accurate information about a potential misconduct, even if you may be later proven to be mistaken.

If you witness behaviour that rises suspicion, or that may represent a breach of the company's Code of Conduct, you have to report the issue promptly. The company will then have the opportunity to deal with the issue and to correct it before it becomes a violation of law or a risk to health and security of your colleagues or to the company's reputation.

The ethical alert procedure

The company should take every reasonable precaution to protect employees reporting in good faith an (alleged or suspected) infringement of the Code of Conduct. Any act of retaliation against an employee who raises an issue in good faith should be itself considered a violation of the Code of Conduct. That an employee has raised a concern in good faith cannot be seen as a justification for a separation, suspension, loss of benefits, harassment, or discrimination. However, knowingly making a false accusation, lying to investigators or refusing to cooperate will probably constitute a violation of the Code of Conduct.

AN EXAMPLE: ALSTOM'S ALERT PROCEDURE

"Employees may use the Group's Alert Procedure, in accordance with the laws and rules applicable in the country where they live or work, if they have reason to suspect a violation of anti-corruption, competition, and securities or accounting laws and regulations.

The Alert Procedure should only be used if the employee has reason to believe that informing his or her direct manager could cause difficulties or has reason to believe that the reported alleged irregularity will not receive the proper follow-up.

In this case, the employee can:

- Use the dedicated secure web platform or hotline phone number to report the matter (…)
- Inform the Country President in any country covered by the International Network or the Country Legal Counsel (…)
- Contact the Group General Counsel or the SVP Ethics & Compliance, who will jointly deal with the matter (…)

Every measure will be taken to respect employees' wishes for confidentiality. Alstom shall honor its commitment that no employee will suffer from retaliation, such as a change of status, harassment or any other form of discrimination as a result of using the Alert Procedure or disclosing information in good faith".

Source: *Alstom Code of Ethics*

Disciplinary Sanctions

The Code of Conduct must clearly indicate that all those who are working for the company – executives, officers, and employees alike – will have to act pursuant to the Code's norms and that all could be disciplined in case of infringement. It should be made clear that there is no place for exceptions, privileges, or immunities.

When a provision of the corporate Code is broken, management should step in to apply appropriate, proportionate and dissuasive disciplinary sanctions and to correct the situation. Whenever a pattern of non-compliance is discovered, measures should be taken to prevent the pattern from recurring. Serious and persistent breaches of the Code that could seriously damage the company's reputation can be punished by the dismissal of the people directly responsible, as well as those with supervisory responsibility.

OTHER TOPICS YOU MAY COVER IN A CODE OF CONDUCT

Privacy

The company should respect the privacy of all its employees, business partners, and customers. All employees should respect the personal dignity, privacy, and personal rights of every individual. The company must handle personal data responsibly and in compliance with all applicable privacy laws.

What do we mean by 'personal information'? While the exact definition of personal information can vary from country to country, it is generally understood to mean any information that directly identifies an individual or could be used to identify an individual. This includes name and initials, date of birth, images, biometric information, contact information, health-related information, genetic information, and personal characteristics. Note, however, that this is not a comprehensive list.

Discrimination and harassment

Workplace harassment is a form of discrimination that is generally defined as any verbal or physical conduct that occurs because of a certain individual's characteristics such as race, gender, sexual preference, age, or religious belief. It includes any action that inappropriately or unreasonably creates an intimidating, hostile, or offensive work environment.

There should be zero tolerance for discrimination and harassment. A company should be committed to a work environment in which every employee is treated fairly and with respect, and where all employees are given an equal chance to succeed. Employees should conduct their work with respect for all people, regardless of differences. A company should not make any employment-related decision, such as a decision about recruitment, selection, development, and advancement of employees, based on a person's race, colour, national origin, religion, sex, age, sexual orientation, marital status, physical or mental disability, or other characteristics protected by law.

> **AN EXAMPLE: A QUESTION-AND-ANSWER ABOUT L'OREAL'S HARASSMENT AND BULLYING POLICY**
>
> "Question: What exactly does L'OREAL mean by 'harassment' and 'bullying'? I don't think we have a law on this in my country.
>
> Answer: The first rule is that L'OREAL respects local law and therefore any employee violating the harassment laws in their country may be sanctioned. But there may be countries where L'OREAL considers that the law on harassment does not prohibit certain behaviours which the Company finds unacceptable. Depending on the circumstances, certain behaviour may be considered inappropriate, such as:
>
> - Actions intended to cause hurt or upset.
> - Deliberately setting a person up to make a mistake.
> - Humiliation or intimidation
> - Physical or social isolation".
>
> Source: *L'OREAL Code of Business Ethics*, 2007

Intellectual Property

Intellectual property rights are crucial to protecting the investments that companies and individuals make in developing new products and ideas. Employees should respect the laws and rules governing intellectual property. In particular, they should comply with the laws and regulations that govern the rights to, and protection of, copyright, trademarks, patents, trade secrets, and other forms of intellectual property.

Employees shall not disclose confidential information, unless expressly authorized to do so by their management. Employees should classify personal information as confidential and limit access to appropriately authorized individuals who have a clear business need for that information.

Health, security and safety

A company needs to be committed to providing safe, secure, and healthy work environments at its facilities for its employees, visitors, and contractors. As a minimum, this should be done by implementing the applicable statutory provisions, monitoring procedures, preventing health risks and occupational hazards, and providing personnel training.

About the author

Dominique Lamoureux is Vice-President, Ethics and Corporate Responsibility, of Thales, a global technology leader for the defense, security, aerospace and transport markets. Mr. Lamoureux is in charge of defining and monitoring Thales's policy for compliance with international trade regulations and, more globally, for the development of a comprehensive company-wide ethics policy. He is involved in various ethics and anti-corruption initiatives led by European and global business organizations. Notably, he is a member of the ICC Commission on Corporate Responsibility and Anti-corruption and chairs ICC France's Corporate Responsibility and Anti-corruption Committee.

ICC ETHICS AND COMPLIANCE TRAINING HANDBOOK

Chapter 8
The Ethics and Compliance Function and Its Interface with Management, Control, and Audit

Carlos Desmet

Ethics and Compliance Officer, Project and Technology, Shell International

Installing an ethics and compliance function does not remove management's duty to oversee operations and ensure that company activities are conducted in full compliance with applicable laws and ethical standards. In this Chapter, we start by highlighting the key elements of an effective ethics and compliance programme. We then describe the main role and responsibilities of the ethics and compliance function. Finally, we define the boundaries between the ethics and compliance function and the respective roles of management, control, and audit in securing the efficient functioning of the programme.

DESIGNING YOUR COMPANY'S ETHICS AND COMPLIANCE PROGRAMME

Emphasis of the programme

The formal emphasis of a corporate ethics and compliance programme is to prevent, detect, and appropriately respond to misconduct. One of the first texts available to define the main elements of an effective ethics and compliance programme was the *United States Federal Sentencing Guidelines*[11]. It still stands today as a global reference point for business. The Sentencing Guidelines first served as a practical guide for enterprises based or having operations in the United States, but they were later used by numerous companies from other parts of the world. In 2012, the Criminal Division of the United States Department of Justice and the Enforcement Division of the United States Securities and Exchange Commission published a *Resource Guide to the U.S. Foreign Corrupt Practices Act*[12] to further guide companies on the application of the United States anti-corruption law.

---

[11] The Federal Sentencing Guidelines are rules that set out a uniform sentencing policy for convicted federal defendants in the US Federal Court system: http://www.ussc.gov/Guidelines/2011_guidelines/Manual_HTML/8b2_1.htm

[12] http://www.sec.gov/spotlight/fcpa/fcpa-resource-guide.pdf

Other authoritative sources of reference include the *OECD Good Practice Guidance on Internal Controls, Ethics, and Compliance*[13] (2010) and the *United Kingdom Bribery Act Guidance* (2010) on "Adequate Procedures"[14]. The *ICC Rules on Combating Corruption* (2011) also provides examples of measures and good practices which companies should consider including as part of their ethics and compliance programme (see box below).

In order to be efficient, a corporate ethics and compliance programme should focus on those areas which are seen as posing the most significant legal and ethical risks for the company. As we have seen in Chapter 5, such evaluation should be made on the basis of a thorough risk assessment. While the risk exposure for a company may vary according to its industry segment(s), geographical markets, and business activities, companies whose operations have a global or multinational footprint will likely direct their compliance efforts towards the following areas:

- Anti-corruption;
- Anti-money laundering;
- Antitrust and competition law; and
- Export and import controls.

Depending on the company structure and industry segment(s), additional focus areas of the ethics and compliance programme may include human rights, disclosure controls, and insider trading.

While ethics and compliance programmes generally focus on legal compliance, they are often complemented in corporate documents by a value-based approach which encourages employees and business partners to commit to the highest standards of ethical conduct in their day-to-day professional activities.

> **ELEMENTS OF AN EFFICIENT CORPORATE ETHICS AND COMPLIANCE PROGRAMME**
> *Excerpt from the ICC Rules on Combating Corruption (2011)*
>
> "Each Enterprise should consider including all or part of the following good practices in its [corporate compliance] programme. In particular, it may choose, among the items listed hereunder, those measures which it considers most adequate to ensure a proper prevention against Corruption in its specific circumstances, no such measure being mandatory in nature:
>
> a) Expressing a strong, explicit and visible support and commitment to the Corporate Compliance Programme by the Board of Directors or other body with ultimate responsibility for the Enterprise and by the Enterprise's senior management ('tone at the top');
>
> b) Establishing a clearly articulated and visible policy reflecting these Rules and binding for all directors, officers, employees, and Third Parties and applying to all controlled subsidiaries, foreign and domestic;

---

[13] http://www.oecd.org/investment/briberyininternationalbusiness/anti-briberyconvention/44884389.pdf
[14] http://www.justice.gov.uk/downloads/legislation/bribery-act-2010-guidance.pdf

c) Mandating the Board of Directors or other body with ultimate responsibility for the Enterprise, or the relevant committee thereof, to conduct periodical risk assessments and independent reviews of compliance with these Rules and recommending corrective measures or policies, as necessary. This can be done as part of a broader system of corporate compliance reviews and/or risk assessments;

d) Making it the responsibility of individuals at all levels of the Enterprise to comply with the Enterprise's policy and to participate in the Corporate Compliance Programme;

e) Appointing one or more senior officers (full or part time) to oversee and coordinate the Corporate Compliance Programme with an adequate level of resources, authority and independence, reporting periodically to the Board of Directors or other body with ultimate responsibility for the Enterprise, or to the relevant committee thereof;

f) Issuing guidelines, as appropriate, to further elicit the behaviour required and to deter the behaviour prohibited by the Enterprise's policies and programme;

g) Exercising appropriate due diligence, based on a structured risk management approach, in the selection of its directors, officers, and employees, as well as of its Business Partners who present a risk of corruption or of circumvention of these Rules;

h) Designing financial and accounting procedures for the maintenance of fair and accurate books and accounting records, to ensure that they cannot be used for the purpose of engaging in or hiding of corrupt practices;

i) Establishing and maintaining proper systems of control and reporting procedures, including independent auditing;

j) Ensuring periodic internal and external communication regarding the Enterprise's anti-corruption policy;

k) Providing to their directors, officers, employees, and Business Partners, as appropriate, guidance and documented training in identifying corruption risks in the daily business dealings of the Enterprise as well as leadership training;

l) Including the review of business ethics competencies in the appraisal and promotion of management and measuring the achievement of targets not only against financial indicators but also against the way the targets have been met and specifically against the compliance with the Enterprise's anti-corruption policy;

m) Offering channels to raise, in full confidentiality, concerns, seek advice or report in good faith established or soundly suspected violations without fear of retaliation or of discriminatory or disciplinary action. Reporting may either be compulsory or voluntary; it can be done on an anonymous or on a disclosed basis. All bona fide reports should be investigated;

n) Acting on reported or detected violations by taking appropriate corrective action and disciplinary measures and considering making appropriate public disclosure of the enforcement of the Enterprise's policy;

o) Considering the improvement of its Corporate Compliance Programme by seeking external certification, verification or assurance; and

p) Supporting collective action, such as proposing or supporting anti-corruption pacts regarding specific projects or anti-corruption long-term initiatives with the public sector and/or peers in the respective business segments".

While all items listed above are recommended by ICC, none should be considered compulsory in their own right. It will be up to your company to select a combination of these various processes and policies, based on its particular circumstances and needs. For instance, no company should feel obliged, unless it is a legal or regulatory requirement, to put into place a whistleblowing system. Nor should a small enterprise feel constrained to opt for one of the above measures, if inappropriate.

Accountability for your company's ethics and compliance programme

Your company, like every other, will have to decide how best to assign accountability between the various players involved in your company's ethics and compliance programme. The matter to decide upon is: who will bear the brunt of accountability for the programme? Should it be management, internal audit, external audit, or the ethics and compliance function? Or should accountability be shared among them all?

In fact, there is no universally applicable formula in this area, just as there is no unique formula for designing and setting up an effective ethics and compliance programme. The sharing of accountability, as decided by your company, will need to fit its overall governance structure (Is it centralized or decentralized? Is it focused on one product line or is it largely diversified?), as well as its particular business circumstances (as for instance, its size, its industry segments, and the countries where it is operating).

For example, companies operating in highly regulated industries often decide to assign policy-setting, implementation, monitoring, and enforcement to a central ethics and compliance function. Others will prefer to assign policy-setting authority to functions which are already in place in the corporate structure (such as legal, finance, or human resources) and hold management accountable for policy compliance, including implementing required controls and procedures. In the latter kind of set up, the ethics and compliance function would typically be assigned a support, advice, and reporting role. But again, there are various types of models which can be effective. The decision to go for one or another model will shape the boundaries (and the conditions for cooperation) between management, control, audit, and the ethics and compliance function.

Reporting line of the Chief Ethics and Compliance Officer

The appointment of a Chief Ethics and Compliance Officer is an important decision for a company. Various organizational structures and options can be considered when establishing such a role, depending on the size and the complexity of the organization. In a smaller enterprise, the ethics and compliance function may be exercised on a part-time basis. In large multinationals, the compliance group may have a headcount of dozens if not hundreds of persons.

To be credible, the Chief Ethics and Compliance Officer should be given a senior enough position within the company so that the incumbent can perform his or her duties with sufficient influence and autonomy. As already touched upon in Chapter 1 (*'A Daunting but Fascinating Task'*) and Chapter 6 (*'The Role of the Board of Directors'*) of this Handbook, consideration should be given to provide him or her with direct access to the Board of Directors and top management of the company. In particular, he or she should be able to provide a regular assessment on the effectiveness of the compliance programme to the Board of Directors or its Audit Committee. These types of decisions will determine the actual impact of the Chief Ethics and Compliance Officer function within the company and vis-à-vis external stakeholders.

Resourcing the ethics and compliance function

It is important to ensure that the ethics and compliance function has sufficient authority and enjoys adequate human and financial resources to perform its duties. To assess the amount of resources required to run an effective ethics and compliance programme, elements to be factored in (and to be revisited on a regular basis) include: the size of the company, the number and diversity of business units, the number and importance of subsidiaries and affiliates, the company's exposure to legal and ethical risks, its corporate culture, the complexity of its business model, the structure of the company's ethics and compliance function, and the extent to which the company uses third parties or business partners to conduct its business operations. An ethics and compliance programme is usually run in-house but may benefit from the support of external third-party service providers in areas which require specific outside expertise.

Skills for the ethics and compliance function

Many people working in ethics and compliance have a legal background. However, compliance departments increasingly include individuals with technical, managerial, and financial skills and experience. Other relevant backgrounds for the compliance function include human resources, information technology, communications, and project management. But first and foremost, an ethics and compliance person should enjoy a high degree of credibility and should be or become truly familiar with the company's products, processes, and daily activities.

THE INTERFACE WITH MANAGEMENT, CONTROL, AND AUDIT

Ethical leadership

As we have seen in Chapter 6 (*'The Role of the Board of Directors'*), top management plays a significant role in shaping, embedding, and spreading authority, norms and culture in the company. In this respect, the role of top management is to set the tone and to lead by example. As leaders, the top of the company should be seen by their colleagues as those who articulate and personify the values and standards of the enterprise. Their leadership is critical for consistently embedding and implementing the ethics and compliance programme in all spheres of the company's activities.

The interface between the ethics and compliance function and management

In any company, the ultimate responsibility for achieving corporate goals, and for ensuring that these goals are achieved in full compliance with applicable laws, corporate policies, and ethical standards, belongs to management. In other words, it is the responsibility of management to define accountability, allocate sufficient resources, and establish adequate processes and structures designed to ensure that:

(i) Policies are followed;

(ii) Adequate procedures and compliance controls are properly implemented; and

(iii) Assurance is obtained via an appropriate blend of monitoring and self-assessment. To be most effective, the processes established for conducting real-time monitoring and periodic self-assessment of compliance controls should be integrated into routine business activities.

The ethics and compliance function may play a role in establishing corporate policies and ethical standards. This may be done, for example, by taking an active part in the development of the company's Code of Conduct. The compliance function is also typically involved in helping management, staff and employees of business partners to understand how these corporate policies and ethical standards address compliance risks in their businesses.

More broadly, the ethics and compliance function is there to support and promote the effective implementation of the ethics and compliance programme. Support activities include the training of management and staff, answering questions, providing advice, and helping to identify where controls and monitoring mechanisms can be embedded in daily business activities.

Another role of the ethics and compliance function is to ensure that systems are in place to allow staff and employees to ask questions, to raise concerns and to ensure that those concerns are properly investigated. Such systems should be designed in a way which reflects the size and governance style of the company. You will find more specifics on how to set up a whistleblowing system in Chapter 11 of this Training Handbook (*'Whistleblowing'*) as well as in the *ICC Guidelines on Whistleblowing* (2008).

In consultation with human resources and legal, the ethics and compliance function supports management in determining consequence management and in identifying lessons learned from incidents, with a view to fostering continuous improvement. Finally, the compliance function is typically responsible for monitoring and reporting on the effectiveness of the ethics and compliance programme. All those activities and functions will require frequent interfaces with management and staff. To perform its duties, the ethics and compliance function must therefore be seen as a business partner: it should not be isolated. On the contrary, it should be visible on the ground.

Management controls

Standards are set by the laws of the various countries where the company operates and by the additional ethical policies and rules which the company has adopted. Evidently, those requirements (including those that support legal and regulatory compliance) are mandatory and need to be communicated to management and staff.

It will be management's duty to insure that these requirements are reflected in the company's operational procedures. Management should also establish regular controls to check that those procedures continue to operate effectively. The ethics and compliance function will interact with management at various stages of this exercise, for instance when updating corporate policies and rules, or when monitoring how those policies and rules are implemented. The depth of the influence of the ethics and compliance function, and its level of activity and pro-activity, will depend on its accountability and on the level of resources it enjoys.

Board governance and oversight responsibilities

Key documents and standards for your company (such as its Code of Conduct) should be subject to the review and approval of the Board of Directors. Members of the Board should be knowledgeable about key ethics and compliance issues facing the company and be regularly informed about specific risks and the effectiveness of the ethics and compliance programme in mitigating those risks. The Chief Ethics and Compliance Officer, as well as your company's assurance providers, should be able to talk and report to the Board of Directors (or a dedicated committee of the Board, such as the Audit Committee) on a regular basis.

The role of internal audit

The first role of internal audit in the compliance context is that of an assurance provider. Internal audit provides the Board of Directors and management with an independent assurance on the design and operation of the system of internal controls in the company. The Chief Ethics and Compliance Officer has a similar independent role when communicating his or her assessment of the effectiveness of the corporate compliance programme to the Board of Directors and management.

The second role of internal audit is to perform compliance audits. The internal audit function develops independently a risk-based assurance plan to cover the key operations of the company. It is responsible for implementing the plan and reporting on its findings. Its scope can be either purely financial or it can be broader to cover strategic, technical and operational risks including those that fall under the umbrella of the ethics and compliance programme.

In the latter case, it is critical for the ethics and compliance function to work closely with internal audit so that testing of the implementation of the ethical and compliance standards of the company is also incorporated into the internal audit programme (using a risk-based approach).

Results from internal audits will provide the Chief Ethics and Compliance Officer and the Board of Directors with precious input to measure the effective implementation of the ethics and compliance programme within the various business lines, subsidiaries and functional departments of the company. These may incorporate testing of the employees' knowledge of the legal and self-regulatory standards, as well as checks of the business controls in place and of the various self-assurance processes implemented to test effectiveness of the ethics and compliance programme. Management is subsequently accountable to implement the audit recommendations to address the gaps found in the control system.

Internal audit can also fulfil a third role: auditing the ethics and compliance function. In particular, internal audit may provide assurance to the Board of Directors on the performance of the ethics and compliance function.

The role of external audit

External audit provides shareholders assurance that the framework of controls established by the company operates effectively and that its financial accounts and mandatory disclosures are a fair reflection of the operations of the business. In that respect, external auditors will also decide to rely on the work done by internal audit, if available, to assess the scope of their tests and to develop and prepare their opinion.

About the author

Carlos Desmet is Global Compliance Officer for Shell International since 2009. Shell is a global group of energy and petrochemicals companies with around 90,000 employees in more than 80 countries and territories. Based in the Netherlands, Mr. Desmet heads the global compliance office for the Shell Project and Technology business. He supports the Projects organization, supply chain, third party services, research and development, safety and environment and technical IT. His team members are based in the United States, Netherlands, Malaysia, China, Nigeria and India. Prior to this role, he was appointed as Upstream compliance officer in 2006. Mr. Desmet is also Vice President of ICC Netherlands' Anti-corruption and Corporate Social Responsibility Working Group and a member of ICC's Commission on Corporate Responsibility and Anti-corruption.

Chapter 9
The Compliance Challenge for Smaller Companies

Annette Kraus

Senior Legal Counsel, Corporate Legal and Compliance, Siemens

Julia Sommer

Legal Counsel, Corporate Legal and Compliance, Siemens

A frequently heard comment is that the drafters of international conventions and national legislation have conceived anti-corruption and antitrust standards with large multinationals in mind. A similar bias would prevail in the guidance developed by business associations and non-governmental organizations. Special attention should be paid, however, to the specific circumstances of small- and medium-sized enterprises, which make up the largest part of the world's economic output. In this Chapter, we analyze what smaller companies should do to comply with anti-corruption and antitrust provisions and what type of compliance model is most adequate to their needs.

COMPLIANCE, AN EVEN BIGGER CHALLENGE FOR SMALLER COMPANIES

Fighting corrupt and restrictive practices represents an immense challenge for any type of business. For companies that do not have the size and the resources of a large multinational, the challenge will be even bigger, as they have to comply with the same legal provisions as their larger counterparts and are often more exposed to corruption and competition risks, while having less human and financial resources to do so.

There is no differential treatment for smaller companies

It is often believed that, when it comes to anti-corruption or antitrust, small companies receive a special and more lenient treatment than larger ones. According to this reasoning, the legal provisions on the criminalization of corruption and the prohibition of restrictive practices would be adapted to the particular circumstances of smaller companies. This is a misperception: the legal standards on anti-corruption and antitrust are the same for everybody, large, medium, and small companies alike.

Even if you try, you will not find any differential treatment between small and large companies in the wording of the key international legal instruments against corruption described in Chapter 2 ('*The International Anti-Corruption Conventions*'). It is not because a company is smaller in size that it is allowed to indulge in malpractice: the size of a company is no defense.

Which companies are we talking about?
But first, let us make sure we understand which companies we are talking about. This Chapter focuses on those companies which have reached a certain size on their national market and which are starting or have already started exporting to other markets. In some cases, they may even have begun creating subsidiaries or affiliates in neighbouring countries. They are not multinationals in the ordinary meaning of the word but are coming in contact with them and often act as their subcontractors.

Not every company has abundant resources
Small companies face a stark challenge when doing business in international markets: they often are an easy prey for solicitation attempts, being newcomers on these markets. With no or little experience in legitimately obtaining contracts overseas, they lack the economic and human weight to counter such pressures. It is clear also that smaller companies do not have the same resources as multinational companies such as Siemens to establish robust compliance systems.

Proportionality in preventive action
The prohibition of corruption and restrictive practices applies to all companies alike. However, in many jurisdictions, legislators, and regulators acknowledge that the preventive measures put in place by companies may be proportionate to their size and risks. Depending on the evaluation of the risks each company is facing, and on its size and resources, a preventive system will have to be established. This system does not have to be slavishly copied on what bigger companies are doing. It should cater for the specific needs of the company at stake.

THE RATIONALE FOR ADEQUATE COMPLIANCE STRUCTURES
Adequate compliance structures will not only help your company to prevent infringements from taking place. Often, they also will serve to mitigate detrimental legal consequences when infringements happen despite the establishment of preventive structures. Increasingly, legislators and regulators give credit to the existence of effective compliance structures when assessing the penalty to be levied on the company where such infringements occurred. The *United States Federal Sentencing Guidelines*[15] for instance are at the forefront of this approach. For the possible mitigating effect of competition compliance programmes in the European Union, see the last paragraph (*'Do Competition Compliance Programmes have a mitigating effect?'*) of Chapter 3 (*'The Global Antitrust Landscape'*).

Furthermore, the national law of certain countries may allow your company to reverse its debarment from public procurement tenders, if it can show that it has established effective compliance structures and remedied the damage caused. The European Union is currently planning to enshrine a cleansing process in an upcoming new directive on public

---

[15] http://www.ussc.gov/Guidelines/2011_guidelines/Manual_HTML/8b2_1.htm

procurement. The benefits of – and requirements for – adequate compliance structures are independent of the size of the company.

Under these legal requirements, your company should, broadly speaking, ensure that infringements are prevented, detected, and remedied. Article 10 of the *ICC Rules on Combating Corruption* (2011) gives an extensive list of good practices (see Chapter 8, *'The Ethics and Compliance Function and its Interface with Management, Control, and Audit'*) which companies may consider adopting to ensure a proper prevention of corruption. None of these practices is mandatory, but you must bear in mind that without adequate compliance structures, your company will have an inbuilt compliance risk.

Elements of an adequate compliance structure

The linchpin of any compliance structure is adequacy. Structures and processes have to be adequate in relation to the vulnerability of a particular business to corruption and to its susceptibility to act in an anticompetitive or other illegal behaviour. As explained in Chapter 5 (*'Risk Assessment'*), each company should conduct a risk assessment to understand which type of risk may arise, in which segment of its business, and in which geographical area(s).

Minimum standards

However, regardless of the specific risks to which a company is exposed, there are certain minimum elements required for a compliance system to be effective. These can be adopted by all companies and are not necessarily resource-intensive:

- First of all, the top management of the company should articulate clearly that corrupt, anticompetitive, and other illegal behaviour will not be tolerated in the company. In other words, the 'Tone from the top' should be clearly pro-compliance.

- In line with the 'Tone from the top', management should set forth explicit corporate compliance rules in writing in order to avoid misunderstandings, as well as to prevent anybody from using the excuse of not having been aware of the rules. The basic set of corporate rules should be applicable to the whole organization.

    These rules can be formulated in a generic way so that they can be applicable anywhere the company does business, despite possible differences in legal systems. Such generic rules include, for example: "Do not bribe", "Act in accordance with applicable local law", "Abide by the rules of fair competition", "Make business decisions in the best interests of the company, not on the basis of your personal interest." This will contribute to a common understanding of the compliance culture of the company and will prevent any misperception and the wrong assumption that the rules do not apply to the entity concerned.

    The *Siemens AG Business Conduct Guidelines*[16] can serve as an example of a generic set of rules applicable to all Siemens entities worldwide. In some circumstances, you may allow local entities to go for 'localized rules'. This means that you can have a general rule for the whole organization but may authorize local entities to add

---

[16] http://www.siemens.com/sustainability/pool/cr-framework/business_conduct_guidelines_d.pdf

something specific to this rule. Such approach can be used when defining rules on gifts and hospitality or when setting requirements for business partners and suppliers. In doing so, you will allow the rule to be better attuned to local requirements and needs.

- To build an effective compliance organization, management should appoint one or several compliance officers. The explicit job responsibility of a compliance officer is to enforce compliance with legal and corporate rules. Management can thus delegate part of its responsibility for compliance issues, provided that it adequately enables compliance officers to fulfil their job requirements by vesting them with the necessary authority, reporting lines and resources. In smaller companies, the compliance officer may very well exercise this function on a half or part-time basis. He or she may be in charge solely of compliance, or perform other duties as well.

- Employees must be enabled and urged to respect corporate rules by way of communication and training. Each employee should become familiar with the rules and should be reminded of them on a regular basis. Otherwise, your company runs the risk that respect for the rules will progressively vanish. Such training does not need to be expensive. It can be combined with networking and social events within the company to boost morale and encourage employees to embrace the corporate culture.

- Management should pay attention to and investigate reports of non-compliant behaviour. Otherwise, they can hardly expect to be exonerated from liability for incidents, which are simply 'put aside'. If you are in a smaller company, a heavy whistleblowing system may perhaps not be suitable, as communication lines will naturally be much shorter, easier, and more flexible than in a large organization. Based on the informal, trustworthy, and close relations prevailing in your company, you should therefore encourage employees to report their concerns to their direct superiors, assuring them that there will be no risk of retaliation, and providing them as much as possible with a protection of their confidentiality. Be careful though not to guarantee too much confidentiality, since this will be more difficult to achieve in a small scale business. At the end of the investigation of an allegation, a proven infringement should be appropriately sanctioned so that the rules are taken seriously.

- Finally, compliance structures have to be regularly reviewed in order to maintain their effectiveness and adequacy in view of the risks your business is facing.

The steps outlined above will contribute to the establishment of a corporate culture in your organization that prevents corruption and other illegal behaviour from taking root. Implement any further methods and means that you consider suitable for building a genuine culture of integrity. None of the elements mentioned above should be left out entirely if you want your compliance structure to be effective.

Your company's compliance organization

There is no 'one size fits all' solution when it comes to designing an adequate compliance organization in a small- or medium-sized enterprise.

The Board of Directors has to decide what kind of compliance organization it needs to establish and ensure an effective compliance structure.

The structure of an adequate compliance organization has to fulfil basic compliance requirements, which means that it should be capable of preventing, detecting, and remediating infringements. The following two models might be considered.

The first model establishes a separate compliance organization:

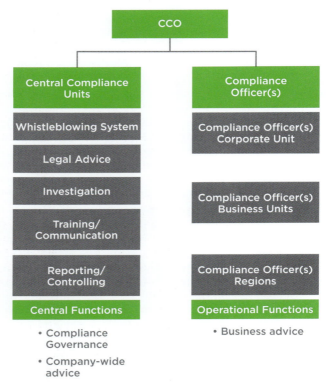

Source: Klaus Moosmayer, Compliance, Praxisleitfaden für Unternehmen, C.H. Beck Verlag, 2. edition 2012, p. 32

Here, the structure is divided into central compliance units and operational compliance functions with responsibility for the business in the home country or abroad. The Chief Compliance Officer heads both units and is therefore responsible for the whole compliance organization. The Chief Compliance Officer reports directly to the top management of the company. This may seem an ideal model, but you may find that it requires considerable personnel and financial resources. Indeed, such a model is probably more suitable for large rather than small companies. Keep in mind, however, that the division between a central functional part and a decentralized operational part may prove effective for any type of organization.

The second model could be more appropriate for small- and medium-sized enterprises:

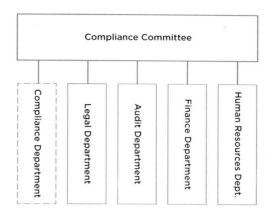

See Klaus Moosmayer, Compliance, Praxisleitfaden für Unternehmen, C.H. Beck Verlag, 2. 2012 edition, p. 33

In that model, the compliance department is responsible for preventive measures only. Responsibility for detecting and responding to non-compliant conduct lies with separate, already-existing departments such as legal, audit, finance, or human resources. A new body, called the Compliance Committee, is responsible for coordinating the compliance function. This committee consists of the Chief Compliance Officer and the heads of the other departments involved. They are responsible for the effectiveness of the compliance structure as a whole and report directly to the top management of the company.

In some scenarios, and especially in smaller organizations, it might be better not to create a separate compliance department at all, but rather to assign the various responsibilities for the compliance function to existing departments or even to designated employees with specific compliance expertise.

MITIGATING THIRD-PARTY RELATIONSHIP RISKS

As a small- or medium-sized company, you will likely need to call upon external forces to help you expand your business. Based on the experience of Siemens in this area, let's explore some general considerations which can also apply in the context of a smaller business.

Siemens, as a multinational company, has implemented a highly differentiated compliance system consisting of tools and methods to fight non-compliant behaviour and to promote compliance worldwide. One of the tenets of this system is the creation of sustainable partnerships with 'clean' commercial partners. For this reason, the company holds itself, its business partners and its suppliers to the highest standard of behaviour. It does so by diligently checking the background of commercial partners and suppliers, by providing them with specific guidelines and information, and by training them.

Working with business partners

When selecting third-party intermediaries, all companies should conduct a thorough, documented due diligence process designed to establish a collaborative, long-term business relationship. One adequate approach is to perform a compliance due diligence prior to the engagement of a business partner following the steps described in the Siemens brochure 'Information for Business Partners'[17]. You will find in this document a wealth of information on how to select your business partners.

In addition, turn to Chapter 14 (*'Agents, Intermediaries and Other Third Parties'*) to learn more about how to design your own due diligence activities not only for low-risk business relationships but also in potentially high-risk and medium-risk circumstances.

Working with suppliers

To ensure sustainability in the supply chain, suppliers should be committed to compliance standards equivalent to those required of your company. Smaller companies also benefit from having their suppliers sign compliance agreements, since companies nowadays are increasingly held responsible for the (non-compliant) behaviour of their suppliers, both legally and from a reputational point of view.

Such compliance standards could take the form of a Supplier Code of Conduct and incorporate the following compliance requirements (see for example the 'Code of Conduct for Siemens Suppliers'[18]):

- Compliance with all applicable laws;
- Prohibition of corruption and bribery;
- Respect for human rights of employees;
- Prohibition of child labour;
- Health and safety of employees;
- Implementation of a management system in order to protect the environment; and
- Active steps to promote adherence among their own suppliers with the requirements of the Supplier Code of Conduct.

To secure the implementation of such requirements, agreements with suppliers should contain the following contractual clauses:

- Commitment to comply with the requirements of the Code of Conduct;
- Performance of a supplier self-assessment;
- Right of termination in the event of a serious violation of the Code of Conduct; and
- If feasible, and taking into account the size and resources of the supplier, specific sustainability audits conducted by external providers.

---

[17] http://www.siemens.com/sustainability/pool/en/core_topics/compliance/business_partner_flyer_en.pdf
[18] www.siemens.com/scm/sustainability

The above measures are targeted at evaluating whether the compliance requirements are acknowledged and implemented by the supplier in order to identify and manage potential compliance risks at an early stage. Such measures also contribute to building up suppliers' long-term skills and thus fostering long-lasting, mutually beneficial business relationships. To achieve this target, a company can also offer training courses aimed at informing the participants of the supply chain about the letter and the spirit of the compliance requirements. Siemens, for example, offers web-based training that provides guidance to smaller enterprises.

BEST PRACTICES IN THE FIELD OF COMPLIANCE

Affiliating with business federations and chambers of commerce is another way for smaller enterprises to receive information on best-practice standards in the field of compliance. There are several networks that provide guidelines and counselling with the ultimate objective of creating a level playing field.

Additional information is available via the following helpful links:

- The ICC Commission on Corporate Responsibility and Anti-corruption provides companies with a wide range of pragmatic tools to help business drive integrity in business transactions[19].
- Companies determined to counter the problem of extortion and solicitation of bribes can train employees to respond appropriately to a variety of solicitations via the training toolkit Resisting Extortion and Solicitation in International Transactions (RESIST)[20].
- Transparency International has developed a special edition of its "Business Principles for Countering Bribery" tailored to smaller companies[21].
- For German speakers, examples of guidelines on providing and accepting gifts and hospitality[22], as well as of Codes of Conduct[23] can be found online.

Whatever the size of an enterprise, it ultimately pays to invest time and effort in preventing, detecting and responding to compliance risks and incidents.

---

[19] http://www.iccwbo.org/advocacy-codes-and-rules/areas-of-work/corporate-responsibility-and-anti-corruption/icc-business-ethics-tools/
[20] http://www.iccwbo.org/products-and-services/fighting-commercial-crime/resist/
[21] http://www.transparency.org/whatwedo/tools/business_principles_for_countering_bribery_sme_edition
[22] http://www.s20.eu/leitfaden_d_250711.pdfx
[23] http://www.zvei.org/index.php?id=4770

About the authors

Annette Kraus and **Julia Sommer** are lawyers in the department Compliance Legal of Siemens, which is part of the Governance function of Siemens Compliance Organization. Compliance Legal is the centre of competence within Siemens for regulatory compliance, criminal law, administrative offenses, and related proceedings ('white-collar crime'). The department aims to prevent infringements by setting worldwide applicable policies, and to detect and investigate alleged infringements.

Mrs. Kraus is Senior Legal Counsel with particular expertise in antitrust compliance. Prior to this activity, she managed projects at Steria Mummert Consulting mainly in the field of capital market compliance in the banking area. She began her legal career at the law firm, Rotter Rechtsanwälte, where she advised and litigated in the area of securities law.

Julia Sommer, LL.M., is Legal Counsel with particular expertise in anti-corruption and anti-fraud compliance. Prior to this activity, she was counsel with the international law firm Freshfields Bruckhaus Deringer with a focus on regulatory and compliance matters.

PART 3

APPROPRIATE MEASURES

Chapter 10
Education and Training

Corinne Lagache

Senior Vice-President, Trade Compliance and Export Control, Safran

Education and training are powerful channels to create an effective culture of integrity in a company. The amount of human and financial resources which an organization allocates to training activities often provides a good indication of its actual commitment to ethical business conduct. This Chapter describes the various tools and training methods that companies can use to make their values and ethical rules known to their employees and other key stakeholders. We stress here the importance of adapting training sessions to their audience by making them directly relevant to the day-to-day professional responsibilities of participants. We also discuss how best to structure an education and training programme and how to improve its effectiveness over time.

INTRODUCTION

Education and training possibly represent your most important line of defense against corruption and other ethical risks. At a time when the pages of regulations governing business practices are piling up, conducting training activities is the best strategy for efficiently communicating compliance messages to your colleagues and other company stakeholders. All major government and industry guidelines on corporate ethics and compliance programmes emphasize the role of education and training in preventing misconduct and creating an effective integrity culture within a company.

ETHICS AND COMPLIANCE TRAINING AND THE B20

Underscoring the importance of education and training to promote a culture of ethics and compliance, the world business community, represented by the B20 Task Force on Improving Transparency and Anti-corruption, designated the development of training materials on anti-corruption compliance and the delivery of a 'train the trainers' programme aimed at compliance officers from the private sector as one of its key priorities for action at the G20 Summit of June 2012 in Los Cabos, Mexico.

WHY PROVIDE EDUCATION AND TRAINING ON ANTI-CORRUPTION?

The advent of a new ethical era

If we go back in time, some will remember a not so distant past when bribing a foreign public official was not forbidden by criminal law and when, in a number of countries, a bribe paid to such official was even deductible from corporate income as a commercial expense. Only a few decades ago, the United States was the only country in the world – with, to some extent, Sweden – that had criminalized international public corruption. It took huge efforts to bring about strong and innovative international conventions, and to transpose their provisions into national law. It took even more time to see these national criminal law provisions being effectively enforced.

The advent of this new ethical era required the acquisition of new reflexes. Abstaining from offering bribes, resisting solicitation or extortion, refusing to create slush funds, rejecting illegal gifts and hospitality, disapproving illegal political contributions: all of these are behaviours that corporate managers and employees have had to integrate in their daily professional life. Practices that were previously considered 'business as usual' had to be replaced with steadfast attitudes that could ensure full compliance with the newly introduced legal and ethical standards.

Making such a 'Copernican' reform effective in the minds of everyone in your organization requires more than producing a glossy leaflet with a corporate Code of Conduct or a colourful poster with company values knitted on office walls. What is required to bring out such revolution is setting up a genuine education and training programme which helps everybody in the company understand and respond to ethical threats and challenges.

> **THE IMPORTANCE OF ETHICS AND COMPLIANCE TRAINING FOR RAISING PRODUCTIVITY AND BOOSTING GROWTH**
>
> In the last quarter of 2012, ICC and the Institute for Economic Research (Ifo) in Munich asked 1,156 experts in 124 countries whether they agreed stronger emphasis on ethics and compliance training for business in their respective countries would help productivity and attract more foreign investment.
>
> Experts in emerging countries overwhelmingly supported the statement. In Africa, 90% of experts agreed and in both South America and Asia the consensus level was 88%. There was also a high level of agreement from experts in Eastern Europe and the CIS countries where the statement was supported by 87% and 85% respectively.
>
> It is interesting to note that the more a country is perceived to be subject to widespread corruption, the greater is the belief that ethics and compliance training is needed to help boost the economy.

The need for a genuine corporate training programme

The goal of education and training activities is to communicate the structure and substance of your company's ethics and compliance programme to its directors, officers, and employees as well as to its business partners, customers, and other stakeholders. The underlying objective is to help everyone understand their individual responsibilities under the ethics and compliance programme and to guide them in making the right decisions when confronted with risky situations.

An effective education and training programme should therefore aim at increasing awareness about ethics and compliance issues by conveying key messages throughout the year about the importance and seriousness of compliance requirements. The key challenge here is to bridge the gap between the sometimes 'dry' legal provisions contained in governmental regulations and corporate policies, and the day-to-day realities of the company's business operations. In other words, trainees should become so savvy about regulatory and ethical standards that they acquire a sense of ownership of the company's ethics and compliance programme.

> **IS TRAINING AND EDUCATION A PRIORITY FOR ALL COMPANIES?**
>
> Not really. According to the results of the Global Anti-Bribery and Corruption Survey 2011 (commissioned by KPMG and conducted with 214 executives of large companies in the United States and the United Kingdom), one in five respondents does not have a training programme and about one in three stated that training for employees is required less than once a year.

To be effective, training activities should be developed in such a way that they provide a 'rehearsal for real world situations'. Explanations about key laws and regulations should be complemented by real-life examples and case studies that mirror the types of circumstances that can be experienced on the ground. This way, training can help employees adopt the right behaviour at all times. In other words, training sessions should not be designed as law classes but deliver practical guidelines for conducting daily work duties.

Education and training also play an important role in feeding your company's risk assessment process. First, training sessions help your colleagues identify, understand, and measure the various ethics and compliance risks which they may encounter on the ground. Second, by providing a platform for open and frank dialogue, they give participants an opportunity to speak up about new risky situations which they may have faced in their work and which may require the introduction of new mitigation measures by your company.

TIMEFRAME OF TRAINING ACTIVITIES

Training activities should be conducted on a regular basis. A reasonable objective is to provide a minimum of basic compliance training to all company employees, through regular information about the evolution of applicable laws and the related internal compliance procedures. As discussed below, longer and more specialized training sessions may be scheduled every year for employees (and if necessary business partners) whose responsibilities expose them to higher risks. In addition, all new employees should be requested to participate in an ethics and compliance training session within approximately 30 days of their hire date or of the effective date of a merger or acquisition. Finally, a comprehensive training programme should be launched following the introduction or revision of the company's Code of Conduct or upon the initial implementation of the company's ethics and compliance programme.

AUDIENCE

All company employees, from top to bottom and regardless of their job function, should follow basic compliance training. You should not stop at the doors of the Board room; your directors also need to be informed about regulatory and ethical requirements. Employees whose job function or geographic location expose them to higher or specific ethical and compliance risks (for example those responsible for international sales or tenders, merger and acquisitions, or offsets) should be requested to participate in more specific and more intensive training sessions. Such enhanced training activities may be provided in the form of one-on-one or on-the-job training to ensure that compliance is integrated into the employee's daily activities and does not remain a theoretical concept. Specialized training should also be given to employees in positions with compliance responsibilities, such as legal, accounting, risk management, control, and internal audit.

> **A NEGATIVE EFFECT OF THE FINANCIAL AND ECONOMIC CRISIS ON CORPORATE ETHICS AND COMPLIANCE TRAINING PROGRAMMES?**
>
> "After years of cost cutting, relatively labor-intensive measures and activities were less frequently cited as examples of anti-bribery/anti-corruption controls in the respondents' businesses. For example, as internal audit and compliance functions are trimmed back, their lower priority areas of responsibility, such as training, also appear to have suffered. As many as 42% of respondents had not received training on anti-bribery/anti-corruption policies. Without adequately trained employees, the ability of companies to identify issues or robustly investigate and act on allegations is also likely to be diminished".
>
> *Excerpt from the 12th Global Fraud Survey by Ernst & Young ("Growing Beyond: a place for integrity") conducted with 1,700 interviews in 43 countries between November 2011 and February 2012*

Business partners, including agents, service providers, distributors, and suppliers, as well as customers and other stakeholders should be informed about the company's corporate policies and ethics and compliance programme through specific communication channels, such as pamphlets, letters, and web-based tools. In certain circumstances, a company may choose to request certain business partners (for example those who interact with government officials on behalf of the company) to participate in the corporate training programme along with other employees or through dedicated training sessions.

DO COMPANIES TRAIN THEIR BUSINESS PARTNERS' EMPLOYEES?

Few companies do, according to the KPMG Global Anti-Bribery and Corruption Survey 2011. The survey shows that three in five companies with compliance programmes that incorporate employee training do not require any third-party representatives to participate in their training sessions.

CONTENT OF TRAINING

Education and training activities are meant both to introduce theoretical concepts and to explain their operational implications for daily business activities.

BASIC COMPLIANCE TRAINING USUALLY COVERS THE FOLLOWING SUBJECT AREAS

1) The body of legal and regulatory instruments guiding the company's compliance programme, including anti-corruption and antitrust laws and regulations;
2) The main provisions of the company's Code of Conduct;
3) The company's ethics and compliance programme: its design, structure, and objectives;
4) Examples of risk areas specific to the company's industry segment(s) and examples of improper practices;
5) Possible legal and disciplinary sanctions for improper or illegal conduct;
6) Red flags to be detected to identify factors or circumstances which pose a high risk of unethical practices;
7) Channels for seeking advice, raising concerns, and reporting suspected violations within the company;
8) Written compliance policies and procedures, and their implementation:
    a. Screening, approval and information of intermediaries and other third parties;
    b. Screening, approval and training of vendors and joint venturers;
    c. Screening and approval of company sponsored gifts and hospitality, travel, and events;
    d. Screening in case of a merger or acquisition;
9) Maintaining fair and accurate books and accounting records.

For employees whose job function calls for additional compliance training, the content of advanced training sessions should be tailored to their specific needs. For example, special sessions dedicated to sales managers may focus on compliance policies and procedures for appointing vendors, giving and receiving gifts or extending hospitality. Other special sessions may be dedicated to antitrust policies. In-house lawyers may benefit from in-depth sessions on conducting anti-corruption due diligence for the appointment of business partners or during the negotiation of a joint venture agreement.

As emphasized above, training activities should as much as possible include case studies and examples which relate to the day-to-day professional activities of participants. A useful point of reference is the training tool RESIST (Resisting Extortion and Solicitation in International Transactions) which develops real-life scenarios and provides practical guidance to company personnel on how to prevent and respond to an inappropriate demand by a customer, business partner or public official in the most efficient and ethical way. Chapter 13 of this Training Handbook (*'Resisting Solicitation'*) provides an explanation of RESIST and of the way it can be used by companies for their training activities.

WHO SHOULD PROVIDE TRAINING?

Frequently the question is asked: "Should my company conduct its own training sessions with its own personnel, or should it call upon external resources to shape, organize, and conduct training?" The market is full of specialized and competent consultants who can provide your company with their training abilities and their vast expertise. Having recourse to a consultancy may indeed be your best option if your company is relatively small and does not have the human resources to cope with the new and demanding challenge of providing up-to-date ethics and compliance training to its personnel.

But as might be expected, this option comes with pros and cons: if you call upon an external service provider (such as a law firm, a human resources specialist, an academic or an anti-corruption specialist), you will miss the down-to-earth touch which only members of your company's personnel can provide. Remember that when organizing ethics and compliance training sessions, a large part of the effectiveness lays in creating the conditions for a real-life dialogue between trainers and trainees. Only your own staff has an intimate knowledge of your company's products and processes, and the risks that may be associated with them. For smaller companies, however, it may be difficult to entrust the totality of their training programme to a specifically designated person. In such circumstances, hiring a consultancy may be an adequate option.

In the context of this Training Handbook, ICC's recommendation is to follow the route of a train-the-trainers programme: specifically, your company could designate a member of its personnel to follow ICC courses based on this Handbook and entrust this person with the task of spreading the knowledge acquired through this training programme to his or her colleagues in the company.

TRAINING METHODS

The learning characteristics of adult learners are varied and may be different from those of younger learners. Some learn through listening, others through seeing, and many by doing. So, to keep education engaging to a diversified audience, the key is to develop a variety of educational formats and supports, such as videos, lectures, webinars, roundtable discussions and 'brown bag' lunches.

Adult learners tend to value problem-centred and results-oriented teaching methods. They usually expect to contribute their own knowledge to the learning experience and seek education that relates or applies directly to their professional needs. The use of case studies and real-life scenarios (which trainees can be invited to share anonymously) often provides for more practical learning and hits home more effectively. The analysis of case studies should include an assessment of possible courses of action and an examination of their corresponding consequences. To avoid embarrassing anyone from the company, it is wise to 'blind' real-life examples by not referring to explicit names or past events.

Face to face training (with an instructor providing the training to a physically present audience) is generally considered the most effective method for delivering educational activities. Live sessions are more interactive and allow participants to raise questions and exchange views with their colleagues. For smaller companies, this will very often be the ideal solution. However, it will not be a realistic option for many companies with several tens of thousands of employees scattered around the globe. Online training courses, also known as e-learning, provide, in such environments, an interesting alternative. There are many benefits to the use of computer-based or web-based training programmes. They can be accessed at any time and any location. They provide a good medium for delivering key compliance messages to a wide audience in a time-effective manner. They also help compliance officers and senior management keep track of who has been trained and who has not.

Many e-learning products with a focus on ethics and compliance are available on the market. Experience shows that e-learning products which are tailored to the specific needs and circumstances of a company are more effective than those simply providing 'off-the-shelf' solutions. Some e-learning providers offer 'customized' solutions, in which a basic template can be altered to meet individual specifications, while others also develop 'custom' solutions, in which the e-learning tool is designed from the ground up to fit the requirements of an individual client. Whatever training method and support is chosen by the company, the litmus test is to design educational and training activities that are directly relevant to your audience.

Another way for companies with very large and geographically widespread workforce to deploy their training activities is to introduce a 'train-the-trainers' programme in which staff members from the enterprise's different business units and subsidiaries develop the skills and knowledge to plan and present effective and interactive training sessions to their colleagues. By training its own trainers, a company empowers its personnel and directly engages them in the mission of promoting ethics and compliance, thereby facilitating the buy-in of employees for the corporate ethics and compliance programme.

EFFECTIVE TRAINING SHOULD BE:

- Delivered in a clear and understandable language (avoid using legal or administrative jargon).
- Based on robust and memorable content.
- Repeated (regularly) without being completely repetitive.
- Interactive (using real-life scenarios, quizzes, role play, evaluation tests)
- It should be fun, or at least not boring (based on games and humor).
- Tailored to the specific needs of each job function.
- Delivered in different languages.
- Based on telling examples and case law from each region but without any finger pointing.

IS YOUR PROGRAMME EFFECTIVE?

As for every part of your company's ethics and compliance programme, education and training activities should be subject to continuous adaptation and improvement based on a regular review of their effectiveness.

How do you measure the effectiveness of your training activities? The first measure of success is of course the absence of violations of your company's ethical rules. However, corrupt practices are often hidden and may sometimes be revealed several years after they have occurred. It is therefore advisable for companies to use a wide range of indicators to gauge the success of their training activities. At the most basic level, the number of questions raised and the degree of active participation during training sessions give a preliminary indication of the impact of the training method employed. Do your colleague employees feel at ease during the sessions, do they trust the trainers, and do they come forward to ask relevant questions? Feedback from participants can also be collected through a survey: to what extent did you find the training useful, interesting and well-organized? Was the content meaningful and clear? Annual or semi-annual performance review sessions also provide excellent opportunities to obtain feedback from your colleagues on their learning experience.

Since the ultimate goal of training is to influence behaviour (helping personnel to act in the right way when confronted with a risky situation), the effectiveness of a company's training programme should also be measured in terms of its concrete outcomes. For example, an increase in the use of the company's ethics hotline or whistleblowing system may be indicative of a stronger awareness of ethics and compliance issues. Some companies also choose to subject their employees, or certain categories of employees, to a comprehensive compliance examination to make sure that they fully grasp the concepts and can identify the correct ethical and compliant path when confronted with 'grey areas' or when facing solicitation and extortion.

Feedback from participants and an analysis of the concrete outcomes of the training programme should help you identify learning gaps and areas for improvement. These may relate to the adequacy of content, the frequency of training, or the effectiveness of the teaching method. Benchmarking one's training programme with those provided by companies from the same segment of industry or services is another useful way to identify strengths and weaknesses and to generate new ideas. Since education and training is above all a human experience – in which participants value spontaneity and seek inspiration – companies should not hesitate to be creative and to innovate by introducing new teaching methods and learning supports.

Finally, in order to ensure employees' knowledge of ethics and compliance issues remains current, companies may wish to introduce regular refresher courses for managers and employees with certain sensitive functions. Monthly newsletters and other corporate communication channels can also help to reinforce compliance messages throughout the year. Indeed, repetition is not only an effective teaching method, it also shows that the company is consistent about compliance and is fully committed to help its employees and other key stakeholders adhere to the highest ethical standards.

About the author

Corinne Lagache is Senior Vice-President for Trade Compliance & Export Control at Safran, a leading high-technology group with three core businesses: aerospace, defense, and security. Operating worldwide, the Safran group has 62,500 employees. Mrs. Lagache joined Safran from EADS, where she was Vice President of Risk Management and Control as well as Group International Compliance Officer. She graduated in finance, economics and taxation from the Political Science Institute of Paris (Sciences Po Paris) and Paris Dauphine University. Mrs. Lagache is an auditor of the French Institute for Higher National Defense Studies and a Member of the Steering Committee of the International Forum of Business Ethical Conduct.

Chapter 11
Whistleblowing

Michael Davies, Q.C.

*Former Vice President and General Counsel,
General Electric Canada*

One of your most important tasks as an ethics and compliance officer will be to organize a group-wide system allowing employees to share concerns, seek advice, and report suspected violations of your company's ethical and compliance rules. This Chapter discusses the essential ingredients of an effective internal whistleblowing system. A prime objective is to ensure that the system is compatible with the various national legislations of the company's countries of operation, including data privacy laws. Other key matters to consider include whether to permit anonymous reporting, whether to make reporting voluntary or compulsory, and how to deal with false or malicious claims.

WHY ESTABLISH AN INTERNAL WHISTLEBLOWING SYSTEM

How can a responsible company become aware, in a timely fashion, of actual or potential wrongdoing – such as corruption, fraud, and accounting improprieties – by one of its employees or agents?

As a matter of fact, it is other employees within the enterprise who are most likely to become suspicious or aware of any proposed or actual unlawful activity, and who are therefore in the best position to bring it to the company's attention. Internal whistleblowing has been proven to be a major source for the detection of fraudulent behaviour in businesses.

> A study conducted by an international accounting firm revealed that more than 25% of the occurrences of fraud discovered in the enterprises surveyed came to light thanks to a whistleblowing system put into place by these companies.
>
> Source: KPMG Forensic, *"Profile of a Fraudster"*, Survey, 2007, p. 26.

However, potential whistleblowers will not report internally if they fear reprisals from within the company or suspect that management may condone or may even have participated in (or approved) the illegal activity. In that event, the company's ability to take appropriate remedial measures will be severely impaired. If it is not perceived as 'safe' to blow the whistle internally, a conscientious employee will either remain silent and allow the illegal activity to occur or, alternatively, will report the wrongdoing to government authorities or the press.

It is, therefore, very much in the interest of an enterprise to establish, as an integral part of its integrity programme, a whistleblowing system, under which employees (and, to the extent possible, any of the enterprise's agents, suppliers and customers) will feel comfortable reporting concerns without fear of retribution. Early reporting, identification, and resolution of potential issues are critical to the success of the process.

Key ICC resources on whistleblowing

ICC RULES ON COMBATING CORRUPTION (2011)

The *ICC Rules on Combating Corruption* (2011) recommend that each enterprise should consider including in its corporate compliance programme, measures "offering channels to raise, in full confidentiality, concerns, seek advice or report in good faith established or soundly suspected violations without fear of retaliation or of discriminatory or disciplinary action".

Such reporting, notes the Rules, may either be compulsory or voluntary and it can be done on an anonymous or a disclosed basis. All reports in good faith should be investigated and an enterprise should, as per the Rules, establish and maintain proper systems of reporting procedures.

ICC GUIDELINES ON WHISTLEBLOWING (2008)

Similarly, in 2008, ICC issued *Guidelines on Whistleblowing* (2008) aimed at helping companies establish and implement internal whistleblowing programmes and encouraging them to put in place, within their organization and as an integral part of their integrity programme, a whistleblowing system, commensurate with their size and resources.

ESSENTIAL INGREDIENTS OF AN EFFECTIVE WHISTLEBLOWING SYSTEM

Once a company has clearly established a policy providing for employees to report concerns about potential violations of corporate policies, including the company's anti-corruption policy, and once it has appointed high-level qualified personnel of undisputable repute to be in charge of the management and administration of the whistleblowing system, its next step will be to define a clear road map indicating what employees should do when they have a concern. The objective is to encourage employees to report promptly and in a way with which they feel comfortable.

The road map should take into account the following provisions:

1. **Variety of reporting channels:** Employees need a number of available reporting channels within the business unit where they can take a concern (for example, to a supervisor, a company legal counsel or to the next higher level of management). This is important because the concern may involve a fellow worker within the same business unit or possibly the employee's own manager. In this regard, a company would be well advised to appoint at least one corporate ombudsperson, outside and possibly also within each major business unit, who is committed to dealing fairly and objectively with all concerns reported to him or her.

2. **External reporting:** In addition to, or as an alternative to, an internal reporting process, a company might also consider designating a firm, external to the group, specialized in receiving and handling whistleblower reports, to which an employee could also report directly. Such firm should be independent, of undisputable repute, and should offer appropriate guarantees of professionalism and secrecy.
3. **The employee should feel comfortable with the reporting channel used:** Employees should be encouraged to use the reporting procedure with which they are most comfortable. Often reporting to someone within their own business unit can be most effective in arriving at a prompt resolution of an issue. Also, reporting channels should reflect the languages spoken in the different countries of operation.
4. **Voluntary or compulsory?** Prompt reporting of a concern about a possible violation of the company's 'no-bribery policy' and other anti-corruption policies is crucial. Delays are likely to allow a problem to grow. Often the potential problem can be averted or the damage minimized if the issue is raised early enough. Companies are therefore increasingly adopting, if the legislation of the country of operation allows it, an affirmative duty to report or, at the very least, are strongly encouraging employees to report any serious concerns and are rewarding them for doing so.
5. **Anonymous reporting permitted?** Although 'open' reports are preferable and should be encouraged, consideration should also be given to allowing an employee to report anonymously (since otherwise some very serious matters could remain unreported). Evaluating the good faith of whistleblower charges, however, is made more difficult when dealing with anonymous allegations. While anonymous complaints should not be rejected out of hand (because whistleblowers may well have legitimate concerns about reprisals), it is also true that the validity of allegations can be determined much more readily when the identity of the whistleblower is known. In addition, company employees against whom allegations are made are also entitled to fair play. Their rights to defend themselves may be impaired when they have to respond to allegations by unidentified accusers.
6. **Confidentiality protected:** Every reasonable effort should be made to respect a reporting employee's desire for confidentiality consistent with the requirements of carrying on an effective investigation. Also, there are circumstances in which the company must disclose the concern and the findings of its subsequent investigation to appropriate management personnel or government authorities. It is not possible, therefore, for an enterprise to guarantee confidentiality in all circumstances.
7. **Prohibition against retaliation:** Company policy must clearly prohibit any form of retribution or retaliation against an employee who reports information about a policy concern in good faith. Appropriate disciplinary action should be taken against any employee who fails to abide by this prohibition. This is a critical element of a successful whistleblower policy, as employees will not report concerns (particularly those relating to those in more senior positions) when they fear their position in the company may be compromised. This does not, however, exclude a company from taking appropriate

disciplinary action (and in such circumstances, they should certainly do so) if an employee abuses the policy by making false accusations against another employee.

8. **If no corrective action taken:** If the reported problem recurs or if the employee feels that no corrective action has been taken within a reasonable time, he or she should be encouraged to raise the matter with one of the other contacts listed in the company guidelines. Clearly, if the situation seems to be recurring or has not been resolved, the employee should raise it again.

9. **Process for dealing with concerns that are raised:** A company needs to differentiate between various problems raised by whistleblowers and establish a process for each. This involves classifying the concern to determine what needs to be done next, assigning appropriate personnel (from ethics and compliance, finance, legal or human resources) to investigate, determining appropriate corrective actions (for instance clarifying the issues, providing education and training or improving procedures) and, where warranted, taking disciplinary action appropriate to the breach. The latter may range from a warning to suspension or an outright dismissal. Each matter should be diligently tracked to ensure prompt close-out. If allegations relate to people at the top of the company, outside investigators should likely be retained.

10. **Acknowledgement of reports and feedback:** In order for the process to be fair and objective, and be seen to be so by all those involved, all whistleblower reports should be diligently acknowledged, recorded, and screened, and the company should also provide feedback about the outcome of the investigation to the employee who reported the concern as well as to the person whose behaviour was reported.

11. **Periodic reports to the Board:** Significant cases identified by the whistleblowing system and statistical summaries relating to the operation of the system should be regularly reported to the Chief Executive Officer (or other top executive) and the Board of Directors.

12. **Compliance with laws:** Finally, the company should at all times comply with all legal requirements relating to the establishment and implementation of whistleblowing procedures, as well as those related to providing notice to relevant governmental authorities. Companies need to be aware that, in certain jurisdictions and cultural environments and, as a result of data protection and labor law concerns, legal restrictions have been imposed on whistleblowing procedures which will have to be complied with.

PROBLEMS IMPLEMENTING AN INTERNAL WHISTLEBLOWING SYSTEM

The experience of companies in establishing internal whistleblowing systems has shown that concerns reported by employees generally fall into one of four categories:

1. **Real problems:** First, there is the reporting by an employee of a concern that turns out to be a real problem, which the company is then able to deal with in a responsive and responsible manner. The reporting of genuine problems is likely to happen often enough to make the existence of an internal whistleblowing system worthwhile.

2. **Perceived problems:** Often an employee, on the basis of limited information, will in good faith report a concern which, upon further investigation by the company, turns out not to be a problem. In these circumstances, it is most important to communicate the conclusions back to the reporting employee in order to preserve the credibility of the programme and to ensure there is no perception of a cover-up by the company.

3. **Employee grievances:** Employees may try to utilize an internal whistleblowing system as a means of securing redress for personal employee grievances that have nothing to do with a breach of laws or of the company's Code of Conduct. These grievances may include issues relating to promotion or compensation or other job-related disputes with managers or fellow employees. These should be appropriately dealt with by some other process, usually within the human resources department. Initially, a large number of calls may fall into this category, but the problem should decrease rapidly as employees come to understand the real purpose of the whistleblowing process.

4. **Abuse of process:** Finally, although this doesn't happen very frequently, complaints made under an internal whistleblowing system sometimes constitute a clear abuse of the process. First, where the local legal system provides protection for whistleblowers, employees may invent or exaggerate a claim to try and protect themselves from an anticipated lay-off or discharge. Due care needs to be taken to diligently investigate these complaints in order to identify their true purpose. Second, false or malicious reporting of a problem can be used by an unscrupulous employee who has a personal grudge (or some other form of personal animosity) against a manager or another employee or for other improper personal purposes. Appropriate disciplinary action needs to be taken against such an employee to effectively deter this type of abuse.

For a whistleblowing system to work effectively, it is important that the ombudsperson (if there is any such function in the company) and others responsible for administering the internal reporting system be of indisputable integrity and have the requisite knowledge, experience, and training to be able to distinguish between these various categories of employee complaints and to deal with them appropriately. Selecting highly respected local employees to perform and explain the whistleblowing system, the reporting process, and the ombudsperson role, will contribute significantly to the success of the programme, particularly in countries where there is a cultural sensitivity with regard to reporting concerns about fellow employees.

PROBLEMS WITH WHISTLEBLOWING

It is important to recognize that a whistleblowing system will inevitably raise tensions in a company. For the whistleblower, there may be conflicting feelings of loyalty towards fellow employees and a sense of obligation to broader corporate interests, as well as to the overall public interest. Potential whistleblowers are likely to be in a very sensitive and potentially precarious position vis-à-vis those whose conduct they criticize. They can be harassed or ostracized by their fellow employees and are susceptible to being demoted or fired by hostile managers. Quite often there will be disagreements about the propriety or the legality of the actions challenged by the whistleblower, and his or her views may prove to be incorrect. There are also some countries (such those in Central and Eastern Europe) where the memory of state-organized eavesdropping and the historical stigma attributed to whistleblowing still prevail.

Notwithstanding all of these concerns, it is very much in the corporate interest to establish an internal whistleblowing system and to deal pro-actively with concerns raised by whistleblowers.

Summary of the essential ingredients of an effective whistleblowing system

COMPANIES SHOULD:

1. Establish an internal disclosure programme ('whistleblowing') which encourages or, if legally permitted, requires employees to identify concerns within the company about what is or could be a possible violation of the company's anti-corruption policy.
2. Not limit the reporting to information relating to actual breaches of the policy, but extend the programme to concerns or suspicions relating to actions which may lead to illegal acts in order that they can be prevented.
3. Require that concerns be reported promptly, again so that the company may stop the illegal activity before it occurs.
4. Establish effective mechanisms, such as hot-lines and ombudspersons, that can deal confidentially with employee reports and with which an employee will feel comfortable.
5. Guarantee that there will be no retaliation or repercussions regarding issues raised or information provided in good faith.
6. Encourage reports to be made openly but allow them to be made anonymously (since a company would be unwise not to pay attention to anonymous reports) and make best efforts to honor an employee's desire for confidentiality.
7. Establish a process within the enterprise for effectively dealing with concerns that are raised.
8. Take appropriate steps to respond to problems that are identified – including education, modifying processes and disciplinary action, when required – and maintain statistical records that identify trouble spots.
9. Provide periodic reports and summaries to the top of the company or to the Board of Directors and comply with laws (including those relating to external reporting to relevant authorities).
10. Ensure that, whenever possible, the reporting employee and the person accused receives appropriate feedback.

About the author

Michael Davies joined General Electric Canada as Associate General Counsel and, in 1987, was appointed Vice President, General Counsel, and Secretary of the company. He retired in 2002. For almost ten years, he was Chair of the Bribery and Corruption Committee of the Canadian Council for International Business and in that capacity has been an active member of the ICC Commission on Anti-corruption. He was one of the founders of Transparency International and was, for many years, a Director and Vice Chair of the Canadian Chapter of Transparency International.

Chapter 12
Internal Investigations
Juan Jorge Gili
Senior Corporate Risk Manager at Novartis International

No ethics and compliance programme, however robust, will ever guarantee a total absence of misconduct. But it is precisely one of the key functions of your company's programme to appropriately respond to allegations of wrongdoing. This Chapter outlines practical steps to conduct an effective workplace investigation in the event of an alleged breach of law or corporate policies by one of your co-workers. Planning an investigation, searching and gathering relevant information, assessing the facts, preparing an investigation report, and taking remedial action are all measures which require special care, as detailed in the following pages.

There may be many valid reasons for conducting an internal investigation. When it comes to misconduct by one of your fellow employees, the duty to investigate arises for you as soon as allegations of unlawful conduct or policy violation become known to your company. The purpose of an internal investigation is to determine what actually happened and decide which remedial action is needed. As these are sensitive matters, that may have severe consequences for your company and your co-workers, the internal investigation process should be handled with a balance of rigor and sensitivity.

AND NOW WHAT?

The investigation of employee misconduct begins with an allegation or initial concern. It could be that management observes such conduct or that the allegedly improper conduct is reported by another employee. It might also be a customer or vendor who reports suspicious or allegedly improper behaviour. In every case, you should make an initial assessment of the allegation to ascertain whether it justifies further investigation or not, as the company may be held liable for failing to investigate and stop misconduct or fraud that it knew (or should have known) about.

What if the matter at hand does not justify any further investigation? If after an initial assessment the matter is dismissed, a good practice is to attach a note to the complaint, stating the decision taken and why no further action was deemed necessary. But you should not dismiss a complaint just because it does not look serious at first sight.

Once it is clear than an investigation is warranted, you will need to decide who is to conduct the investigation. It is critical that the person designated as the investigator approaches the matter objectively and is perceived as doing so. As each and every situation is different, the same person may not be suitable to conduct every kind of investigation. You should consider the subject matter, the respective positions of the complainant and of the suspected person, the potential impact of the investigation, the outcome on your business operations, and any perception of bias a potential investigator might generate.

Depending on the circumstances, it is sometimes advisable to bring in an external investigator. In complex situations, it could be convenient to appoint a sophisticated multifunctional investigation team.

Investigators should conduct a fast yet thorough examination of the facts and circumstances, without violating the legal rights of any person involved.

PLAN THE INVESTIGATION

One of the most important components of an effective internal investigation is preparation.

You should know what you are investigating and develop a plan for achieving your objectives. Careful planning of the investigation is important to reach a fair outcome. Planning is a step which should not be neglected, no matter how urgent the situation may be.

Some of the questions to be considered before beginning the investigation include:

- Do applicable national laws or industry branch collective agreements subject your company to obligations that you should be aware of, before starting or during the investigation?
    - Consider for example matters like the statute of limitations; meaning in practice: "Is the alleged infringement already time barred or is it going to be time barred very soon?"
    - Special care must also be taken not to breach relevant privacy or personal data protection laws and laws governing an employer's right to monitor employees' communications. Consequently, it is crucial to have a plan to address these potential legal issues from the earliest stages of the investigation.
- You should also consider if you first should obtain specialized assistance from internal or external legal counsel or from a human resources specialist to ensure that you are taking the right course of action. Ensure that you are sufficiently familiar with relevant company policies and, especially, with the rules for searching an employee's workspace, computer, and personal belongings.
- Which persons, if any, have to be interviewed? Which order should you follow for conducting interviews?
- What documents should you look for?
- Should any interim actions be undertaken? Consider if such interim actions may be appropriate and necessary based on the situation. One of the interim actions may be removing the suspected person from the workplace and placing this person on paid leave pending the investigation. Likewise, you should consider restricting the person's access to computers, files, or certain areas of the workplace.

It is important that your company demonstrates that it takes alleged misconduct in good faith or fraud complaints seriously. Waiting too long to conduct an investigation could be perceived as not taking complaints seriously and may prompt the complainant to pursue a formal complaint through the authorities or the courts. Likewise, while you leave the alleged misconduct unaddressed, it could continue to occur, worsening the situation. Another risk of waiting too long to investigate is that the outcome of the investigation can be negatively impacted either because evidence may be destroyed or altered or because, as time goes by, it becomes more difficult to get facts straight, as people may forget the details of the matter.

SEARCH FOR AND GATHER INFORMATION

What, when, who, where, why, and how?

Once an investigator is designated and goals are set, the next step will be to conduct a thorough review of relevant documents.

The investigator should conduct the assignment keeping in mind that the matter may ultimately be debated in court or have to be disclosed to outside parties such as government agencies. For this reason, it is crucial to pay serious attention to documenting the process and to gathering evidence, as the manner in which evidence is obtained and retained may determine its admissibility in court.

First, the investigator should review the allegations in depth and draft a precise chronology of the most relevant facts.

Then, the investigator could continue by studying the background of the matter under investigation, review the suspected person's professional history and the person's position on the company's organizational chart. This will help clarifying relationships and identifying potential biases. It could be helpful to draft a chart of key individuals along with their positions and contact details. In certain cases, it could also be useful to visit the company's websites.

The next step will be determining which persons should be interviewed as well as establishing in which order to proceed with the interviews. Generally, the complainant should come first, followed by reliable witnesses, and then, once the investigator has gathered all reasonably available information, the suspected person. Of course, as said already, every situation is different, and the order of interviewing may vary based on the particular circumstances of each case.

Interview the complainant (unless you are investigating an anonymous complaint)

It is advisable to meet with the complainant in a private location and explain to this person the investigation process. Likewise it is important to discuss confidentiality (avoiding making far reaching promises) as well as to emphasize the no-retaliation policy of the company.

Ask the complainant if there are any relevant documents which are not yet known. The investigator will request the complainant to share additional facts or documents, if any of these come to light after the interview.

Likewise, the complainant will be asked to identify witnesses who may support his or her allegations. Moreover, the investigator should request the complainant to inform on the existence of evidence and of other similar past and present situations.

The investigator should make sure that the questions asked are clear so that an answer can easily be given. If no answer is provided, insist (if possible) by reformulating the question.

On occasion, the complainant may be asked to provide a written statement based on his or her personal knowledge. If this is not possible, ask if the complainant is willing to sign a statement based on the notes of the interview. At a minimum, the investigator should draft the written statement during the interview and verbally recap in the complainant's presence to make sure that the interview notes are accurate.

Interview witnesses

In this context, a 'witness' means any person who may have reliable information about the facts and events under investigation. The interviewees should be appraised of the purpose of the interview. It is important for the investigator to emphasize that he or she does not want to hear speculation, hearsay or the expression of opinions, but is interested in facts that witnesses know of first-hand.

Once the investigator has finished interviewing witnesses, he or she may ask them to identify other persons who may contribute additional factual knowledge, and then proceed with the interview of these persons.

As with the complainant, it may on occasion be necessary to obtain a written statement. If not, the investigator should recap the notes verbally to make sure that they accurately reflect the witnesses' statements.

Search and gather all relevant data

Relevant data the investigator should search for and gather may, depending on the circumstances, include the following. In doing this research, the investigator should be particularly careful to comply with the legal provisions protecting personal data and their conservation:

- Electronic documents and logs. This may include e-mails, electronic diaries, and files. To preserve the data gathered, it could be convenient to make a mirror image of the hard-disk or any other electronic storage media.
- Paper documents. Documents to be reviewed may include company policies and procedures, expense reports, checks, invoices, personnel files, performance appraisals, correspondence, and contracts. All paper documents should be referenced with a unique number and stored securely. In certain circumstances, it is advisable to digitally scan relevant documents.
- Telephone logs (numbers dialled and calls received).
- Security system logs (for example, video surveillance analyses). One may need to collect the names of those who had access to certain areas of the company's premises at a particular time.

To perform the investigation under the best possible conditions, the investigator should also bear in mind the following:

- When conducting a search, a designated person should be present to observe how the search is conducted and to take note of what is found. This will help you and the investigator answering, for instance, any possible complaint about non-respect of the personal data protection laws.
- Another practical concern that may arise when conducting a cross-border internal investigation is language and communication. If the investigation requires reviewing documents drafted in local language or conducting interviews with local associates, the investigator should arrange early on for adequate translation.

Interview the suspected employee

The investigator will want to confront the employee concerned in a non-adversarial manner by sharing with this person the allegations, and allowing to offer an answer and to listen to this person's version of the facts. Meeting with the suspected employee should take place as soon as possible after having gathered the necessary information from other sources. Note that in certain jurisdictions, a meeting with an employee that may lead to disciplinary action will require proper notice to the employee concerned and to the company's works council representatives.

It is advisable to have another person, such as a manager or a human resources representative, present during the interview to take detailed notes and to prevent disputes about what was stated during the meeting. Also consider having a witness observe how the interview was conducted to avoid allegations that the suspected person was intimidated during the interview.

At the start of the interview, the investigator should try to create an atmosphere of mutual trust and confidence. At the same time, appropriate disclosure should be made to the person concerned about what the investigation is about. The employee should be provided a sufficiently detailed description of what the person is said to have done or what the concern is. One should explain that the interview is designed to give the employee an opportunity to relate his or her version of the facts, to respond to the allegations made, and to communicate any other information that should be considered during the investigation, as well as to reveal the possible existence of witnesses who could confirm the concerned person's story.

If the suspected employee refuses to participate in the interview, one will try to ascertain why and remind the suspected employee that he or she has a duty to reasonably cooperate with the company, whilst employed. Advise that company management, in the absence of any cooperation in the interview, will have to base its decision on other information gathered through the investigation. On the other hand, if the suspected employee requests to leave the interview, this request should be granted and duly documented.

One will start with broad, open-ended questions ("Tell me about ..."). It would be unwise to start with tough interrogations, as this may cause the person to become defensive or non-cooperative. Then, move to narrower, pointed follow-up questions, and keep unfriendly or possibly embarrassing questions for the end of the interview. Ensure the employee is given a reasonable opportunity to provide a full response and explanation.

If an interviewee declines to answer one or more questions, the person should be asked the reasons for such attitude and one will record that explanation. One should see, in case of refusal if it is possible to ask the same question(s) in a different way.

One will carefully observe the interviewee; nonverbal cues can be as important as verbal responses. Attention should be paid to how the suspected employee is reacting to difficult questions, and what does his or her body language tell you.

If the concerned employee denies the allegation, the investigator will ask for an explanation of the facts from his or her point of view and ask for names of witnesses who could support this version.

One should also determine if the suspected employee has knowledge of the company's policies as, if not, it could be a mitigating circumstance.

The investigator will ask the interviewee if there is any other matter he or she wants to tell about and that should be considered. The interviewee will be told that if he or she remembers additional information after the interview, the investigator will welcome the sharing of these additional facts.

At the conclusion of the interview, the investigator should confirm the accuracy of the information gathered. To do so, the investigator will summarize the interview by repeating the most relevant points and asking the interviewee to confirm that the information is accurate and complete. If this is not the case, questions will be asked for clarification purposes.

Finally, one should inform the suspected employee that the company will be continuing the investigation in order to reach a conclusion, that the employee will be advised of the outcome, and that this process may lead, if the company reaches a negative conclusion, to disciplinary action. Moreover, one should stress the confidentiality of the investigation and request the suspected employee not to discuss the matter with other employees. Last but not least, the suspected employee will be warned that the company will not tolerate retaliation or reprisals against the complainant or anybody else involved in the investigation.

If the suspected employee asks detailed questions about the allegation under investigation that could damage the investigation, the investigator is not obliged to answer. However, one should answer reasonable questions that allow the employee to provide a full response or allow him or her to better understand the investigation process.

Confidentiality

If any of the participants in the investigation requests confidentiality, remember that one cannot promise absolute confidentiality. Depending upon the result of the investigation, disclosure may be required, and failure to uphold confidentiality may result in lawsuits or acts of retaliation against those involved in the investigation. Explain that the information will only be shared on a need-to-know basis in the interest of everyone involved.

Record the results of the interviews

It is preferable that the investigator takes notes during the interview but if he or she feels that it may take his or her attention away and impede his or her ability to listen attentively, one will try to have the help of another person to take notes. If this is not possible, one will prepare the interview record immediately after the interview is completed, because memory recall is often at best incomplete and at worse inaccurate.

It will be necessary to always indicate the place, date, and time of the interviews as well as the names of all those present. One will not forget to date and sign the notes, and ask interviewees to review and sign them.

Compliance with law and collective agreements

It is fundamental to ensure full compliance with applicable laws and relevant collective agreement provisions along the entire investigation. Violating fundamental obligations of procedure under a collective agreement or relevant labour law during an investigation, no matter how innocent, can result in disciplinary measures being disallowed by a judge. In turn, it might raise responsibility in case the concerned employee files a complaint alleging a breach of his or her privacy rights, or raising defamation or emotional distress issues.

ASSESS THE FACTS

The investigation process is intended to provide you with a clear picture of the facts.

One of the major challenges for those in charge of conducting an investigation is to determine credibility as they are often confronted with different stories.

When attempting to determine whether a person is relating accurately a story, they should look to the following factors for assistance:

- What is the interviewee's conduct like? Did the interviewee tell the story in a convincing manner?
- Was the story reasonable? Did the story have internal consistency? Did the different pieces fit together, or were there things out of place?
- If the story was told more than once, did the story remain consistent?
- Did the interviewee have a bias or self-interest which might taint the story?
- Is the story told by the interviewee probable or not?

The more serious the offence, the more convincing must be the evidence.

Sometimes, the outcome of the investigation will be inconclusive and it will not be possible to determine whether the alleged wrongdoing occurred. When this happens, the complainant and the suspected employee should be so informed in a neutral manner and clearly advised that any kind of retaliation or reprisal will not be tolerated. Invite the complainant to report any future violation. Consider if it would be worthwhile conducting individualized or department-wide training.

THE INVESTIGATION REPORT

Usually the findings of the investigation will be documented in writing. The investigation findings are not the investigator's opinions, but summarize the facts that were learned during the investigation and that can be supported.

It may be worthwhile asking an in-house or external legal counsel to draft the report if this would give this document legal privilege. In any case, the investigation report should be written assuming that it may have to be disclosed to parties other than the addressee.

Bear in mind that the investigation report should only address topics that are within the scope of the internal investigation. It should be written in a clear, concise, factual, and objective manner, leaving no room for ambiguity or speculation.

TAKING REMEDIAL ACTION

"What did you do when you found out about it?"

That is a crucial question. Once the investigation is completed and the investigation report has been issued, management should determine what kind of action, if any, should be taken.

Do not take action against the suspected employee unless the outcome of the investigation is clear. In case of doubt, you should consider either investigating further or, if you deem continuing the investigation not feasible or unreasonable, bring the matter to an end.

When the allegation is substantiated, management should determine the appropriate remedial action. Disciplinary measures may include oral or written warning, suspension or even termination, as detailed in the company's Code of Conduct. Each instance should be carefully reviewed and several factors should be considered including:

- The severity of the proved misconduct;
- The concurrence of aggravating or mitigating circumstances;
- The accused employee's employment record;
- How similar situations have been handled in the past to ensure consistency; and
- Whether or not there is any provision in relevant legislation, collective agreements, policies, or regulations.

Any disciplinary action should be properly documented.

It is important you provide clear guidelines for future misconduct and establish severity of future discipline in the event of repeated conduct.

If the disciplinary action does not include termination, the situation should be properly monitored to identify potential signs of retaliation as well as recurring misconduct of the disciplined employee.

Additionally to taking disciplinary measures, as part of the remedial action plan, you should consider adopting general preventive measures like re-circulating the policy that has been broken and conducting additional training.

Notice to the parties

- **Communication with the complainant:** Inform the complainant of the investigation results and that appropriate remedial action is being taken without going into unnecessary detail. Likewise, tell the complainant what to do if this person experiences retaliation or becomes aware of additional misconduct, and reiterate the message about the confidentiality of the investigation.

- **Communication with the disciplined employee:** Management should inform the disciplined employee of the conclusion reached and provide this person with sufficient explanation. Inform the person concerned about the remedial action, if any. Warn him or her against any type of reprisal. If appropriate, warn that future misconduct will result in additional discipline, up to termination. Finally, reiterate once again the confidentiality of the investigation.

- **Communication with witnesses:** There is no need to inform others about the details of the investigation. Remind them, if need be, that the investigation is confidential.

Additionally, you may consider communicating to colleagues and associates of the disciplined person or even, if necessary, to third parties that a compliance investigation was conducted and that, as a result of the findings, management took appropriate action to resolve the matter. Seize the opportunity to reinforce the policy in question and remind the persons concerned of the no-tolerance principle for misconduct. This will help stop rumours and set the right tone.

Bad faith reporting

If the outcome of the investigation determines that the complainant made the allegations in bad faith, management should determine what type of disciplinary action, if any, would be appropriate for the complainant.

About the author

Juan Jorge Gili is Senior Corporate Risk Manager at Novartis International since April 2013. With global headquarters in Basel, Switzerland, Novartis is a multinational healthcare company with operations in over 140 countries. Prior to this position, Mr. Gili served as Global Compliance and Risk Management Officer for the Novartis Over-the-Counter (OTC) Division, being a member of the Novartis Compliance Leadership Team. Mr. Gili graduated in 1985 from the University of Navarra, Spain, and holds a Master in Company Law (LL.M.) from the Instituto de Empresa Business School in Madrid. He is a member of the Barcelona Bar since 1988.

ICC ETHICS AND COMPLIANCE TRAINING HANDBOOK

Chapter 13
Resisting Solicitation
Iohann Le Frapper
Chief Legal Officer at GBI

This Chapter focuses on the demand side of bribery. We explore here the role of business in resisting and denouncing all forms of bribe solicitation and extortion. Demands for bribes can come in many forms. They typically occur at the pre-sales and bidding stage of a project, but also in the context of project implementation and day-to-day operations. We stress the importance of training, notably through the use of the RESIST scenarios, a practical tool designed to help employees prevent and respond to inappropriate demands in the most efficient and ethical way. The B20 proposal for a High-Level Reporting Mechanism, if appropriately implemented, could constitute another useful resource for companies to rely on when faced with bribe solicitation.

INTRODUCTION

Fighting corruption is one of the core components of corporate responsibility and good corporate governance. Companies have an important role to play in supporting government initiatives to combat corruption and taking appropriate steps to prevent illicit and unethical business practices from taking place.

The strengthening of anti-corruption and anti-money laundering laws, the increase of public investigations, the growing number of shareholder and competitor suits coming on top of government bribery prosecutions, the risk for managers of spending time in jail or losing their jobs and, last but not least, the reputational and brand impact of media coverage of bribery-related developments (with immediate and worldwide coverage in our digital society) make a compelling case for companies to work against passive as well as active corruption.

The role of business in the fight against corruption revolves around two distinct but complementary priorities:

(i) The design and implementation of robust corporate compliance programmes, aimed at preventing all forms of active corruptive practices; and

(ii) The development of strong internal policies rendering companies capable of resisting and denouncing all forms of solicitation and extortion.

This Chapter focuses on the latter aspect of the business fight against corruption, namely how to resist solicitation and extortion.

COMPANIES CONTINUE TO BE VICTIMS OF SOLICITATION

Many companies, including those that have implemented robust compliance programmes, report that they continue to face direct or indirect demands for bribes. While they generally resist such attempts, some companies admit being tempted at times to acquiesce in these demands due to their frequency and the insistence of bribe-askers. They think, often erroneously, that giving in to bribe demands under these circumstances can be justified as an acceptable response to extortion.

A demand for a bribe may or may not be accompanied by a threat. But it is important to bear in mind that if a bribe demand or request is accompanied by a threat, this will only be a valid defense to a bribery prosecution if one was acting under necessity or duress, or when the health, security, or safety of a company employee or agent was at risk. In other words, a purely verbal or psychological threat, not accompanied by any pressure on the health, safety, or security of the person concerned, will not be considered as a sufficient defense by a judge or a prosecutor.

WHAT DO WE MEAN BY SOLICITATION OR EXTORTION?

In Chapter 4 (*'Glossary'*), we have examined the definitions of solicitation and extortion, while taking note of the relevant provisions from the *ICC Rules on Combating Corruption* (2011).

Certain legal instruments refer to solicitation and extortion as 'passive corruption'. This expression gives the wrong impression that the person requesting or demanding a bribe is just at the receiving end of the transaction. In many instances, however, the 'passively' corrupt person will often be very active and may even make strenuous efforts to obtain a bribe.

It is also worth noting that both extortion and solicitation are criminally sanctioned but the sanctions applicable to extortion may differ from those applicable to solicitation.

REGULATORY AND ENFORCEMENT TRENDS

Although bribe solicitation and extortion are daily challenges for business, they received only minimal attention in the early international anti-corruption instruments. The *OECD Convention* (1997), which was structured on the *United States Foreign Corrupt Practices Act* (1977), is mainly directed against the 'supply side' of bribery. The idea of the drafters of the *OECD Convention* was that if they succeeded in stopping the supply side of corruption (mainly originating from Western developed countries), demand would naturally taper off.

Things have changed, however, in the years following the adoption of the *OECD Convention*. Several explicit provisions of the *United Nations Convention* (2003) prohibit 'passive' corruption in both the public and the private sector. Even before 2003, requests or demands for bribes were widely prohibited by national laws. It should also be stressed that the frequency of prosecutions for requesting or demanding a bribe has dramatically increased in recent years.

This evolution towards embracing both the supply and the demand of bribes is reflected in the recent OECD document entitled *Good Practice Guidance on Internal Controls, Ethics, and Compliance*, also referred to as *Annex II to the OECD Recommendation of the Council for Further Combating Bribery of Foreign Public Officials in International Business Transactions* (2010)[24]. The Guidance calls the business community:

- To provide companies – in particular, small and medium-sized enterprises – with general advice and support on resisting extortion and solicitation; and
- To implement measures to address major risk areas, including solicitation and extortion, as part of companies' ethics and compliance programme.

SOURCES OF SOLICITATION AND EXTORTION

Regardless of their size, many companies face solicitation or extortion when doing business abroad. Although endemic corruption is often associated with emerging markets, media reports show that industrialized countries are not immune from corrupt practices. In particular, the funding of political parties remains a cause of corruption in many OECD countries.

In certain countries, the demand side of corruption may not stem from greed but from the need for low-level officials with low wages to maintain a decent standard of living. In today's challenging economic times, the temptation for a public official to solicit a kickback (to increase or maintain his or her family's standard of living) may even increase. Likewise, it will be particularly tempting for a sales manager to pay a bribe in order to meet yearly sales targets (and secure bonus entitlements, if not a career move or promotion).

BRIBERY AS A 'COST OF DOING BUSINESS'

Unfortunately, recent surveys show that a significant number of managers, including company executives, still believe that paying a bribe can be justified as a necessary evil to win business in certain countries. They see bribes as a 'cost of doing business', particularly if the business transaction at stake is needed to reach strategic corporate objectives.

The lack of a level playing field in many industries raises very valid concerns when competitors (eager to gain market share or to enter new markets) use bribes to secure the award of a project or to lock in a preferred business relationship. Bribes also sometimes are paid to influence bidding requirements, whether technical or otherwise.

As a compliance officer, in the course of your ethics and compliance training sessions, you will often hear comments like: "Our competitors are doing it" or "We just lost a strategic project in a key market because our competitor bribed the decision-makers." It will be your task to explain in crystal clear terms why your company refuses to pay bribes and has chosen to resist solicitation and extortion.

In doing so, you should not restrict yourself to a mere 'rules-based' position ("Paying a bribe to a public official is against the law"). Try to

---

[24] http://www.oecd.org/daf/ca/corporategovernanceprinciples/31557724.pdf

explain the reasons why the company rejects all forms of corruption, including under the guise of solicitation. It will be particularly telling for your audience to hear concrete examples of the dire consequences stemming from unethical business practices for your company and your industry at large. Using examples will not only allow you to capture the attention of your audience, but also to make sure that your colleagues understand that paying a bribe can lead to serious consequences for the company as well as for themselves as individuals.

VARIOUS FORMS OF SOLICITATION AND EXTORTION

At the bidding stage of a project, a company that declines solicitation will be faced with the risk of losing a specific business opportunity or facing a de facto ban from a particular customer, if not outright exclusion from the market or country at stake. We will see in Chapter 17 (*Managing the Transition to a Clean Commercial Policy*), how to face the risk of losing business.

Solicitation may also occur at the implementation stage of a project. Once a company is awarded a contract, it needs to invest significant resources to deliver the products or services promised to the customer. In such a context, it may be exposed to various types of pressure from different stakeholders. For instance:

- Your company may face the threat of delays in the issuance of a permit that is required to meet the project's time schedule. Such delays can result in high liquidated damages being assessed against the company or may even entitle the customer to terminate the relationship for a breach of contract.
- Your company may face unreasonable delays in approving the payment of its invoices or a refusal to sign an acceptance certificate, despite the fact that the equipment was supplied or the services were provided in accordance with contractual specifications. This may jeopardize the company's ability to collect receivables from the customer.

With the return on project investment at stake, it will be very challenging for a field project manager to reject a demand for a bribe, knowing that he or she is accountable for the timely and successful commissioning of large infrastructure, such as a power plant, or the implementation of an important service package, such as a software solution. Pressure on managers to achieve results may further increase when the variable portion of their compensation is significant.

SMALLER COMPANIES CONFRONTED WITH SOLICITATION

Business leaders, regulators and commentators generally agree that companies need to be proactive in their efforts to combat corruption. The companies that are known to have a strong policy against bribery tend to experience less extortion and solicitation than others. A refusal to deviate from such firm standing may be relatively easier to achieve for a large company than for a small- or medium-sized enterprise, whose financial credit worthiness might be at stake if the collection of one large outstanding payment is critical to meet its financial commitments towards its banks.

As we have seen in Chapter 9 ('*The Compliance Challenge for Smaller Enterprises*'), smaller businesses are more vulnerable to solicitation than larger companies, in part because they tend to have fewer resources to prevent corruption. They are often newcomers in exposed international markets who have not yet established a track record of resistance to solicitation. As smaller companies generally have less diverse income streams than their larger counterparts, the threat that may come with a bribe solicitation can be extremely destabilizing.

SHOULD YOUR COMPANY WITHDRAW FROM A PROBLEMATIC COUNTRY?

Several companies have acknowledged that, when confronted with endemic corruption in certain markets, they came to the conclusion that doing business in a specific country was no longer a worthwhile option. Such assessment is based on a thorough analysis of business benefits versus legal, financial, and reputational risks. Some companies have chosen to withdraw from certain countries, although they were aware that by doing so they opened the door to competitors with lower ethical and compliance standards.

A decision to stop doing business in an excessively 'high-risk' country is not necessarily a permanent one. A company may be able to capitalize on its withdrawal when, several years later, it comes back to that country and touts its 'no-bribe policy' as a competitive advantage, while stressing its ability to sell products and services based solely on pricing and innovation, quality or reliability, without hidden costs.

TRAINING WITH RESIST

For many years, ICC has urged companies to resist demands for bribes and stressed the benefit of using training tools such as RESIST (*Resisting Extortion and Solicitation in International Transactions*)[25] to identify practical ethical responses to dilemmas.

Based on real-life scenarios, RESIST is designed to provide practical guidance for company employees on how to prevent and respond to an inappropriate demand by a customer, business partner, or public official in the most efficient and ethical way, recognizing that such a demand may be accompanied by a threat.

Within companies, this training tool is mainly directed to:
- Those, like yourself, in charge of organizing ethics, compliance, and integrity training; and
- Individual employees involved in sales, marketing, and operations.

RESIST is the result of a successful partnership among four major international organizations involved in the fight against corruption:
- The International Chamber of Commerce;
- Transparency International;
- The United Nations Global Compact; and
- The World Economic Forum/Partnering Against Corruption Initiative.

---

[25] http://www.iccwbo.org/products-and-services/fighting-commercial-crime/resist/

In addition to these four sponsors, it is worth noting that the main contributors were anti-corruption specialists from European, North American, and African companies. Since the launch of this joint initiative in 2007, RESIST has gained growing visibility and traction beyond the rather closed circle of anti-corruption experts and organizations involved in the fight against corruption. RESIST is available in six languages: English, French, Spanish, Mandarin, Arabic, and German.

TWO PHASES OF THE CONTRACTUAL LIFETIME

Reflecting the normal life-cycle of projects, the RESIST tool is made up of two sections:

- Phase 1 covers the pre-contract stage and the business development period until the project award; and
- Phase 2 covers the contract implementation;

RESIST consists of:

(i) Seven scenarios of solicitation which may arise during the procurement process (at the pre-bidding or bidding stage until the award of a project to a company);

(ii) 15 scenarios of solicitation or extortion attempts which may arise during the course of the project implementation; and

(iii) An annex listing generic recommendations to prevent and resist solicitation and extortion, which are applicable to the 22 scenarios.

Each of the 22 scenarios addresses two basic questions in a concrete and specific manner:

- How can the enterprise prevent the demand from being made in the first place? and
- How should the enterprise react if the demand is made?

The Annex includes a series of good practice recommendations that can apply to most situations. Users of RESIST should study the generic recommendations before reviewing the individual scenarios. Responses to the dilemmas that are presented in the toolkit usually comprise individual company responses as well as some form of collective action.

The RESIST toolkit was designed as a 'Public Good'. As such it has the following features:

- The RESIST materials are subject to a joint copyright of the four sponsors;
- The agreed approach was, and remains, to facilitate the global dissemination of the materials made available, on a free of charge basis, on each of the sponsors' websites; and
- Any use of the materials for commercial purposes is expressly prohibited.

THE TRAINING TOOLKIT 'ERESIST'

On the initiative of ICC France, several companies contributed to the design and development of 'eRESIST', an on-line training toolkit based on the RESIST scenarios. This free of charge, interactive online training tool meets the needs of companies that seek to train their teams on the risks of corrupt practices and to prepare them to resist inappropriate requests. This training tool includes an initial programme of 10 modules chosen from the 22 RESIST scenarios. It offers a modern method of training that emphasizes proximity, interactivity, and accessibility to all teams, wherever they are located. The toolkit is available on the ICC France website (http://www.icc-france.fr/). It will be released initially in two languages (French and English) but the application will enable translation into other languages.

PREVENTIVE MEASURES

The *ICC Rules on Combating Corruption* (2011) recommend that each enterprise choose, as part of an efficient corporate compliance programme, the procedures that are the best adapted to its particular circumstances. Each enterprise also is urged to ensure proper prevention against corruption and to support collective action, for example by proposing or supporting anti-corruption pacts relating to specific projects, or by taking part in anti-corruption initiatives with the public sector and industry peers.

Although the responses provided in the RESIST toolkit may apply to all companies, the solutions proposed should not be implemented 'as is' in the field. As for any proper compliance programme, each company should determine how each recommendation can be adapted to its needs, taking into account its size, industry, countries of operation, and the exact nature of the solicitation or extortion attempt.

Cultural considerations should not be ignored. The way a staff member negatively responds to a bribe demand, which may have been expressed in a more or less subtle manner by an intermediary, does not have to be the same and depends on the country's culture. A standard and straightforward "no" answer, without proper explanation, may be perceived as very offensive if, for example, the solicited manager lives in the country concerned and feels exposed to retaliation such as physical threats. Again, if there is a demonstrable risk of physical retaliation, there will be virtually no risk of prosecution under the main anti-corruption laws.

The recommendations provided in the RESIST toolkit, whether generic or specific to a scenario, emphasize the need to explain to the soliciting person why solicitation and its acceptance can expose both persons and their organizations to prosecution. Moreover, the safety of your colleagues, agents or representatives either living in the country or on a business trip should be of paramount importance to the company and its stakeholders.

There are multiple real-life examples where a project manager or field engineer may be stopped on the road by police or military officials who may request a small cash payment in exchange for the release of their confiscated passports or other personal belongings. Such a threat will normally not qualify as a defense to a bribery prosecution or discourage a bribery prosecution from being initiated in the first place. However, in some extreme situations the threat may expose an employee's life or physical integrity, and in that case it will be possible to invoke a defense to prosecution.

COLLECTIVE ACTION

It is also worth noting the recent and growing trend of 'collective action' initiatives either through specific industry initiatives or multi-industry coalitions with a view to:

- Addressing the 'demand' side of bribery; and
- Emphasizing the need for best practices and robust compliance programmes to ensure a 'level playing field' for all companies globally.

Competing bidders intending to cooperate in resisting solicitation should first seek legal advice to ensure that such cooperation does not violate applicable antitrust or procurement laws. 'Integrity pacts' were developed by Transparency International to enhance a level playing field and record the undertaking by all bidders and the customer not to offer or pay bribes to win a call for tenders.

Some real-life examples of solicitation and extortion:

- A small enterprise, specialized in chemicals, has sold its product for the last seven years to a giant textile mill in an emerging country. The mill's new purchasing manager mentions to the enterprise that a competitor offered substantial gifts and wonders if the enterprise can match these.
- A company has a manufacturing subsidiary in an emerging country. One day an employee of the local power supply company informs the company of impeding power cuts. The power company signals that this problem might be avoided with a little 'extra help'.
- A company has finished construction of a chemicals production plant. All that remains is to recover a 15% retention bond after a successful start-up. The company is informed that it would help to pay 8% to Mr. X. Once this is done, the start-up of the plant will run smoothly and a protocol confirming the successful start-up will be signed.
- A businessman from a country, that produces first-class raw materials, offers a company interesting qualities of these raw materials at prices substantially under the world market level. However, the company is asked to pay significant amounts into a Geneva bank account to ensure a second delivery.
- Having made an in-depth study of costs, availability of qualified staff, and local suppliers, a company decides to set up a factory in country X. When construction comes to an end, it asks the local telephone company for 30 outside lines. One evening, one of the telephone company's staff pays a visit and asks if the company needs these lines within three days, three months, or two years.

REPORTING SOLICITATION THROUGH APPROPRIATE CHANNELS

Companies have a duty to prevent corruption. Now the question is: Do they also have an obligation to denounce the solicitation or extortion of bribes? The answer to this apparently innocent question is not easy. Companies may be reluctant to name individuals or groups since their attempt to solicit or extort can only be evidenced in very rare circumstances.

The past few years have witnessed a multiplication of proposals to create channels to report on bribe solicitation via different means. Such proposals were initiated by:

- The Ministry or Department of Justice of certain countries. In such circumstances, special care should be given to the use made of reports to a public administration and the possible business implications for the reporting company;
- Market regulators, such as stock exchange bodies;
- Dedicated public agencies, such as the anti-corruption agency of the European Union (OLAF), the Serious Fraud Office in the United Kingdom, the Central Service for Corruption Prevention in France, or the Independent Commission Against Corruption in Hong Kong;
- Civil society stakeholders, including non-governmental organizations and media, such as the http://ipaidabribe.com/ website in India; and
- Internal reporting or alert systems set up by companies (the so-called 'hotlines').

HIGH-LEVEL REPORTING MECHANISMS

The business community has continuously expressed its strong interest in finding concrete, appropriate and effective means to address the demand side of corruption. It therefore comes as no surprise that the B20 Working Group on Improving Transparency and Anti-Corruption repeatedly called on G20 Leaders to support the development of collective action and sector-based initiatives to combat solicitation. One concrete proposal has been to establish an appropriate form of a High-Level Reporting Mechanism to address allegations of solicitation of bribes by public officials.

The High-Level Reporting Mechanism proposed by the B20 offers an efficient answer to address the issue of bribe solicitation. This is going to be one of the most challenging topics on the global anti-corruption agenda for the years to come. The proposed specifics of the High-Level Reporting Mechanism are as follows:

For governments:

- The reporting mechanism should be established by governments at a sufficiently high level to enlist the support of government agencies engaged in procurement and regulation of business. Separating the reporting mechanism from the procurement agencies should also alleviate concerns about retaliation against whistleblowers.
- The reporting mechanism should be available to domestic as well as foreign companies to present allegations of solicitation of bribes by government officials and intermediaries.

- Governments should design a mechanism, consistent with applicable legal requirements, with the objective of facilitating the speedy resolution of allegations:
    - Whenever possible, informal means should be used to determine whether there is a reasonable basis for the allegations and whether improprieties can be effectively eliminated. For example, when bribe solicitation is directed to more than one bidder, contacting other bidders can provide a simple way to confirm the reality of the allegations made.
    - Bribe solicitation is often conducted through intermediaries. Inquiries by the reporting mechanism may be sufficient to cause bribe requests to be dropped.
- Even though the primary objective of the reporting mechanism is preventative, governments would have full discretion to take disciplinary action, disqualify companies, or initiate criminal proceedings.
- The reporting mechanism should not be regarded as the exclusive way to deal with solicitations of bribes. For example, governments that use their commercial 'attachés' to help companies deal with bribe solicitation by foreign officials should be free to continue to do so.

For companies:
- The use of the reporting mechanism by companies should remain voluntary. Companies would be expected to submit adequate information to support their allegations. The decision to submit an allegation should be approved by senior management after a serious investigation;
- The name of the company submitting the allegation would have to be disclosed;
- The reporting mechanism should be used when it becomes apparent that a bribe is being solicited; and
- The reporting mechanism is most likely to function successfully in countries where there is high-level government commitment to curb corruption.

The proposed reporting mechanism represents an innovative approach to dealing with the demand side of bribery. Unfortunately, while this reporting mechanism is an interesting solution to prevent corruption, companies reporting solicitation may still face retaliation in the form of harassment, threats, or firing and it will always be possible that their disclosures will be ignored.

Moreover, some countries are still unwilling to introduce comprehensive whistleblower legislation to protect those who speak up and to ensure that their claims are properly investigated. In such circumstances, companies, public bodies, and non-profit organizations should introduce adequate mechanisms for internal reporting.

It should be noted, however, that the proposed High-Level Reporting Mechanism has also raised some serious and legitimate objections:

- From a business perspective: There is a risk that the reporting mechanism may be misused by competitors to raise unsubstantiated allegations against a successful competitor to cancel the award of a project, or to delay for years the ability of such bidder to deliver a project and receive the related business and financial benefits; and
- From the perspective of national regulators or enforcement agencies: The recourse to the reporting mechanism should not be seen as a substitute for appropriate disclosure and reporting mechanisms, as provided by existing legal and regulatory frameworks.

About the author

Iohann Le Frapper is the Chief Legal Officer of GBI, a Gulf-based telecom carrier. Prior to his current position, Mr. Le Frapper was the General Counsel Networks group at Alcatel-Lucent. Since 2004 he has gained significant experience in designing and implementing compliance policies. In 2009, Mr. Le Frapper was appointed chair of the RESIST project, a business ethics training toolkit jointly sponsored by the International Chamber of Commerce, the World Economic Forum/Partnering Against Corruption Initiative, Transparency International and the United Nations Global Compact. In 2013, Mr. Le Frapper became Vice-Chair of the ICC Commission on Corporate Responsibility and Anti-corruption. He is also a member of the global Board of Directors of the Association of Corporate Counsel.

PART 4

MANAGING BUSINESS RELATIONSHIPS

Chapter 14

Agents, Intermediaries, and Other Third Parties

Richard J. Battaglia

Senior Counsel, Steptoe & Johnson and Former Senior Counsel, Regulatory Compliance, at BP America

Lucinda A. Low

Partner, Steptoe & Johnson

WHO ARE THE 'THIRD PARTIES' YOU NEED TO BE CONCERNED ABOUT?

In this Chapter, we address the corruption risks posed by persons and entities that act for, or provide services or goods to, your company and who are not its employees.

Third parties are most everyone who provides your company with services or goods to one degree or another.

These 'third parties' include the persons your company hires to act as agents or representatives of the company in its outward dealings, such as its dealings with government agencies, whether in the sales and marketing function or in other areas. They can be brokers, finders, or business development consultants or accountants, attorneys or other professional advisers. They can also include vendors and service providers of all types including suppliers of equipment and materials, distributors, customs agents, ship brokers, port agents, freight forwarders, 'formalities' agents who assist with corporate filings and obtaining visas and work permits, architects and engineers and construction contractors, zoning and land use consultants, environmental consultants, and teaming partners or joint-venture partners (for the latter category of third parties, see Chapter 15).

All these third parties (also referred to as 'business partners' in this Chapter) can present a risk to your company from an anti-corruption perspective, because of who they may be (government officials or their close relatives or associates; companies owned or controlled by a government official or persons associated with them), or because of who they may interact with and how they will do so. Your company's liability for the actions of such business partners may depend in part on the nature of your company's relationship with them, but they all create some degree of vicarious liability risk.

This Chapter is meant to help you identify and minimize those risks, while maintaining courteous and productive relationships with your business partners.

WHY ARE THEY A RISK?

A legal reason

Under agency law, you may be held liable for the actions of your agents during the course of their performance of services for you. Statutes that prohibit transnational corruption expand the scope of vicarious liability beyond your agents, particularly to all providers of services and, in some cases, to vendors and suppliers of goods. The *United States Foreign Corrupt Practices Act* (1977), for example, treats approval or furtherance of improper payments as an offense: This can include your approval and payment of an invoice for a shipment of goods if you know or are deliberately ignorant of the fact that the shipping party or freight forwarder paid bribes to deliver the goods to you in time and is seeking reimbursement or compensation for the improper payment. The *Foreign Corrupt Practices Act* prohibits improper payments made 'indirectly' by 'any person' on your behalf, with or without a contractual relationship. Mitigating this risk requires principals to take steps to prevent and detect improper payments by their business partners.

Accounting rules

For companies subject to the accounting requirements of the *Foreign Corrupt Practices Act*, the statute also requires that you have internal controls in place to provide "reasonable assurance" that the company's books and records fairly and accurately reflect the nature of each transaction, including each payment to your business partners. Other national anti-corruption statutes include similar or analogous requirements. The *United Kingdom Bribery Act* (2010) imposes strict liability for bribery by associated persons or service providers unless a company has "adequate procedures" in place. This creates a strong incentive to take affirmative steps to prevent any act of bribery by your business partners (as well as your employees) in the context of their relationship with your company. Hence, the *ICC Guidelines on Agents, Intermediaries and Other Third Parties* (2010) encourages companies to put in place anti-corruption compliance procedures to vet, train, control, and monitor their business partners in the context of their relationship with the company.

A psychological reason

Most people understand that they are not allowed to pay bribes. However, many people do not understand that they may be liable if so-called 'independent contractors' pay bribes in connection with performing services for, or executing a contract with them. Without appropriate training, some of your colleagues may mistakenly believe that the independent contractor's methods are none of their concern, and that they have no business telling an independent contractor how to act. This view is often rationalized when the independent contractor is able to produce rapid results when dealing with the local 'red tape'. The employees' responsibilities to prevent corruption in the context of their dealings with third parties often are not instinctive and they certainly require communication, training, procedures, and control to be assimilated into a 'best practices' or 'adequate procedures' anti-corruption compliance programme.

A pragmatic reason

If nothing else, a good reason to focus on your business partners to mitigate your exposure to corruption is that intermediaries appear in many reported foreign bribery cases. Implementing adequate anti-corruption procedures for the appointment of business partners, and maintaining appropriate oversight and control over these business partners, can be the 'weakest link' in an otherwise robust corporate compliance programme. The government agencies in charge of enforcing anti-corruption statutes know that third parties are a key risk area for many companies and a key area to control through corporate compliance programmes.

DECIDING ON A BUSINESS RELATIONSHIP

1. Justifying the relationship: Do you need this new party or this new risk?

Among the many relationships listed above, some may be integral to conducting business in a certain location and practically unavoidable. Most companies cannot internalize all operations up and down their supply chain, from purchasing consumables, spare parts and equipment to procuring specialized services such as accounting, tax, and legal advice. Furthermore, in some countries, local law requires that you have a local business partner in order to operate in the country. In others, local law requires the use of specialized, licensed, independently registered service providers to perform certain acts (such as a law firm to appear in court, an architect to design certain types of constructions, registered customs brokers to clear goods, licensed insurance providers). In certain industries, the state may grant a concession or license to operate on the condition that you partner with a local entity, often a state-owned or state-controlled entity, to operate the concession or engage in the business.

Where local law requires you to establish a relationship with a third party, and where it might even impose certain criteria to guide your choice of entity, you will want to carefully and completely understand any such requirement to justify the existence of the third-party relationship and possibly the choice of business partner. Within the limitations set by local law, you would further justify your final selection through the vetting or due diligence process described later in this Chapter.

While you need to deal with some forms of business relationships by law or business necessity, you may be able to reduce your company's risk before even starting the due diligence process, or by examining whether you need the service from an outside entity in the first place. It is not the purpose of this Training Handbook to dissuade you from using common, legitimate business services from agents, intermediaries, and other third parties, but insofar as they carry anti-corruption risk, you may want to weigh whether such services may not be better performed in-house, where the service providers (your own employees) might be better known and more capable of being closely monitored and controlled.

2. Identifying red flags

How does a third-party risk manifest itself? The circumstances in which improper business behaviour arises are as varied as the business environments in which your company operates. While we list here some classic avenues to explore, you should let yourself be guided throughout the due diligence process by your knowledge of the business practices in the country or industry and by your own common sense. At every stage, put yourself in the shoes of the party under review and ask yourself whether the element you are considering (ownership structure, business practice, and compensation) makes sense, whether it is common and expected or unusual and surprising, and when the latter, whether there is a legitimate explanation for it.

The following are examples of elements or 'red flags' that may increase the risk in a relationship:

- The country in which the third party will act (if it has a low Transparency International Corruption Perceptions Index score or is known for the prevalence of corruption in business practices);
- The nature of the services requested of the third party (government relations, lobbying, customs clearance, obtaining visas, work permits, and other licenses or permits to operate, and other services which are aimed at getting some form of needed government approvals or actions, including reductions in taxes, duties, and fees);
- The timing and urgency of such services (in connection with critical steps for the business, for instance obtaining a fire inspection or occupancy permit for a new construction project, obtaining an environmental impact approval or clearing urgently needed goods through customs);
- The identity and ownership of the third party (where there is an opaque ownership structure, or ownership or close association with a public official);
- The qualifications of the third party (if the individual's main qualification is its address book or family connections, if the individual has no training for, or record of, having performed the services being contracted for, or no record of operating in the country in which the proposed services would now be rendered);
- The reputation of the third party, particularly in areas relating to fraud or corruption (allegations of unethical conduct, past or current investigations, proceedings, or judgments);

- Terms requested by the third party (for example, requests for payment to an offshore account or in another name, or for payment in cash or in kind, or if the third party asks for a 'success bonus' or 'success fee' in lieu of being paid a reasonable fee for work documented and actually performed); and
- The third party's control environment and response to requested controls (for example, a refusal to sign your anti-corruption contract clause, refusal to attend your proposed ethics and compliance training, or a lecture on "How business is done in this country").

The vocabulary of corruption is equally diverse, cultural, colloquial, contextual, and above all, unspoken or implied. Some expressions and body language are cross-cultural, and direct questions may elicit some of the information you seek. Nonetheless, your due diligence will be immeasurably more solid if you can involve someone who is sensitive not only to the words written or spoken but also to the cultural context and references they may suggest.

The risk factors, or red flags, cited above, and others you may encounter, will rarely constitute, on their own, violations of law that would warrant dismissal or non-engagement of the proposed third party. Some (such as the country or sector risk) are 'generic' and cannot be eliminated. In many situations, you may not have a practical commercial alternative but to work with a business partner even though the due diligence raises a red flag or two.

The purpose of due diligence is to identify the risks, particularly those specific to the parties and the transaction, so that you may evaluate in the most informed manner whether those risks can be appropriately controlled and improper behaviour prevented in the context of a future relationship with your company, and if so, how. If not, you will have the basis to make an informed decision to find another option.

The appearance of red flags in due diligence should lead you to gather more facts about the flagged areas to assess their significance, and, assuming the transaction goes forward, to design and effectively implement tailored compliance safeguards (whether in the form of contract clauses, written statements, trainings, or close monitoring during the relationship), so that you can fairly conclude that the red flag situation is appropriately mitigated and controlled to the point that you do not believe corruption is likely to occur.

3. Vetting the new third party
a) **Communicating about the process: Setting expectations, involving all parties**

The biggest difficulty you may face in implementing your due diligence programme could be the reticence of your own business colleagues as well as the third parties under review, even if they are conscious of the importance of the process and willing to cooperate.

You will want to streamline and tailor the vetting or due diligence programme, justify its steps by illustrating its purpose and importance, and educate people about timing considerations. You might directly ask your business colleagues some of the questions that the process is designed to answer, to impress upon them the importance of knowing the answer: "When the auditor comes, how will you demonstrate that your company complies with this legal obligation? How did you find this agent? What objective assurances can you give that this new agent will not implicate your company in an act of bribery?" This exercise may also help you to keep sight of the purpose of the due diligence exercise, and design appropriate tools to accomplish it.

You may also have to contend with your colleagues' reluctance to spend time on new procedures in general: In addition to periodic training (discussed below), you will want to walk employees through their first due diligence exercises, until they are comfortable conducting the process alone, and have made it part of their routine.

Finally, you should anticipate that the practice of due diligence may be considered (genuinely or not) highly disconcerting and even insulting to some outside parties, particularly non-Western parties or those in senior business or government positions. You will want to pre-empt any misunderstanding by highlighting that due diligence is a standard procedure for your company, not a sign of mistrust of, or concern with, the particular third party under review. You will want to ensure that the practice of due diligence and what it entails is socialized as early as possible in the relationship. As an example, some companies publish and regularly communicate to the business world, via their websites, forums or chambers of commerce, their terms and conditions of doing business.

You will want to present and construct the process as a team exercise in which each party has a specific role to play. Involving more than one actor in the process increases your chances of obtaining all the relevant information on a timely basis, minimizes outcomes based on conflicts of interest, and places responsibility for an accurate and reasonably complete result on all the actors concerned.

The sponsoring employee or department within your company, who is generally the one primarily in contact with the third party, is typically best positioned to bring to the due diligence file information about the need for that party, how it was identified, a critical evaluation of the third party's technical competence and expertise, and the commercial justification for the amount and form of compensation.

Other information may be obtained by research conducted by the department in charge of the due diligence. This department may want to involve a due diligence service provider or a professional investigator to add information regarding the proposed third party's business reputation or ownership structure, especially if the information is otherwise not readily accessible.

Finally, your company may want to have the third party itself contribute to its due diligence file with completed self-descriptive questionnaires, documentation, statements, and guarantees about itself and its business practices, thus causing the third party to take active responsibility for its future behaviour.

b) **Defining the scope of the due diligence**

How much information is enough, and how long will it take? These will be the questions most frequently asked as you implement your due diligence procedures. Unfortunately, your answer can almost never be expressed in terms of standard timelines. It will depend on a number of variables, and the most precise answer to the timeframe question may be to present and briefly analyze these variables on a case-by-case basis with the person asking.

The most recurring variables will be the resources at your disposal to conduct due diligence, the category of risk posed by the proposed new relationship, the possibility of compound risk (the first layer of due diligence uncovers a red flag, which when investigated reveals additional red flags, also to be investigated), the degree of difficulty in obtaining the information (existence or not of complete and up-to-date public databases and other sources of information, cooperation you receive from the party under review), and the layers of internal reviews and approvals that you will chose to implement at the end of the process.

As you develop and tailor your procedures for identifying and controlling third-party risk, keep in mind that you are doing this in order to be able to answer questions from company directors, auditors, regulators, enforcement authorities, the press and the larger public, and potentially other stakeholders as well, and that the auditors and enforcement authorities will be looking not so much at how good your policies and procedures are on their face as how well you implement them. Be realistic about the resources at your disposal to control the risk. Build in adequate periods of time for the process. Well implemented and understood policies and procedures allow you to give more definitive answers on what risks exist and how you are in control of processes than 'paper policies' that are inconsistently or hurriedly applied. In order to be adequate, compliance procedures must be effectively and consistently implemented with the application of suitable resources.

c) **Defining and tailoring the elements of the due diligence**

The purpose of implementing third-party policies and procedures is to ensure that your business partners adhere to the same ethical and legal standards that you do in the context of their work with or on behalf of your company. You also want to ensure that you meet the standards laid out in applicable laws controlling your relationship with your business partners.

In some cases, being able to meet these goals will be relatively simple, few red flags will come up, and the due diligence process will require only documentation of the basic facts about the third party, in whatever format you will have chosen. In other cases, however, red flags may arise in the initial rounds of your due diligence that will require more in-depth consideration. When that happens, how you complete the due diligence will be unique to each new party, bearing in mind your goal: To put yourself in a position where you can demonstrate that you gave appropriate consideration to all the identified risks associated with the relationship and took reasonable steps to control and eliminate those risks.

The basic information – Your first round of information gathering will include basic information about the prospective service provider, such as name, legal status, status of any licenses and permits required for the entity to provide the goods or services under consideration, ownership, credit history, judicial and litigation history, qualifications and past experience of providing the goods or services expected, and general reputation. You may want to gather these basic facts for the entity and its owners and senior management from the outset, especially if faced with an owner or manager who is known to the public independently or who is closely associated with the company in the public eye.

In all first rounds, you want to try to determine whether any public official has a connection with or interest in the entity or its income, profits, or dividends (as owner, principal, lender, or close relative or business associate). Finally, in all first rounds, you want to note the circumstances in which the idea of a relationship arose and document the legitimate commercial purpose for hiring the services or purchasing the goods.

By contrast, if you find that the idea was rooted in a government official's suggestion that paying for the services of entity X or the goods of entity Y could be helpful to your company winning a government tender or obtaining needed permits, this would be considered as a red flag. You would then want to be prepared to justify that you did have a legitimate and independent commercial need for the goods or services provided, that other vendors or service providers had a fair opportunity to work for you, and that entity X or entity Y was indeed the best qualified to provide the services or the goods, that it did indeed provide the services or goods in question in a good, merchantable, and workmanlike manner, that the compensation paid to entity X or entity Y was commercially reasonable, that the ownership and management of entity X or entity Y was independent of the government official rather than a conduit for improperly enriching the official, and that there was a proper explanation for the official's recommendation.

Heightened due diligence by level of risk – After the first round of review, what would warrant additional due diligence, and potentially, additional compliance safeguards?

- **Country** – If you or the third party will be operating in a country known for a prevalence of corruption in business relationships, you will want to research the manner in which this could arise in your relationship, and review how the prospective business partner has handled the perceived risks of corruption in the past. While country risk cannot be eliminated in the short term, it may be able to be managed.

- **Know your counterparty** – When researching your prospective business partner your degree of presumed knowledge and oversight of the partner's behaviour leads to potentially increased responsibility for any future improper behaviour. You cannot avoid this, however, by 'self-blinding' or 'putting your head in the sand'.

- **Type of service rendered** – If the services involve representation of your company before government agencies, courts, or legislative personnel, or clearing goods or vessels through customs or ports, obtaining work permits or visas, or obtaining any of many types of government permits, licenses or approvals, you would also want to conduct more than basic due diligence before engaging the third party that would provide such services, not only on the entity, but on key personnel who will be involved in performing the services.

The Internet? – The process of collecting information may be done in large part online. Additionally, there are a number of companies who will undertake to carry out anti-corruption or reputational due diligence for you and provide you with a report that you can review. They may also advise you on identifying common red flags, and creating a series of questions specific to each. Naturally, as with all your other service providers, you will have to run that due diligence company through a due diligence process as well. These services are not inexpensive, but they can provide useful information and analysis if you do not have the resources within your company to gather and review the relevant facts yourself. There are some shared services options as well as companies that screen prospective third parties against lists of politically exposed persons and other lists of blocked or restricted parties.

Privacy considerations – Certain types of information requested during the due diligence process, particularly regarding individuals, may implicate privacy or data protection laws of the country where personnel are located. Companies may want to seek legal advice about what is permitted and try to tailor questions to get the necessary information while avoiding data protection or privacy law issues.

4. Deciding on a new business partner: Who makes the decision to hire, and how?

One of the strategic decisions you will have to make is how to bring the vetting process to a close. Who will do so, and on what basis?

One option is to have the results of the due diligence rest with the legal and/or compliance departments and give those departments veto rights. Or, you may choose to give the final decision to a committee that will have no direct relation (or a more diluted relation) to the third party going forward, or to company management, on the basis of the data assembled and recommendations made by both the sponsoring and legal and/or compliance departments.

These various options need not be mutually exclusive: You may, for example, want to leave a hiring decision for low-risk candidates primarily in the control of the sponsoring department with consultative input from the legal or compliance departments, and elevate the levels of approval required and the involvement of the legal and compliance departments as the risks identified with the third party increase.

5. How to pay your new business partner?

Your company, when contracting with a business partner, is free to negotiate the reasonable, arms-length form and amount of compensation to be paid for the services of the new business partner. There may be good and sufficient business justifications for many different types of compensation arrangements, including so-called success fees or similar incentive payments.

You will note, however, that compensation unrelated to hourly fees for documented time worked, such as a success or bonus fee can constitute a red flag. While there may be cases where success fees are appropriate and justifiable from a commercial point of view, we recommend that you give special consideration to the reasonableness and the commercial justification for such success fees or other similar lump sum compensation not tied to fees for hours of work. Keep also careful documentation of the legitimate business case for the engagement of the intermediary and of the nature and extent of the compensation.

MANAGING A BUSINESS RELATIONSHIP

1. Controlling the terms of the relationship

a) **Sign the contract before services or goods are provided or payments are made**

Written engagements should be entered into with the business partner. These will generally require, among others, the business partner to do the following: Acknowledge and agree to comply with applicable anti-corruption laws and your company's Code of Conduct and policies on anti-corruption and compliance with laws (or maintain their own, consistent Code of Conduct and policies), affirm that these will be followed in the course of the relationship, and affirm that the party has not engaged in improper practices in the past in connection with the subject matter of the contract.

These undertakings act first and foremost as a test of the third party's approach to anti-corruption. If your prospective business partner is threatened, annoyed, suspicious, or otherwise resists making such commitments, this constitutes a red flag and is best dealt with at an early stage. While such commitments may seem like a check-the-box exercise, they serve to demonstrate attention to the issue, and that the parties have an affirmative understanding regarding the avoidance of illegal practices in their business relationship, in case the issue comes up in an audit or court case against you or the other party or in a commercial dispute between you. In the latter case, they define the standard of conduct, and can justify the remedies you choose to impose for any breach, whether that is withholding of payment, termination of contract, making official reports or disclosures or other remedial actions you may choose.

b) Written anti-corruption contractual provisions

For the same reasons and purposes described for entering into binding written contracts, you will want to introduce detailed anti-corruption clauses in your contracts.

Contractual rights to verify the other party's compliance with your policies or other measures to ensure compliance will often be helpful. As an example, you could require that other party's staff assigned to the relationship take annual trainings prepared by the company, or you could require the right to conduct spot audits of their businesses or books and records.

You will also want to lay out clearly what will constitute a violation, what level of knowledge or certainty you must have in order to impose remedies, and what those remedies will be. You may want to oblige the third party to notify you in case there are changes in its ownership and control during the life of the contract that would bring additional risks. You may want to limit where and how payments can be made.

Different business or legal cultures have different approaches to contracts. What terms need to be defined, what elements the agreement has to cover, to what degree unlikely scenarios need to be addressed, may vary from one country or legal system to the other. 'Common law' lawyers are generally trained to pre-empt as many disputes as conceivable in the contract, so as to map out the future relationship under the contract with as much predictability as possible. This can draw impatient reactions from your prospective business partner and its legal counsel. If you see this being an issue, you may want to prepare to reassure your business partner and its counsel that your purpose in setting out anti-corruption clauses is merely to recognize what you are sure is a shared commitment to proper business practices, and that this is a standard practice for your company, not a suspicion raised against the prospective partner's past or present practice.

c) Elements of anti-corruption contract provisions

As set out in the *ICC Guidelines on Agents, Intermediaries and Other Third Parties* (2010), you may wish to consider contract clauses that include the following matters:

- The third party (if a sole proprietorship or individual) is not a public official (if it is an entity, the focus will likely shift to owners and key managers or personnel), and does not have any official status and you will be notified if this changes;

- The third party does not (and its principals do not) have any close personal or business relationship with a current official or any close relative or close associate of an official who would be in a position to influence a decision in your favour, and you will be notified if this changes;

- The third party will comply with all applicable anti-corruption and anti-money laundering laws;

- The third party and its principals is not and has not been the subject of an anti-corruption or other similar type of investigation, and has not been convicted or plead guilty to fraud, bribery, corruption, money laundering, or for violations of similar laws;
- The third party will comply with your company's Code and guidelines, in particular, your rules on gifts and hospitality or has its own Code of Conduct or guidelines with equivalent standards and will maintain and comply with them during the course of the relationship;
- The third party represents that no payments, offers, or promises to public officials or other third party beneficiaries have been, or will be made, promised, offered, or authorized directly or indirectly, for an improper purpose (note that a substantive anti-corruption clause is generally more effective than one that represents that there have been no violations of particular national laws);
- The third party agrees to comply with your business ethics and anti-corruption guidelines (including matters of documentation) and limits for reimbursement of expenses;
- You have the right to suspend payment or terminate the contract immediately upon unilateral good faith determination that there has been a violation of any applicable anti-corruption law or provision of the agreement without paying any compensation to the third party, and the third party agrees to indemnify you, as far as law permits, for your expenses related to violations of the anti-corruption laws;
- The third party agrees to a clearly defined scope and a clear and specific description of the services to be provided;
- The third party agrees to regularly report on its activities on your behalf, and to provide detailed invoices and detailed supporting documentation for its expenditures;
- The third party agrees to provide audit rights to you related to activities undertaken on your behalf (but note that, having secured such rights, you may need to invoke them);
- The third party agrees not to subcontract the work or to submit the retention of subcontractors or other persons or entities designated to perform similar services to you for prior approval;
- The third party is prohibited from assigning the contract or the compensation to be paid;
- The third party agrees to transparent and commercially reasonable payment provisions and commercially justifiable compensation;

- The third party is required to maintain accurate books and records and appropriate internal controls; and
- The third party is required to cooperate with any investigation into alleged breaches of the compliance provisions, including the requirement to provide access to documents and personnel.

Enterprises facing higher risks in connection with third parties may wish to consider additional safeguards such as:

- A requirement that the third party submit certain actions to you for prior approval (for instance interactions with public officials or certain levels of gifts and entertainment or engagement of other third parties);
- Provisions that limit the third party's ability to act on your behalf in relation to government contracts or tenders; and
- Provisions, as appropriate, for transparency of the relationship with local authorities.

You may wish to review the *ICC Anti-Corruption Clause* (2012) which is presented in Chapter 16 of this Training Handbook for additional background on anti-corruption contractual provisions.

2. Training of Business Partners

Should you also train your business partner's personnel? Again, you may want to adopt a calibrated approach to this. Where you have requested and obtained copies of the business partners' own compliance policies, training materials, and training records, and it appears the business partner has its own robust compliance programme and is committed to maintaining it, retraining by your company may be unnecessary. However, in all cases, you will want to confirm that the other party's training programme has been fully and effectively implemented, and that the individuals working on your account have been trained.

Moreover, if you have specific compliance provisions you require the business partner to follow, or if you are uncertain as to the third party's own programme or appreciation of the governing conduct standards, training may be necessary. Where the business partner is low-risk for other reasons (such as providing its services in a low-risk environment, not having any connection with government entities in the context of its work for your company, or because of the magnitude of the relationship), the nature and content of any anti-corruption training you provide can also be calibrated to this lower risk scenario.

Where this is not the case, however, training may be a valuable added assurance and compliance procedure, as well as an additional opportunity to discover and discuss corruption-related questions with the business partner that would not have arisen in other contexts. When you are at risk of being liable for any improper actions of your business partners, it makes good common sense to take steps to ensure that their personnel have been trained in anti-corruption compliance and general business ethics and compliance topics and that they know and understand your compliance with law and anti-corruption policies and procedures.

The anti-corruption training should include the business partner's personnel assigned to the contract with your company and the business partner's management. It could be conducted by your own qualified employees (such as in-house legal counsel or compliance officers) or by outside lawyers or other qualified experts, especially if the latter are used to train your company's own staff.

3. Monitoring/Auditing

The training of your staff should allow you to rely on them as a first level of control on the actions of your business partners. However, you may want to conduct occasional in-depth reviews of a third-party's behaviour, asking the third party to produce all of its required licenses and permits, asking to see relevant sections of their books, records and accounts, asking to interview key personnel to review their process for performing a particular service and asking to examine their compliance programme and training records.

As we have discussed in other parts of this Chapter, such requests may strain your relations with the party in question. That is when it will be useful to be able to refer back to contractual agreements or written statements dating back to the beginning of the relationship. It will also be in your interest to limit your requests to reasonable inquiries, and explain the reason for your request.

Whether or not you audit, the third party relationship needs to be monitored for changes or requests that could raise new red flags and risks. Invoices, additional payment requests, changes in ownership or control, new information about the operating environment including changes in the host government, can all produce conditions that need to be addressed from a risk standpoint.

4. Keeping records

What should your records on a third party contain? As with any other part of your business, your books and records should be an accurate, fair and reasonably detailed reflection of your business transactions with any party. In addition, in order to show that you have not looked away from the other party's business practices but actively took steps intended to understand and control them, you will want to keep the records of your due diligence methodology, searches, and findings on the other party prior to the engagement (including searches that do not yield responsive information as well as searches that do), and records of the certifications, trainings and any monitoring that takes place in the course of the relationship. You will want to keep those at least as long as the relationship is in existence, and perhaps for some period of time thereafter, depending on your company's general records retention policy and any applicable statutes of limitations.

About the authors

Richard J. Battaglia was Senior Counsel, Regulatory Compliance, for BP for many years with global responsibility in the anti-corruption, trade sanctions, and export controls areas. He has over 35 years of experience in the international petroleum industry both as in-house legal counsel and with his own consulting business. Mr. Battaglia is a member of the ICC Commission on Corporate Responsibility and Anti-corruption and was instrumental in drafting the *ICC Guidelines on Agents, Intermediaries and Other Third Parties* (2010). In 2012, he became Senior Counsel in the Chicago office of Steptoe & Johnson LLP.

Lucinda A. Low is a partner in the Washington, DC office of Steptoe & Johnson LLP where she heads the firm's anti-corruption practice. She advises clients on United States and international anti-corruption laws; counsels on joint ventures, mergers and acquisitions, and other business transactions and foreign operations issues; conducts internal investigations; and represents clients in enforcement matters before the Department of Justice, the Securities and Exchange Commission, and in World Bank and other International Financial Institutions sanctions proceedings. Ms. Low also represents investors in a broad array of investment disputes with commercial partners and host governments, including disputes involving issues of fraud and corruption. She is a member of the Board of Directors of Transparency International-USA.

APPENDIX – Due Diligence Sample Checklist

For the Sponsoring Department
- Memorialize the purpose of the relationship. Include justification for choice of an outside party over an in-house department resource.
- Describe the method for choosing the entity (open bid, restricted bid, recommendation, direct contact).
- Evaluate the reputation and qualifications of the proposed third party (technical expertise, prior experience, size, location, and reputation in the industry) and any key personnel.
- Evaluate and confirm that proposed payment amount is justifiable and payment process is straightforward and vetted.
- List the contact person within the company who will oversee the proposed third party.
- List the following information for the proposed third party:
  - Business information. Attach copies of documentation obtained (as for instance the record of incorporation).
  - Ownership information. Include any known presence of or connection to a foreign official.
  - Compliance information. Attach copies of any policy, certification or other document obtained.

For the Legal and Compliance Department
- Complete any information above that the sponsoring department was unable to obtain.
- Run a conflicts check.
- Check proposed third party and principals against lists of sanctioned entities, and in legal databases for any legal history or ongoing dispute.
- Confirm and comply with local law regarding hiring of agents.
- As needed, make inquiries with other customers and business community.
- Prepare template compliance language for the contract; prepare payment terms and conditions for the contract.

For the proposed third party
- Complete company questionnaire.
- Provide documentation proving that the company is in good standing to perform the services contracted for (registrations, licenses and permits).
- Complete certifications regarding the identity of owners, directors, personnel; absence of conflict of interest; adherence to company compliance policies.

Chapter 15
Joint Ventures

Massimo Mantovani
General Counsel and Senior Executive Vice President of Eni

Joint ventures are vital for business. Your company, like all the others, cannot do everything on its own and, as we have seen in Chapter 14, it will sometimes need input from agents, intermediaries, and other third parties. In other circumstances, it will make good business sense for your company to join forces with other companies to pursue a specific project or activity. This will give rise to the formation of an incorporated or unincorporated joint venture. Creating a joint venture is a commonly accepted business solution but may raise new corruption risks, which should be carefully managed. This Chapter provides an overview of the policies and procedures which your company should put in place before entering a joint venture agreement, and which it should enforce during the life time of the joint venture, in order to keep clean from corruption.

INTRODUCTION

In certain circumstances, joint venture partners may be held criminally liable for acts of corruption carried out for the benefit of the joint venture. Companies should therefore take measures, within their power, to ensure that joint ventures in which they participate enforce effective anti-bribery and antitrust rules and establish adequate internal control systems.

Joint venture arrangements come in many forms. As a general rule, companies planning to enter into a joint venture implement policies and procedures to effectively guard against corruption risks. In this Chapter, we refer to this systematic framework of policies and procedures as the company's joint venture policy.

The aim of a joint venture policy is to ensure that:

- The company only enters into joint venture agreements with partners who have the right reputation for integrity;
- The negotiation and implementation of a joint venture agreement is carried out with diligence, transparency, and honesty, and in full compliance with applicable anti-corruption and antitrust laws;
- An adequate anti-corruption and antitrust programme is established to regulate the joint venture's future activities; and
- The activities of the joint venture are appropriately monitored, especially in areas that are prone to corruption and competition risks.

A joint venture policy covers four basic areas:

- First, it sets forth the due diligence process that a company should follow before deciding whether or not to enter into a joint venture agreement with a potential partner and how often such a due diligence process should be renewed;
- Second, it determines the clauses, representations, and warranties that should be included in contractual documentation relating to the setting up and activities of the joint venture;
- Third, it defines the procedures and control systems that should be implemented once the joint venture is established in order to prevent corruption and other criminal offences; and
- Fourth, it outlines the role and responsibilities of the company's representatives in monitoring the activities of the joint venture.

A joint venture policy should clearly define at the outset which internal corporate functions are to be involved in the negotiation and management of the joint venture, as well as in the conduct of preliminary anti-corruption and antitrust controls. It is particularly important to make clear which input will be expected from the compliance and the legal functions.

It is advisable to involve at least two separate internal corporate functions. This normally includes the business unit proposing the joint venture and the company's legal and compliance function, including anti-corruption and antitrust legal support, where available. For the purpose of this Chapter, we assume that such legal support (the Anti-corruption and Antitrust Support Unit) already exists in the company.

Finally, a company should provide – as part of its broader compliance programme – a framework for bringing all joint ventures that pre-date the adoption of the joint venture policy into compliance with its basic requirements.

1 DUE DILIGENCE ON POTENTIAL PARTNER(S)

Before a company enters into a joint venture agreement, it should conduct due diligence on its potential partner(s). The responsibility for leading the due diligence normally sits with the business manager (the Manager) promoting the participation in the joint venture.

The joint venture policy should describe the normal procedure for conducting due diligence on potential partners (the standard due diligence) and indicate the cases where such due diligence may be reduced or even omitted (the reduced due diligence). For instance, a reduced due diligence may be sufficient when the potential partner has an excellent ethical reputation or has a long-standing relationship with the company and is positively known to be honest and reliable.

When the Manager believes that a reduced due diligence should be conducted on a potential partner, he or she should submit a written request to the Anti-corruption and Antitrust Support Unit specifying the reasons for this request. After evaluation, the Anti-corruption and

Antitrust Support Unit shall specify in writing whether it believes that: (i) it is necessary to conduct a standard due diligence, or that (ii) a reduced due diligence will be sufficient, in which case it should specify which of the due diligence requirements listed in Section 2 below can be modified or waived, or that (iii) a due diligence is not necessary.

2 STANDARD DUE DILIGENCE REQUIREMENTS

A standard due diligence procedure should be based on the following steps and requirements:

Step 1: The Manager asks the potential partner to fill out a due diligence questionnaire in order to gather information and documentation about its corporate ownership, business history, and other relevant facts.

Step 2: The Manager collects further information on the potential partner from available sources, including public records. The amount of information to be gathered will depend on the particular circumstances of the situation at stake, such as the company's knowledge of the partner based on prior dealings; the importance of the project for which the joint venture is being established; the specific risks associated to the country where the joint venture will operate; the role that the partner will have in the management of the joint venture; and, in general, the perceived level of risk (also from a competition perspective) associated with the joint venture.

Step 3: Information and material collected from the potential partner are checked and confirmed as appropriate against publicly available information, Internet searches, and external sources (including embassies, consulates, international exchange agencies, and chambers of commerce). Appendix A at the end of this Chapter gives an example of due diligence guidelines which could be used as a basis for reviewing and verifying the information collected through the due diligence questionnaire and other means.

Step 4: The Manager should watch for specific red flags, meaning instances which suggest a strong corruption risk. Appendix B at the end of this Chapter gives a list of common red flags to look after.

The data and information gathered through the due diligence exercise should be adequately documented and collected in a note (the Note) to be signed by the Manager and submitted to the Anti-Corruption and Antitrust Support Unit.

The Note should indicate:

- The reasons for which the creation of the joint venture is deemed necessary (or at least useful) for the pursuit of the company's strategic objectives.

- How the potential partner's name came about; which external entity, if any, recommended the potential partner; which corporate area or business unit within the company received the recommendation and gave the potential partner's name to the Manager.
- A declaration that due diligence was completed and that verifications were conducted in compliance with the principles contained in the joint venture policy and other applicable internal policies.
- A description of any red flags or particular risks identified during the due diligence process.
- If due diligence was reduced or omitted, a clear statement of the due diligence activities that have been conducted along with a description of the guidance received by the Anti-Corruption and Antitrust Support Unit about the appropriate level of due diligence to be undertaken (or not).
- The name(s) of the person(s) chosen (see Section 3 below) to conduct the negotiations with the potential partner on the company's behalf.
- A declaration that the person(s) who personally interviewed the partner's representative(s) concluded that there were no reasonable grounds for believing that the partner would violate or would cause the joint venture to violate applicable anti-corruption and antitrust laws.
- Information on any current or past relationship between the company (or its subsidiaries and affiliates) and the potential partner.
- A specific description of the structure of the joint venture and of the activities that the joint venture will be carrying out.
- A list of the sources that have been used to verify the information provided by the potential partner in the due diligence questionnaire and throughout the due diligence process.

The Note, signed by the Manager and including all supporting documentation, should be sent by the Manager (or by another person delegated to act on the Manager's behalf) to the Anti-corruption and Antitrust Support Unit.

The Anti-corruption and Antitrust Support Unit shall then evaluate the results of the due diligence on the basis of the due diligence guidelines and the existence of red flags. It may then make its decision known and, if necessary, suggest to the Manager possible actions to address red flags that may have been identified.

3   NEGOTIATION PROCESS AND REQUIREMENTS

Once the choice of the partner has been finalized, the negotiation of the joint venture agreement can begin.

The Manager should appoint at least two individuals to carry out the negotiation of the joint venture agreement. These individuals should belong to separate corporate functions and should not have a hierarchical relationship with each other.

- If your company is going to exercise control over the joint venture: Your company should cause the joint venture to adopt an internal compliance programme, including anti-bribery and antitrust policies and procedures, in line with those it has adopted. An adequate internal control system should be also adopted and implemented, taking into account the specific risk factors related to the country of incorporation of the joint venture and the country in which the joint venture will operate.

- If your company is not going to exercise control over the joint venture: Your company shall use its influence, to the extent reasonable under the circumstances, to cause the joint venture to: (a) adopt principles of ethical conduct, including anti-bribery policies and procedures as well as antitrust principles, in line with those adopted by your company; and (b) meet the standards set out in your company's internal control system, by adopting and maintaining an adequate system of internal accounting standards and controls consistent with the requirements established by the relevant applicable anti-corruption laws.

In negotiating the joint venture agreement, the joint venture partners will make their best efforts to include into the agreement provisions, clauses, representations, and warranties along the following lines:

a) The joint venture should adopt and maintain an effective internal control system and a compliance programme for the prevention of (i) corruption, money laundering, and other corruptive practices. and (ii) of any forms of restrictive practices by the joint venture itself or between its partners, as long as they are actual or potential competitors on one or more related markets. It is recommended that the agreement explicitly refers to the anti-corruption provisions laid down in the *ICC Rules on Combating Corruption* (2011).

b) Each partner should supervise and monitor the implementation and effective operation of the joint venture's internal control system and compliance programme, and promptly inform each other partner of any potential deficiency or red flag that is identified.

c) The joint venture should provide that it (i) will act in compliance with applicable anti-corruption and antitrust laws, the joint venture's internal control system, and the joint venture's compliance programme; and (ii) will not pay directly or indirectly bribes to public officials or their family members or to shareholders, partners, or members of the corporate bodies of the counterparts with which the joint venture proposes to operate.

It is recommended that the joint venture systematically makes use of the *ICC Anti-corruption Clause* (2012) in its commercial contracts (see Chapter 16 of this Training Handbook).

d) Each partner should commit that its principals, who will carry on activities directly or indirectly related to or on behalf of the joint venture, (i) will act in compliance with applicable anti-corruption and antitrust laws, the joint venture's internal control system and the joint venture's compliance programme and, (ii) will not pay directly or indirectly bribes to public officials or their family members or to shareholders, partners, or members of the corporate bodies of the counterparts with which the joint venture proposes to operate.

e) Each partner[26] should give a statement or commitment:

- that neither this person, nor its family members, nor its principals, are public officials, who are directly or indirectly related to the activities to be carried out by the joint venture;

- to promptly inform the other partner if, after the signing of the joint venture agreement: (i) the person, or any of its family members, or any of its principals are appointed as public officials and, as public officials, they will be directly or indirectly related to the activities to be carried out by the joint venture; and (ii) of any event that could influence the circumstances pertaining to the person's own position or that of its family members or that of its principals as represented to the company. Written confirmation of the above should be provided on a yearly basis or on the company's request.

f) Each partner should ensure that no public official who is directly or indirectly related to the activities to be carried out by the joint venture, or its family members, will be appointed as a director of the joint venture or be hired by the joint venture as an employee, consultant or external consultant, intermediary, or agent.

---

[26] When implementing this statement/commitment, one will take into account whether such statement/commitment is given on behalf of a privately held or a government-owned company.

g) There should be a veto right for the company over the joint venture's decisions concerning the execution of agreements with, or otherwise the use or hiring of, intermediaries or business partners that (i) will perform lobbying activities on behalf of the joint venture, (ii) will endeavour to obtain regulatory approvals, or (iii) will in any way deal with public entities or will have contact with a public official for or on behalf of the joint venture.

h) Each partner should designate one or more person(s) who shall act as the partner's representative(s) in the joint venture or should undertake to designate such representative(s); such representatives should have an outstanding reputation for integrity, have an appropriate level of seniority, and possess the necessary skills in the field of internal control systems.

i) Each partner should cause its representative(s) to sign and adhere to the ethical commitments contained in the joint venture agreement.

j) There should be a right to perform an audit on the joint venture, or on the joint venture's operator, in the event the company has a reasonable belief that the joint venture or the joint venture's operator (in its activities directly or indirectly related to the joint venture) may have violated any relevant anti-corruption and antitrust laws or any of the anti-corruption commitments set out in the joint venture agreement.

k) There should be appropriate provisions to protect the company against the risk of violation of the anti-corruption clauses in case of a change of control of any of the partners.

l) The non-transferability of the joint venture agreement, or any of the obligations or rights contained therein, by the partner to third parties without the company's prior written approval.

m) The right of the company to terminate the joint venture agreement and to obtain compensation for damages in case of breach by the partner of the anti-corruption obligations, representations and warranties contained in the joint venture agreement, or in case of violation of anti-corruption laws.

Depending on the circumstances of each transaction, the Manager should seek the advice of the Anti-corruption and Antitrust Support Unit before modifying or waiving any of the provisions, clauses, representations and warranties listed above. If the Manager is proposing any such modifications or waivers, he or she shall specify the reasons in writing for evaluation by the Anti-corruption and Antitrust Support Unit which, if necessary, shall suggest possible actions to alleviate specific concerns.

The final draft of the joint venture agreement should be sent by the Manager to the Anti-corruption and Antitrust Support Unit, which shall check that it complies with the requirements set forth in the joint venture policy and applicable anti-corruption laws. Only then can the joint venture agreement be signed.

4 IMPLEMENTATION OF THE JOINT VENTURE AGREEMENT

The company's representative(s) are responsible for the implementation of the joint venture agreement. They will have received comprehensive training on anti-corruption compliance.

The company representative(s) should be appointed for a limited period of time, ideally no longer than three years. Any decision to keep the representative(s) in place for longer than the regular period should be documented and the reasons clearly stated.

The representative(s) are responsible for:

- Ensuring that the joint venture and the joint venture's partners operate the joint venture with diligence, transparency, honesty, integrity, and in compliance with applicable laws, and in line with the joint venture's internal control system and its compliance programme;
- Monitoring – with the support of the Anti-corruption and Antitrust Support Unit – the effectiveness, efficacy and adequacy of the internal control system and compliance programme adopted by the joint venture and, if necessary, proposing changes to the compliance programme in order to maximize effectiveness and help ensure continued compliance;
- Monitoring the relationships with the joint venture's customers and counterparts, especially when they are public entities;
- Monitoring that the joint venture shall not act as a device for facilitating collusion between the partners in the related markets, where they are actual or potential competitors; and
- Monitoring – in particular – the relevance, necessity, legality, and correct execution of any agreement with intermediaries or business partners that act for or on behalf of the joint venture.

The representative(s) should promptly report to the Anti-corruption and Antitrust Support Unit any red flags that are identified in relation to the activities carried out by the joint venture or to the activities carried out by its partner(s), the partners' representatives, directors, managers, and employees in connection with the joint venture. They should immediately alert the Anti-corruption and Antitrust Support Unit of any inadequacies, gaps, or suspected violations.

In addition, the representative(s) should be required to submit a periodic report (at least annual) to the Anti-corruption and Antitrust Support Unit on the activities carried out to fulfil the responsibilities indicated above. This report should be submitted to the Anti-corruption and Antitrust Support Unit which will evaluate it and, as appropriate, provide assistance, and suggest actions to address specific concerns.

About the author

Massimo Mantovani is General Counsel and a member of the Executive Committee of Eni, the largest Italian corporation and one of the largest integrated energy companies in the world, with 79,000 employees and activities in 85 countries. He graduated in Law at Università Statale di Milano and gained a Master's in Law from King's College, University of London. He is admitted to practice law in Italy (avvocato) and England (solicitor). Since 2011, Mr. Mantovani participates in the B20 Working Group on Improving Transparency and Anti-Corruption and is a regular speaker at national and international conferences and in postgraduate courses on compliance issues. From 2005 to October 2012 he was a non-executive member of the Board of Directors of Snam, an Italian listed company, and is currently an independent member of the Board of Directors of University of Bologna 'Alma Mater'.

APPENDIX A - Due Diligence Guidelines

The following guidelines may be used as a basis for reviewing and verifying the information collected through the due diligence questionnaire and throughout the due diligence process. They will also serve to identify and document any unethical or suspicious conduct of a potential joint venture partner. Additional investigations may be required in certain circumstances.

- **Relevant names and identification:** As a first step, start by reviewing the potential partner's registrations and other documents to identify its full name, related entities (for instance parent company, subsidiaries, branches, and affiliates) and principals (including owners, directors, and officers representing the partner).
- **Official registry of organizations:** Most official registries of companies and other organizations make their records available to the public in some form. Check the ownership of potential partner's companies, its directors, accounts, and other relevant official documentation. Furthermore, if the owner is a trust company, check, to the fullest extent possible, the ownership of this company.
- **Financial references:** Request that the official registries provide the financial statements (including the balance sheet and profit and loss statements) for the last three years of the potential partner and its related entities (in particular, the holding company and the subsidiaries) and verify, when possible, their completeness and accurateness. If audited financial records for the previous three years are not available, an independent third party may be requested to certify the potential partner's reliability, financial capabilities, and probity.
- **Qualifications and membership of professional bodies:** Review the curricula vitae of the principals, executives, managers, or key employees related to the contractual activity to be performed by the potential partner and verify, when possible, the information disclosed; in particular the experience and qualifications of the individuals concerned should be verified through relevant professional associations, Internet or by contacting their former employer, when deemed useful or necessary.
- **Electoral records, local government business records:** Local government offices and business libraries usually make available to the public records of individuals (for instance from electoral rolls) and businesses (for instance from local business directories). Verify that the potential partner is recorded at the address given.
- **Criminal records:** Check criminal records of the potential partner, of its related entities (parent company, subsidiaries, branches, and affiliates), and (if legally permissible in the country concerned) of its principals and key management personnel.

- **Debarred or restricted parties lists:** Information about companies and individuals barred from bidding on local, national, or international contracts can be found through media and Internet searches. For example, the World Bank's website[27] provides a list of debarred companies and individuals that have been sanctioned under the World Bank's fraud and corruption policy for bribery or corruption in bid processes.
- **Credit rating:** There are a large number of international and local commercial organizations offering credit rating services on individuals and organizations on a fee-paying basis. Other facilities, including public registers and online listings, also provide information about bankruptcy or insolvency of individuals and companies.
- **Business history:** Identify through Internet, financial statements and other sources, the business history and experience of the potential partner. Use business references provided by the potential partner in the due diligence questionnaire to verify the information found.
- **Past experience with your company:** Review the list of joint venture agreements that the potential partner currently has, or had in the past, with your company. Subsequently, contact relevant personnel in your company to request documentation relating to previous due diligence efforts conducted on the potential partner, as well as information regarding the potential partner's conduct in performing such agreements, including any red flags and other issues.
- **Media and Internet:** The use of free or subscription databases provides a simple and cost-effective way to find relevant information about a potential partner. Use a reputable search engine, search each name associated with the potential partner and narrow the search using appropriate terms such as: bribe, crime, charge, corruption, fraud, slush fund, black money, or money laundering. Review the results, identifying and printing any articles (i) that implicate the potential partner, its related entities or principals in an inappropriate activity; (ii) that indicate government services/employment or ties to the government or to public officials; or (iii) that provide information that appears to be inconsistent with the information obtained through the due diligence questionnaire. Verify, if possible, such information through other sources (including embassies, consulates, chambers of commerce).
- **Anti-corruption measures:** Check the official website of the potential partner and of its related companies and search for codes, policies, and procedures addressing business ethics, anti-corruption compliance, and gifts and hospitality policies.
- **Antitrust decisions:** Competition authorities usually provide on their websites details about pending cartel investigations and final decisions. From these sources, a track record of the partner's attitude towards antitrust compliance can be drawn.

---

[27] http://www.worldbank.org/html/opr/procure/debarr.html

APPENDIX B - Red Flags

The following are some of the red flags to watch for during the due diligence process and throughout the negotiation and implementation of a joint venture agreement. The presence of one or more red flags does not mean that improper conduct by the potential partner has already occurred or will occur. It does mandate, however, greater scrutiny and the implementation of appropriate safeguards.

- The circumstances in which the potential partner (called hereafter 'it') was identified or introduced are unusual or abnormal (for instance it was the only available partner; it was introduced by someone who may have a conflict of interest; it was strongly suggested by a government customer or a public official).
- It carries out its business in a country or in an industrial sector with a reputation for corruption.
- It, or any of its principals, is domiciled or is a resident of a so-called tax haven or of a country with a perceived high rate of corruption.
- It, if a company, has an unusual corporate structure or was only recently incorporated.
- It is involved or has been proposed for no apparent good reason.
- It is duly registered but has no activity, it has no or only limited staff and its business address appears to be only a letter box.
- It is owned by or employs a public official or a family member of a public official.
- It, or any of its principals, has a conflict of interest, has a questionable reputation, has been debarred or blacklisted, or has been investigated, prosecuted or convicted (especially in the case of corruption related offences, money-laundering or fraud).
- It presents a history of unexplained or inadequately explained breakup of association with other companies.
- It has a desire to keep the relationship secret or requires its identity not to be disclosed.
- It insists on having sole control of any host country government approvals.
- It (or a third party representative) suggests that it can make special arrangements with regard to the decision-making or action process at stake.
- It refuses to commit to compliance with the anti-corruption laws.
- It does not have an adequate internal control system nor adequate procedures for the prevention or identification of corruptive practices or refuses to implement them.
- It refuses to provide information requested during a due diligence review process.
- Its business scope does not appear to be consistent with the scope of the joint venture.

- It does not have adequate resources to support the joint venture or has a questionable financial situation (for example: annual turnover and net assets are less than the services provided, significant losses, financial statements not subjected to an independent audit, discrepancies, or inconsistencies in the financial statements).
- It has no or only poor experience in relation to the contractual activity.
- It requests that the returns under the joint venture agreement be paid: (i) in cash; (ii) to an entity or individual other than itself; (iii) into a bank account registered in a country that is not the country where it resides or where the joint venture operates; or (iv) into a ciphered bank account.
- It requests an unusual transaction structure or wishes to include incorrect or unnecessary cost items or false documentation.
- It requests unusually large payments, or payments that appear excessive and not justified.
- It gives incomplete or inaccurate information in required disclosures for invoices or other documentation.
- It is regularly involved in large cartel investigations in countries where antitrust laws apply.

This list is not exhaustive. Other circumstances may arise suggesting that a corrupt or anti-competitive activity is about to occur. These should also be immediately reported to the Anti-corruption and Antitrust Support Unit.

FRANÇOIS VINCKE

Chapter 16
The ICC Anti-corruption Clause (2012)

François Vincke

Member of the Brussels Bar,
Former Secretary General and General Counsel of PetroFina

Experience shows that, during contractual negotiations, it is not easy to confront an existing or potential business partner with the vexed issue of corruption. It is however an increasingly important issue to address, and one which requires special care. ICC therefore took the initiative to develop a model Anti-corruption Clause, based on international best practice, which corporate lawyers and commercial negotiators are encouraged to include systematically in their contracts. In doing so, companies make the difficult but necessary step from 'corporate compliance' to 'contractual compliance'. This Chapter introduces the *ICC Anti-corruption Clause* (2012) whose full version can be found in Annex 2 of this Training Handbook.

ANOTHER BOILERPLATE CLAUSE?

Let's imagine the following situation: Commercial colleagues of yours have embarked on a sensitive contractual negotiation. They are drafting an important agreement with international ramifications to be concluded with a new and promising industrial partner. Everything happens according to plan and the negotiators are making headway. You hear them say that they have reached the stage of what is erroneously called the 'legal clauses' or 'boilerplate clauses', which in practice means these end-of-the-contract provisions, such as the 'Choice of law and jurisdiction', 'Arbitration', and 'Entire agreement' clauses. It is now time to decide whether the parties will include or not an anti-corruption clause in the contract.

In fact, your company is relatively confident with its future counterpart, having gone through the usual due diligence procedures. However, nobody in the company has practical experience of doing business with this new partner. You, as a compliance practitioner, should raise the question: "Shouldn't we introduce in the contract a provision giving the company (and in fact all the parties involved) sufficient assurance about the parties' integrity?" Even though the candidate partner's record has been reviewed and everything looks fine, you feel the need to protect the future of the contractual relationship. In introducing an anti-corruption clause, you will protect your company's integrity record and will ensure a flawless implementation of the contract, free from any corrupt and other fraudulent practices for which your company may be held (indirectly) liable.

YOUR CLAUSE – MY CLAUSE?

Once the question of the inclusion of an anti-corruption clause has been answered positively, the next question will be: Which provision will you introduce in the contract?

You may try to 'impose' the standard clause your company has developed over the years. But in such case, you run the risk of confronting your future counterpart, who may feel overrun and may have the impression that you consider his business conduct model inferior to yours. For instance, a small- or medium-sized enterprise may, not totally without reason, consider that a larger company uses the issue of anti-corruption to pressure it into practices that seem to restrict its freedom of action.

Alternatively, you may decide to opt for the model clause which your new partner is proposing. But the problem there will be that your company has no experience of how such clause will be effective in different (and sometimes difficult) contractual circumstances and you too will be reluctant to 'submit' to your partner's unilateral solution.

Your best option will finally be to use a clause, which is available off the shelf and can be seen as neutral, since it has been developed by the International Chamber of Commerce on the basis of the experiences gained by a great many of companies from different segments of industry and services, and which are active in all parts of the world: the *ICC Anti-corruption Clause* (2012).

A CLAUSE FOR ALL SEASONS

The *ICC Anti-corruption Clause* (2012) is an ideal neutral ground on which any party in all contractual relationships should be able to meet. It was prepared by two ICC policy commissions (the Commission on Commercial Law and Practice – which produced the worldwide known Incoterms® Rules – and the Commission on Corporate Responsibility and Anti-corruption) with the straightforward aim of providing the business world with strong and simple contractual provisions, shielding contractual parties from corruptive practices, while at the same time preserving, as much as possible, the continuity of their contractual relationship.

The Clause can be used by large, medium, and small companies alike. It is usable between equals (for instance between two producers) or amongst parties with dissimilar economic strength (such as a principal and an agent or a purchaser and a supplier in a supply chain). Thanks to its neutral character, no party will feel that its integrity model is challenged or considered inferior to the one of the other parties.

Indeed, the ICC Clause should not be perceived as the product of one of the negotiating parties, nor should it be seen as belonging to one defined culture or to one specific legal system or jurisdiction. The Clause should rather be looked upon as the result of the best internationally accepted, up-to-date, and commercially viable integrity practice.

FROM 'CORPORATE COMPLIANCE' TO 'CONTRACTUAL COMPLIANCE'

Many leading companies all over the world have made considerable efforts to build up their own corporate compliance system, with a view to shielding themselves from the huge damage corruption can inflict. We have described in the successive Chapters of this Ethics & Compliance Training Handbook which measures companies should take to establish an efficient corporate compliance programme. But all these costly, time-consuming efforts could be ruined by a single contractual relationship that turns sour due to non-compliance by one of the parties.

To avoid such kind of damage, 'corporate compliance' has to find its logical development in 'contractual compliance'. Companies should invest not only in their own internal compliance efforts but also in securing compliance by their contractual partners.

These partners, by adopting the *ICC Anti-corruption Clause* (2012), have to commit expressly to comply with anti-corruption provisions – and in particular with the provisions of Part I of the *ICC Rules on Combating Corruption* (2011) – and to develop, maintain, and implement a genuine corporate integrity programme.

A CLAUSE BUILT ON TWO PILLARS AND THREE OPTIONS

By introducing the Clause in their contracts, the parties state that they have not and will not use bribes in the context of the contract. If this were to happen, the non-infringing party can bring the matter to the attention of the non-compliant party and require remediation. Failing remediation, the contract can be suspended or terminated at the discretion of the non-infringing party.

The *ICC Anti-corruption Clause* (2012) is built on two pillars: (i) the determination expressed by parties to ensure anti-corruption compliance in their contractual relationship and (ii) the will to preserve, in that context, the sanctity of contracts through maintaining trust between parties throughout the lifetime of the contract.

In practical terms, three options are open to the drafters of an agreement for including the *ICC Anti-corruption Clause* (2012):

Option I consists of a shorter version of the Clause. This version incorporates by reference the provisions of Part I of the *ICC Rules on Combating Corruption* (2011), which expresses the prohibition of all forms of corruptive practices. This Option, which contains four relatively short paragraphs, has the advantage of not overburdening the text of the contract and will therefore be better suited to shorter and less complex agreements.

Option II is based on the incorporation in full of the provisions of Part I of the *ICC Rules on Combating Corruption* (2011). This Option lists explicitly the whole text of Part I of the ICC Rules. Option II will be preferred by parties who wish to make explicit all the commitments they undertake and will be the optimal solution in longer, more elaborate and complex contracts.

Option III differs from the two preceding Options, as it is built on another type of commitment. Here the parties declare that they have put in place (or are about to do so) a corporate anti-corruption compliance programme, as described in Article 10 of the *ICC Rules on Combating Corruption* (2011). The commitment by the contractual parties is of another nature than the one under Options I and II but should reach the same objective: Maintaining integrity throughout the lifetime of the contract (and even thereafter).

A USEFUL COMMENTARY

The parties may incorporate the Clause by referring to its full name but any reference in their contract to the 'Clause' or related variations shall be deemed to be a reference to the *ICC Anti-corruption Clause* (2012).

A useful, explicit and detailed commentary is attached to the Clause, giving precise guidance as to how to interpret the provisions of the Clause in specific circumstances.

To give two examples, the commentary explains which type of evidence a party should produce in case an infringement of the anti-corruption provisions is alleged or which kind of remedial action can be undertaken by the non-complying party to repair the situation.

WHAT ABOUT SANCTIONS?

Setting up a new contractual anti-corruption compliance system would be meaningless without the introduction of a serious sanction in case of infringement.

And what would be, in the context of a contractual relationship, a more efficient deterrent than the suspension or termination of the contract at the discretion of the non-infringing party? Hitting the infringing party in the wallet, through the suspension or termination of the contract, is probably the most effective civil penalty one can inflict in these circumstances. But this will be allowed only after having given the non-complying party the opportunity to remedy the situation.

A BALANCE BETWEEN CONTINUITY OF CONTRACTS AND BUSINESS INTEGRITY

The harshness of the sanction imposed in case of infringement should not, however, change the parties' perception of the *ICC Anti-corruption Clause* (2012): The aim of the Clause is not sanctioning in itself but is, very much to the contrary, the promotion of integrity in contractual relations (before the entering into force of the contract, throughout the course of the contract, and thereafter) between all the parties (including subcontractors, agents, and other third parties).

In other words, the drafters of the Clause were aware that there should be a balance between the genuine efforts of the parties to fight corruption and the treatment of corruption as a breach of a contract justifying its termination.

OPTIONS I AND II

This balance between the principle of continuity of contracts and the strong commitment to actively ensure integrity in contractual implementation is underlined by the following elements, contained in Options I and II of the Clause:

(i) An infringement under the Clause will only be considered relevant if it consists of material or several repeated breaches of the provisions of Part I of the *ICC Rules on Combating Corruption* (2011);

(ii) Such infringement should be concerned with the very contract itself and not with other contracts concluded between the same parties, or any other contracts;

(iii) Evidence of an infringement can be brought (a) through the conclusions of a contractually-provided audit of the other party's accounting books and financial records (b) or by bringing other evidence, which does not have to be corroborative but which should be sufficient to prove that suspicions are not invoked in a vexatious or otherwise unjustified manner;

(iv) The allegedly infringing party will be allowed to take the necessary remedial action curing the situation in a reasonable time after having been notified by the other party; and

(v) The allegedly infringing party may invoke a defense by proving that, by the time the evidence of breach(es) had arisen, it had put into place adequate anti-corruption preventive measures, as described in Article 10 of the *ICC Rules on Combating Corruption* (2011).

OPTION III

Similarly, in Option III, the following items are indicative of a fair balance between the parties' desire to give the contract its full effect and their wish to maintain integrity throughout the contractual term:

(i) The parties declare that they have put in place a corporate compliance programme, as described in Article 10 of the *ICC Rules on Combating Corruption* (2011);

This programme should be adapted to each party's particular circumstances and should be capable of detecting corruption and of promoting a culture of integrity in the organization of the party concerned;

(ii) The corporate compliance programme has to be maintained and implemented by each party at least throughout the lifetime of the contract and each party will have to inform the other party on a regular basis about the programme's implementation through statements prepared by a qualified corporate representative, whose name will have been communicated to the other party;

(iii) If a party becomes aware that the other party's qualified corporate representative's statements contain material deficiencies, undermining the efficiency of that party's programme, it will notify the latter party accordingly;

(iv) A party invoking a deficiency in a qualified corporate representative's statements must bring evidence that either such statements are missing or that a statement contains materially untrue, false, or incomplete declarations;

Such evidence does not have to be corroborative but must be sufficient to prove that suspicions are not invoked in a vexatious or otherwise unjustified manner; and

(v) The party, whose statements are alleged to be deficient, will be allowed to take the necessary remedial action curing the situation in a reasonable time after having been notified by the other party.

Necessary remedial action might include providing a new, accurate, complete, and sincere statement, giving a full and fair picture of the implementation by such party of the provisions of the corporate compliance programme, as well as any corrective action this party will take to improve such implementation.

A CLAUSE FOR MORE INTEGRITY IN CONTRACTS

It is ICC's hope that the *Anti-corruption Clause* (2012) will become general practice, as is the case of the many other model contracts and clauses produced by ICC over the years, such as the ICC Force Majeure Clause and the ICC Model Confidentiality Agreement.

Compliance practitioners, company lawyers and other corporate officers in charge of audit and control should encourage their colleagues in charge of managing their company's industrial or commercial relations to adopt the Clause as a matter of routine in all significant contracts executed by their company.

This will help anti-corruption not being restricted to law books, corporate Codes of Conduct or statements by Chief Executive Officers and becoming a daily business reality.

About the author

François Vincke is a Member of the Brussels Bar. He worked 26 years for PetroFina, a European oil, gas and petrochemicals company, including 11 years as Secretary General and General Counsel. Since 1994, he is the Head of Anti-corruption at ICC, first as Chairman of the Anti-corruption Commission and later as Vice-Chair of the Commission on Corporate Responsibility and Anti-corruption. He wrote a number of articles and gave numerous conferences on matters related to ethics and compliance.

Chapter 17
Managing the Transition to a Clean Commercial Policy

Max Burger-Scheidlin
Executive Director, ICC Austria

In this Chapter, we analyze step by step, and in very concrete terms, how your company should prepare, organize, and communicate on its transition from a bribe-prone to a bribe-free corporate policy when dealing with its customers. Your mission as an ethics and compliance officer will consist in changing the mindsets of your colleagues, while paying heed to a number of legal, tax, commercial, human resources, and internal communications considerations. You will also need to take into account your customers' perspective when explaining and implementing your new clean commercial policy – the ultimate goal being to achieve this transition without losing your customer base.

INTRODUCTION

Until 1999, year of the entry into force of the *OECD Convention*, many companies doing business across borders were inclined to 'persuade' customers to give them business in exchange for bribes. At the time, this practice was still legal in many countries, even though it was widely regarded as unethical. ICC warmly welcomed the *OECD Convention* as a historic milestone in global efforts to achieve a level playing field for international business. However, some in the business world only reluctantly accepted this new reality. Several resounding cases, such as the Siemens case, served as a wake-up call but, even in 2013, one still comes across companies which stand by their belief that they cannot run their business without paying bribes.

Some enterprises are simply still stuck in their old habits. Following decades of business relations based on corruption, they simply do not know how to break the vicious cycle of corruption. They fear that the current smooth running of their business might come to an end if bribery were to be abandoned.

Generally, it will be easier for your company to become clean if it sells relatively unique or differentiated products (tailor-made, for example), since your customer will have less competitors to turn to. If your company is not presently at this stage, aim at further differentiating your products. This should be a key strategy in your efforts to extirpate corruption.

WHEN AND HOW SHOULD YOU START THE TRANSITION?

Try to have change coincide with an external stimulus, such as the change of your company's Chief Executive Officer, the appointment of a new chairman of the Board of Directors, a major change in your company's ownership, or the occurrence of disrupting external events like a visible corruption case, the voting of a new law in your home jurisdiction or in certain key markets, such as Russia and China. Highlight the impact of said change and use it as a starting point for your company's transition to a clean commercial policy.

In companies where bribery has long been used as a tool for winning contracts, corrupt practices may have become a 'second nature' to sales managers. This means that while they have acquired the skills to negotiate a bribe, they have long neglected the actual skills of selling your company's products or services. To remedy this situation, have your company send your sales managers to training courses on sales skills and negotiation tactics. Set up internal working groups to identify your company's unique selling propositions or niches. Your sales force needs to understand what differentiates your company's products or services from those of your competitors.

Additionally, try to analyze and match the personality of your company's sales people to that of the purchaser in the buyer's company and to the specific identity of your company's products. A street-wise salesperson, say in the mining machinery industry, may be a superb bribe negotiator but poorly skilled in highlighting the unique technical features of the products.

INSTALLING AN ETHICS AND COMPLIANCE SYSTEM IS NOT ENOUGH TO CHANGE YOUR COMPANY'S INTEGRITY CULTURE

It may be tempting for management to believe that a top-down approach will be sufficient to change a company's culture from corruption-prone to corruption-free overnight. What frequently happens is that management wants a 'recognized' ethics and compliance system to be introduced by external experts from outside the company, and then expects this move to operate some kind of automatic change. Such an approach is ill conceived. Instead, you should seek to nurture change from within the company.

Admittedly, a frequent complaint from your sales people will be that "To obtain business in countries like Russia and China, we need to bribe". That "bribing is an offence" cannot be your only answer. The challenge here will be to explore with your sales people some of the possible alternatives to corrupt business, namely, the means for them to sell without having to pay a bribe. Keep in mind that sales managers are often technicians and not lawyers. Experience tells that they are success-driven and often conduct business under the motto: "I do everything to get my contract signed." Their remuneration system often reinforces this attitude. Therefore, a change to a 'clean business' model should involve demonstrating the personal risks of paying a bribe and should shed light on successful case studies of clean business in very corrupt countries. Remember also to inform your sales people about external resources available for support, such as ICC national committees or ICC's specialized division in detecting and fighting economic fraud, ICC Commercial Crime Services[28].

DRIVE CHANGE IN HUMAN RESOURCES MANAGEMENT

Performance targets set by management should move away from short-term success criteria to focus on long-term achievements. Many job descriptions in the marketing and sales divisions will have to be rethought: Your company's sales philosophy must clearly aim towards achieving long-term market shares and stable profits. The approach for landing new business will be different: It will need to move from "Go and get a contract tomorrow" to "Explore the environment for solid and stable business." Sales managers will have to bear greater responsibility for the selection of sales partners and their performance over the medium term. Bonuses and stock options will have to be adapted accordingly. Since bribery is no longer permitted, sales managers should upgrade their technical abilities and become significantly more service-oriented, notably by tailoring the product to the customer's wishes. This will be especially important in a context where your competitors still use bribes to obtain business.

SELL CHANGE WITHIN YOUR COMPANY

First, you will need to convince your company's owners and shareholders of the need for change. They should be informed that the new anti-corruption policy may reduce business in the short or medium term but will, on the other hand, yield a more stable, long-term business profile with solid profits and a lower risk rate (which should itself improve the stock market valuation, as the company is demonstrating solid risk management). Then you will need to talk to your Supervisory Board or Board of Directors and, finally, to your staff.

Ultimately, all company stakeholders will have to be informed, trained, and convinced to embrace the new company culture. This includes contractors, subcontractors, technical consultants, parts suppliers, agents, and intermediaries. Only start re-educating stakeholders once you are at an advanced stage of delivering anti-corruption training to your own staff. Try convincing your stakeholders, such as your suppliers, that the change to a robust anti-corruption culture will benefit them as well. Your suppliers should see that they stand to gain from convincing their own suppliers (your sub-suppliers) to follow suit and adopt a similar clean commercial policy.

SHOULD YOU INFORM THE GENERAL PUBLIC?

It will probably not be a good idea to talk openly about your company's past corruptive practices when presenting and justifying your new reform agenda. However, to make a successful anti-corruption stand, your company should be in a position to demonstrate its anti-corruption efforts in the media. This will make your company policies more credible in foreign markets. Try to combine your new anti-corruption policies with other company initiatives relating to corporate social responsibility,

---

[28] http://www.icc-ccs.org/

environmental issues, or compliance with new laws. Inform the public that your owners desire stable, long-term business. Your sales managers can use such media reports to convince old business partners and bribe-takers that your company has now changed course.

COMMUNICATE THE NEW ANTI-CORRUPTION POLICY TO YOUR CUSTOMERS

Start the implementation of your new policy at a point in time when there are no key contracts up for negotiation: Try to identify a 'relaxed' moment in your business relationship. You might for instance seek to re-negotiate smaller contracts first, and observe the results. At first, your old customers may stall: They may threaten to stop buying from you, and may even make a small purchase from one of your competitors to show how serious they are about the situation. If relationships have been difficult in the past, you might lose some of your customers. If, however, your technology is unique, and your business relationship has been frictionless over the years, many (but perhaps not all) of your customers will return and continue to do business with you.

MANAGING THE LEGAL TRANSITION

One of the major hurdles your company will face in its transition to a zero-bribe policy is the fact that laws differ from country to country. This is true of anti-corruption legislation, but also of tax, accounting, and anti-money laundering legislation. In certain countries, it will be possible to 'confess your old sins' to the judicial authorities but that will not necessarily mean that the tax authorities of the same country will take the same attitude as their colleagues of the Department of Justice. To successfully manage your legal transition, you will need to consider the laws and regulations of:

(i) All relevant jurisdictions: Those of the bribe-giver's country, those of the bribe-taker's country, those of the country where the bribe transits, those of the country where the bribe is paid, and maybe those of the countries which are indirectly involved, such as the United Kingdom pursuant to the *Bribery Act* (2010) or the United States through the *Foreign Corrupt Practices Act* (1977); and

(ii) The various legal disciplines: Criminal law, civil law, accounting law, and tax law.

It will be important to find out if under these different laws a voluntary disclosure by your company of its past misconduct may shield it from disproportionate liabilities. Analyze if and how you can correct the accounts, reintegrate slush funds into the regular accounts, and how you can regularize your tax situation. You may come to the conclusion that confessing to the authorities is not your best option. Unfortunately the international legal environment is not yet ready to help companies that are becoming clean. A disclosure may seriously damage your customer's business and ruin your bilateral business relationship. However, while it is still difficult to report past offences to the authorities, nothing stands in your way of becoming clean in your future business dealings. If your partner disagrees, you may have to stop the relationship altogether.

RETAINING YOUR CUSTOMER

Most people resent change. It is most likely that you will hear former bribe-takers tell you: "Our arrangement worked so well in the past." As you want to retain your old customer, changing from the old illegal relationship to a clean new one will require great tact and care. You will receive two types of advice. Your lawyers will probably tell you to become clean overnight. Your sales team, on the other hand, will tell you that "This is an excellent customer" and that "The profitable long-term relationship with this customer should not be disturbed." You should pay heed to both arguments.

The first reaction of the old bribe-takers will likely be: "Well, we fully understand your new policies, and we have come across well-publicized cases in the media. However there are wonderful covert and secret ways to get around all these new laws and regulations. Surely you want to remain in business, don't you?" At this point you must stand your ground. If you have not yet spoken to your customer's owner (or Chief Executive Officer), it is time to do so. This will not always be possible, especially if you are a small- or medium-sized supplier and your customer is a giant company, but do try. Be aware that your customer's corrupt purchasing manager will do everything to prevent you from contacting the company's owner (or Chief Executive Officer). You will hear many excuses. External organizations like your ICC national committee may help you in these circumstances.

NEGOTIATING THE TRANSITION

Your legal anti-corruption experts will tell you to stop all bribes immediately, to dismiss the bribe-givers and bribe-takers on the spot, and to inform the authorities of any wrongdoing. While this may be considered the optimal solution, you should try to find a legal and practical way to become clean without upsetting exceedingly your business relationship. Not all customers will agree to your new anti-corruption policy. Many will threaten to withdraw their business. In anticipation of this, many may contact your competitors.

The line prescribed by your lawyers might also be hampered by twists and conflicts of interest. Let us imagine various hypotheses. The purchasing manager of your customer may be opposed to your new policy as past bribes from your company represented a vital source of income. The customer's general manager may be a recipient of part of the bribes. This might give this person leverage over the purchasing manager. The owner of the customer's company, on the other hand, may have a totally different view on how to conduct business than the general manager and the purchasing manager. In some instances, the owner may be fiercely opposed to corrupt practices, as they reduce the company's profit margin. In other circumstances, an owner may not oppose corruption because the company's purchasing manager may demand higher salaries in return for abandoning an additional income previously derived from bribes. Additionally, in high-tax countries, even the owner may be an indirect recipient of bribes and be happy to receive money in an off-shore tax haven. When the bribe-takers are public officials or politicians, the situation becomes even more complicated and involves many interests.

WHAT ARE THE KEY ARGUMENTS FOR YOUR NEW POLICY?

Concluding corrupt deals often results in purchasing subpar raw materials or machines, or obtaining suboptimal services. Over time, this may result in a significant fall in the performance and competitiveness of the corrupt company. Your argument should be that without bribes being included in the sales price, the customer's company will become more competitive and profitable and less exposed to risk in conducting its business. More specifically, you can show your customer (and its owner) how they will directly benefit from your new anti-corruption policy: as prices can be lowered, after-sales services will increase. You could also deliver higher quality goods at the same prices as before and give better technical training to your customer's staff. Time saved on lengthy and lousy bribe negotiations will make both companies more competitive.

Still, many customers may be reluctant to follow your arguments, especially if you are a small- or medium-sized enterprise with little leverage on the market. What will follow is a longer series of negotiations, battles, and threats during which you should stay firm about your new anti-corruption policy.

In developing your negotiation technique, always try to take into account the bribe-taker's perspective. Presently, the bribe-taker makes a good additional income by accepting bribes. But to go on like this, he or she has to hold sway. Everyone has competitors and opponents. This means that a bribe-taker must be outwardly successful to keep opposition at bay. This person cannot risk being continuously responsible for mismanaged, technically inferior, non-performing, or loss-making operations. So, if he or she wishes to survive, simply going for the highest bribe is a dangerous path. You should therefore research your counterpart's overall position. Is there an opportunity to make your corrupt counterpart more successful? Finding 'face-saving' support for the manager concerned would create more willingness to support your policy change, and this without compromising your anti-corruption standards.

Also, when conducting these negotiations, think about reshuffling your sales team by reallocating responsibilities. If you send your old sales manager (the one who has negotiated bribes in the past) along to negotiations, put this person as a second-in-command in your company's delegation. It must be clearly visible that this individual is no longer in charge and comes along only to provide advice. If you can make an appointment with the owner of the corrupt customer's company, the top echelon of your company (or at least a member of your Board) should attend. The message should be clear, strong, and simple: "We want to support you, to make your business more competitive, but there will be no more bribes." Do not yield to temptation; do not negotiate a "bribe only for the next six months", a "reduced bribe", or any other form of circumvention of your new policy. Price reductions, however, are possible.

Be patient in your negotiations. You might have to fly in several times to retain your customer. Give your old partners time to get accustomed to the new situation, to ponder the difficulties as well as the new opportunities which are now on the table. If possible, give examples of old but rejuvenated business relationships, and show that this was a successful process. In situations where you have a relatively unique product or service, and have enjoyed a good, frictionless business relationship for an extended period of time, there is a good chance that you will be able to retain your customer. Be aware, however, that in a number of instances the negotiations will end inconclusively.

PUTTING INTO PLACE THE NEW ANTI-CORRUPTION POLICY

The threat and fear of losing business or a customer must not paralyze you in your move towards a clean commercial policy. Keep your company's global picture in mind. Provided your products and services are somehow unique or special, your new policy should lead to less risk and higher profits. Stay firm. Do not let corrupt buyers and other business partners interfere. Communicate your new policy to all local stakeholders known to you and show them the potential advantages for themselves. Where possible have your top management see your customers (and their owners) in person, explain the situation (past and future) and promote your new anti-corruption policy.

Offer to conduct anti-corruption training workshops at the premises of your bigger customers. Or invite customers to an annual meeting at which all kind of new business is discussed, but which includes, for example, a two-hour anti-corruption workshop. Wherever necessary, have your lawyers meet your customers and provide them advice about the validity and continuity of the contracts concluded with your company. Past corrupt business relationships should be no hindrance to future business dealings.

Let them also ascertain that your company is not blacklisted, for instance by a municipality or another important buyer, an export credit agency, an international lender (such as the World Bank, the Asian Development Bank, or the European Bank for Reconstruction and Development). Should anything look amiss, seek contact with the institution, be proactive and transparent. Do not wait until they contact you. It is much easier to prevent facing the issue than having your company removed from a blacklist. Should trouble loom due to past mistakes, try to have your new anti-corruption compliance system certified by a well-known international auditor (as for instance SGS, one of the big four auditing firms or any specialized certification firm.).

Try to introduce in all your agreements the *ICC Anti-corruption Clause* (2012), as suggested in Chapter 16 of this Training Handbook. If you and your customer have an ethics and compliance officer, have both of them meet and suggest they install a hotline to handle possible incidents.

MANAGING THE FIRST SHIPMENTS UNDER THE NEW CLEAN FORMULA

Even when negotiations have remained inconclusive, business must go on. Under the contract, you still may be obliged to deliver parts and services or find yourself under the threat of no payment, or face the risk of your customer simply not confirming receipt of your goods and services.

Even if you have not received the corrupt customer's explicit consent, start implementing what you had promised when negotiating the move to a clean policy. For instance, start lowering prices on spare parts or give extra services at reduced or no cost. Behave as if your partner had consented to the policy change and ensure that not only the old corrupt purchaser but also his superiors and the company owner take note of the new policy and your new practice. There is no need to brag about your new conduct; take a low profile but remain clear and clean while signalling your new behaviour to all other stakeholders involved.

For your first shipments, select items which are non-essential and of low value. Select shipments which can be delayed at customs and are not easy to damage. To be on the safe side, have somebody from your side (a member of your staff, an independent consultant or an inspection company) at the receiving end of the first shipments to independently document the receipt of goods or the implementation of services. Make sure that your company performs exceedingly well.

Although success never is guaranteed, there is a strong likelihood that your policy change will be well received, the more so if your company has experienced an extended and well-functioning business relationship in the past, and where the experts from both sides trusted each other. Should, however, your business partner still insist on receiving a bribe, let him go, but do not rule this partner out for future opportunities. Keep a positive contact, like with any other potential customer. This partner may come around eventually: times change, managers retire, and others come up with new ideas and a different outlook. Globally, the pressure mounts for stricter ethics and compliance standards, and a new global level playing field is slowly emerging.

The most important trend in your favour (at least in the context of private-to-private business) is that many companies are moving to some forms of profit-sharing agreements. Through this, formerly corrupt buyers and managers receive higher rewards in the absence of corruption, as slowly everyone realizes that the days and weeks needed to negotiate a bribe is time wasted and that buying suboptimal raw material or underperforming machines strongly reduces possible rewards in profit-sharing agreements.

CONCLUSION

The transition from past corrupt practices to 'clean' business is a stony path. If properly prepared, you will be able to retain the majority of your existing customers, especially when dealing with other business entities. However, this may be more difficult to achieve with customers from the public sector.

About the author

Max Burger-Scheidlin is Executive Director of ICC Austria. He consults companies on foreign trade contracts, the prevention of commercial crime (corruption, counterfeiting, import-export fraud, and espionage), global competitive challenges to business, cross cultural negotiation tactics, and the prevention of international disputes. He is a lecturer at several universities in Austria and events and conferences internationally, including China. Mr. Burger-Scheidlin has published extensively on anti-corruption, anti-money laundering, corporate compliance, and macroeconomic topics. He has lived 16 years in Asia and the Middle East.

Annex I
ICC Rules on Combating Corruption
2011 edition

Prepared by the ICC **Commission on Corporate Responsibility and Anti-corruption**

The 2011 edition of the ICC Rules for Combating Corruption consists of three parts:

- **Part I** states the Rules proper;
- **Part II** deals with policies which Enterprises should enact to support compliance with the Rules;
- **Part III** lists the suggested elements of an effective corporate compliance programme.

First published in 1977 by ICC

Copyright © 2011

International Chamber of Commerce (ICC)

All rights reserved.

ICC holds all copyright and other intellectual property rights in this collective work. No part of this collective work may be reproduced, distributed, transmitted, translated or adapted in any form or by any means, except as permitted by law, without the written permission of ICC.

Permission can be requested from ICC through pub@iccwbo.org.

Preface

Jean-Guy Carrier, *ICC Secretary General*,

François Vincke, *Vice-chair of the ICC Commission on Corporate Responsibility and Anti-corruption*, and

Jean-Pierre Méan, *Chair of the Task Force on the Revision of the ICC Rules on Combating Corruption*

The International Chamber of Commerce (ICC) has always been at the forefront of the drive for more integrity in business transactions, because only a corruption-free system makes it possible for all participants to compete on a level playing field.

ICC emphasizes the critical role of compliance by enterprises with self-imposed rules, while recognizing the basic responsibility of international organizations and national governments in the fight against all corrupt practices, including extortion, solicitation and bribery.

Enterprises' adherence to strict rules will help them fulfil their legal obligations in a more natural, effective and sustainable way. The adoption and implementation by businesses of their own corporate compliance programmes is therefore strongly recommended, as it is made compulsory in an increasing number of jurisdictions.

ICC was the first business organization to issue anti-corruption rules with the publication as early as 1977 of its Rules of Conduct to Combat Extortion and Bribery. It has updated these Rules in 1996, 1999, and 2005 to reflect the adoption of key international legal instruments, such as the Convention on Combating Bribery of Foreign Public Officials (1997) of the Organisation for Economic Cooperation and Development and the United Nations Convention on Corruption (2003). These instruments, which are major milestones in the fight against corruption, have been actively supported in their adoption, implementation and enforcement by the business community. ICC will continue to actively contribute to these organisations' anti-corruption programmes.

The present 2011 revision of the ICC Rules on Combating Corruption mirror-images the impressive evolution of the ethics and compliance practice of leading enterprises. It is based on numerous contributions made by ICC national committees, member companies and experts of the Commission on Corporate Responsibility and Anti-corruption. It provides a compliance model applicable to large, medium and small-sized enterprises. It builds on other documents ICC has prepared such as the ICC Handbook "Fighting Corruption, a Corporate Practices Manual" and on various ICC Guidelines on specific integrity matters.

Fighting corruption, which is at the core of corporate responsibility and good corporate governance, is never finished. Sustained efforts will continue to be necessary in the future. A better awareness is necessary among public officials, in board rooms and in all layers of the corporate world. ICC is committed to continue to bring its contribution to this daunting task.

Introduction

These ICC Rules are intended as a method of self-regulation by business against the background of applicable national law and key international legal instruments. Their voluntary acceptance by Enterprises will promote high standards of integrity in business transactions, whether between Enterprises and public bodies or between Enterprises themselves. These Rules play an important role in assisting Enterprises to comply with their legal obligations and with the numerous anti-corruption initiatives at the international level. They also provide an appropriate basis for resisting attempts at extortion or solicitation of bribes.

These Rules are of a general nature constituting what is considered good commercial practice. They reflect, and should be read in accordance with the key international legal instruments [...].

All Enterprises should conform to the applicable laws and regulations of the countries in which they are established and where they operate, and should observe both the letter and the spirit of these Rules.

ICC Model Contracts contain references to Part I of the present Rules. Enterprises are equally urged to incorporate, in full or by reference, Part I of the present Rules in their commercial contracts, in order to prevent their contractual relationships from being affected by any form of corruption.

Enterprises are advised to collaborate with each other as well as with relevant international, regional and sectorial initiatives to promote and develop the practices reflected in these Rules; they are further encouraged to cooperate with national and foreign law enforcement authorities conducting corruption related investigations. Enterprises are also urged to resist extortion or solicitation for bribes e.g. by using tools such as RESIST [...].

For the purposes of these Rules, the term "Enterprise" refers to any person or entity engaged in business and other economic activities, whether or not organized for profit, including any entity controlled by a state or a territorial subdivision thereof; it includes a parent and its controlled subsidiaries. Although these Rules do not differentiate according to the size of an Enterprise or the nature of its activities, their implementation will have to be adapted according to a risk assessment and notably to the nature of the business conducted by small and medium size Enterprises. The success of these ICC Rules will depend on the "tone at the top": there should be a clear message from the Chair of the Board of Directors (or other body with ultimate responsibility for the Enterprise) and/or the Chief Executive Officer of the Enterprise that corruption is prohibited and that an effective corporate compliance programme will be implemented. Buy-in by all employees of the Enterprise is also essential.

These ICC Rules consist of three parts. Part I states the Rules proper, Part II deals with policies which Enterprises should enact to support compliance with the Rules and Part III lists the suggested elements of an effective corporate compliance programme. [...].

Part I – Anti-Corruption Rules

Article 1
Prohibited Practices

Enterprises will prohibit the following practices at all times and in any form, in relation with
- a public official at international, national or local level,
- a political party, party official or candidate to political office, and
- a director, officer or employee of an Enterprise,

whether these practices are engaged in directly or indirectly, including through Third Parties:

a) **Bribery** is the offering, promising, giving, authorizing or accepting of any undue pecuniary or other advantage to, by or for any of the persons listed above or for anyone else in order to obtain or retain a business or other improper advantage, e.g. in connection with public or private procurement contract awards, regulatory permits, taxation, customs, judicial and legislative proceedings.
Bribery often includes (i) kicking back a portion of a contract payment to government or party officials or to employees of the other contracting party, their close relatives, friends or Business Partners or (ii) using intermediaries such as agents, subcontractors, consultants or other Third Parties, to channel payments to government or party officials, or to employees of the other contracting party, their relatives, friends or Business Partners.

b) **Extortion or Solicitation** is the demanding of a bribe, whether or not coupled with a threat if the demand is refused. Enterprises will oppose any attempt of extortion or solicitation and are encouraged to report such attempts through available formal or informal reporting mechanisms, unless such reporting is deemed to be counter-productive under the circumstances.

c) **Trading in Influence** is the offering or solicitation of an undue advantage in order to exert an improper, real, or supposed influence with a view of obtaining from a public official an undue advantage for the original instigator of the act or for any other person.

d) **Laundering the proceeds of the corrupt practices mentioned above** is the concealing or disguising the illicit origin, source, location, disposition, movement or ownership of property, knowing that such property is the proceeds of crime.

"Corruption" or "Corrupt Practice(s)" as used in these Rules shall include Bribery, Extortion or Solicitation, Trading in Influence and Laundering the proceeds of these practices.

Article 2
Third Parties

With respect to Third Parties subject to the control or determining influence of the Enterprise, including but not limited to agents, business development consultants, sales representatives, customs agents, general consultants, resellers, subcontractors, franchisees, lawyers, accountants or similar intermediaries, acting on the Enterprise's behalf in connection with marketing or sales, the negotiation of contracts, the obtaining of licenses, permits or other authorizations, or any actions that benefit the Enterprise or as subcontractors in the supply chain, Enterprises should:

- instruct them neither to engage nor to tolerate that they engage in any act of corruption;
- not use them as a conduit for any corrupt practice;
- hire them only to the extent appropriate for the regular conduct of the Enterprise's business; and
- not pay them more than an appropriate remuneration for their legitimate services.

Part II – Corporate Policies to Support Compliance with the Anti-Corruption Rules

Article 3
Business Partners

Business Partners include (i) Third Parties and (ii) joint venture and consortium partners as well as contractors and suppliers.

A. An Enterprise should, with respect to a Third Party, and to the extent that it is within its power:

   a) make clear that it expects all activities carried out on the Enterprise's behalf to be compliant with its policies; and

   b) enter into a written agreement with the Third Party:

   - informing it of the Enterprise's anti-corruption policies and committing it not to engage in any corrupt practice;
   - permitting the Enterprise to request an audit of the Third Party's books and accounting records by an independent auditor to verify compliance with these Rules; and
   - providing that the Third Party's remuneration shall not be paid in cash and shall only be paid in (i) the country of incorporation of the Third Party, (ii) the country where its headquarters are located, (iii) its country of residence or (iv) the country where the mission is executed.

B. The Enterprise should further ensure that its central management has adequate control over the relationship with Third Parties and in particular maintains a record of the names, terms of engagement and payments to Third Parties retained by the Enterprise in connection with transactions with public bodies and state or private Enterprises. This record should be available for inspection by auditors and by appropriate, duly authorized governmental authorities under conditions of confidentiality.

C. An Enterprise should, with respect to a joint venture or consortium, take measures, within its power, to ensure that a policy consistent with these Rules is accepted by its joint venture or consortium partners as applicable to the joint venture or consortium.

D. With respect to contractors and suppliers, the Enterprise should take measures within its power and, as far as legally possible, to ensure that they comply with these Rules in their dealings on behalf of, or with the Enterprise, and avoid dealing with contractors and suppliers known or reasonably suspected to be paying bribes.

E. An Enterprise should include in its contracts with Business Partners a provision allowing it to suspend or terminate the relationship, if it has a unilateral good faith concern that a Business Partner has acted in violation of applicable anti-corruption law or of Part I of these Rules.

F. An Enterprise should conduct appropriate due diligence on the reputation and the capacity of its Business Partners exposed to corruption risks to comply with anti-corruption law in their dealings with or on behalf of the Enterprise.

G. An Enterprise should conduct its procurement in accordance with accepted business standards and to the extent possible in a transparent manner.

Article 4
Political and Charitable Contributions and Sponsorships

a) Enterprises should only make contributions to political parties, party officials and candidates in accordance with applicable law and public disclosure requirements. The amount and timing of political contributions should be reviewed to ensure that they are not used as a subterfuge for corruption.

b) Enterprises should take measures within their power to ensure that charitable contributions and sponsorships are not used as a subterfuge for corruption. Charitable contributions and sponsorships should be transparent and in accordance with applicable law.

c) Enterprises should establish reasonable controls and procedures to ensure that improper political and charitable contributions are not made. Special care should be exercised in reviewing contributions to organizations in which prominent political figures, or their close relatives, friends and Business Partners are involved.

Article 5
Gifts and Hospitality

Enterprises should establish procedures covering the offer or receipt of gifts and hospitality in order to ensure that such arrangements (a) comply with national law and applicable international instruments; (b) are limited to reasonable and bona fide expenditures; (c) do not improperly affect, or might be perceived as improperly affecting, the recipient's independence of judgement towards the giver; (d) are not contrary to the known provisions of the recipient's code of conduct; and (e) are neither offered or received too frequently nor at an inappropriate time.

Article 6
Facilitation Payments

Facilitation payments are unofficial, improper, small payments made to a low level official to secure or expedite the performance of a routine or necessary action to which the payer of the facilitation payment is legally entitled.

Facilitation payments are prohibited in most jurisdictions.

Enterprises should, accordingly, not make such facilitation payments, but it is recognized that they may be confronted with exigent circumstances, in which the making of a facilitation payment can hardly be avoided, such as duress or when the health, security or safety of the Enterprise's employees are at risk.

When a facilitation payment is made under such circumstances, it will be accurately accounted for in the Enterprise's books and accounting records.

Article 7
Conflicts of Interests

Conflicts of interests may arise when the private interests of an individual or of his/her close relatives, friends or business contacts diverge from those of the Enterprise or organization to which the individual belongs.

These situations should be disclosed and, wherever possible, avoided because they can affect an individual's judgment in the performance of his/her duties and responsibilities. Enterprises should closely monitor and regulate actual or potential conflicts of interests, or the appearance thereof, of their directors, officers, employees and agents and should not take advantage of conflicts of interests of others.

If their contemplated activity or employment relates directly to the functions held or supervised during their tenure, former public officials shall not be hired or engaged in any capacity before a reasonable period has elapsed after their leaving their office. Where applicable, restrictions imposed by national legislation shall be observed.

Article 8
Human Resources

Enterprises should ensure that:

a) human resources practices, including recruitment, promotion, training, performance evaluation, remuneration, recognition and business ethics in general, reflect these Rules;

b) no employee will suffer retaliation or discriminatory or disciplinary action for reporting in good faith violations or soundly suspected violations of the Enterprise's anti-corruption policy or for refusing to engage in corruption, even if such refusal may result in the Enterprise losing business;

c) key personnel in areas subject to high corruption risk should be trained and evaluated regularly; the rotation of such personnel should be considered.

Article 9
Financial and Accounting

Enterprises should ensure that:

a) all financial transactions are adequately identified and properly and fairly recorded in appropriate books and accounting records available for inspection by their Board of Directors or other body with ultimate responsibility for the Enterprise, as well as by auditors;

b) there are no "off the books" or secret accounts and no documents may be issued which do not fairly and accurately record the transactions to which they relate;

c) there is no recording of non-existent expenditures or of liabilities with incorrect identification of their objects or of unusual transactions which do not have a genuine, legitimate purpose;

d) cash payments or payments in kind are monitored in order to avoid that they are used as substitutes for bribes; only small cash payments made from petty cash or in countries or locations where there is no working banking system should be permitted;

e) no bookkeeping or other relevant documents are intentionally destroyed earlier than required by law;

f) independent systems of auditing are in place, whether through internal or external auditors, designed to bring to light any transactions which contravene these Rules or applicable accounting rules and which provide for appropriate corrective action if the case arises;

g) all provisions of national tax laws and regulations are complied with, including those prohibiting the deduction of any form of bribe payment from taxable income.

PART III - Elements of an Efficient Corporate Compliance Programme

Article 10
Elements of a Corporate Compliance Programme

Each Enterprise should implement an efficient Corporate Compliance Programme (i) reflecting these Rules, (ii) based on the results of a periodically conducted assessment of the risks faced in the Enterprise's business environment, (iii) adapted to the Enterprise's particular circumstances and (iv) with the aim of preventing and detecting Corruption and of promoting a culture of integrity in the Enterprise.

Each Enterprise should consider including all or part of the following good practices in its programme. In particular, it may choose, among the items listed hereunder, those measures which it considers most adequate to ensure a proper prevention against Corruption in its specific circumstances, no such measure being mandatory in nature:

a) expressing a strong, explicit and visible support and commitment to the Corporate Compliance Programme by the Board of Directors or other body with ultimate responsibility for the Enterprise and by the Enterprise's senior management ("tone at the top");

b) establishing a clearly articulated and visible policy reflecting these Rules and binding for all directors, officers, employees and Third Parties and applying to all controlled subsidiaries, foreign and domestic;

c) mandating the Board of Directors or other body with ultimate responsibility for the Enterprise, or the relevant committee thereof, to conduct periodical risk assessments and independent reviews of compliance with these Rules and recommending corrective measures or policies, as necessary. This can be done as part of a broader system of corporate compliance reviews and/or risk assessments;

d) making it the responsibility of individuals at all levels of the Enterprise to comply with the Enterprise's policy and to participate in the Corporate Compliance Programme;

e) appointing one or more senior officers (full or part time) to oversee and coordinate the Corporate Compliance Programme with an adequate level of resources, authority and independence, reporting periodically to the Board of Directors or other body with ultimate responsibility for the Enterprise, or to the relevant committee thereof;

f) issuing guidelines, as appropriate, to further elicit the behavior required and to deter the behavior prohibited by the Enterprise's policies and programme;

g) exercising appropriate due diligence, based on a structured risk management approach, in the selection of its directors, officers and employees, as well as of its Business Partners who present a risk of corruption or of circumvention of these Rules;

h) designing financial and accounting procedures for the maintenance of fair and accurate books and accounting records, to ensure that they cannot be used for the purpose of engaging in or hiding of corrupt practices;

i) establishing and maintaining proper systems of control and reporting procedures, including independent auditing;

j) ensuring periodic internal and external communication regarding the Enterprise's anti-corruption policy;

k) providing to their directors, officers, employees and Business Partners, as appropriate, guidance and documented training in identifying corruption risks in the daily business dealings of the Enterprise as well as leadership training;

l) including the review of business ethics competencies in the appraisal and promotion of management and measuring the achievement of targets not only against financial indicators but also against the way the targets have been met and specifically against the compliance with the Enterprise's anti-corruption policy;

m) offering channels to raise, in full confidentiality, concerns, seek advice or report in good faith established or soundly suspected violations without fear of retaliation or of discriminatory or disciplinary action. Reporting may either be compulsory or voluntary; it can be done on an anonymous or on a disclosed basis. All bona fide reports should be investigated;

n) acting on reported or detected violations by taking appropriate corrective action and disciplinary measures and considering making appropriate public disclosure of the enforcement of the Enterprise's policy;

o) considering the improvement of its Corporate Compliance Programme by seeking external certification, verification or assurance; and

p) supporting collective action, such as proposing or supporting anti-corruption pacts regarding specific projects or anti-corruption long term initiatives with the public sector and/or peers in the respective business segments.

Annex II
ICC Anti-corruption Clause

Copyright © 2012

International Chamber of Commerce (ICC)

All rights reserved.

ICC holds all copyright and other intellectual property rights in this collective work. No part of this collective work may be reproduced, distributed, transmitted, translated or adapted in any form or by any means, except as permitted by law, without the written permission of ICC.

Permission can be requested from ICC through pub@iccwbo.org.

Foreword

by Jean-Guy Carrier, ICC Secretary General

The International Chamber of Commerce has prepared over the years a large number of model contracts and clauses. These documents reflect best international corporate practice in transactional work, facilitate business negotiations and improve the drafting of the numerous contractual documents companies are processing.

At the same time, ICC has been concerned about the devastating effects on business of corruptive practices. It has become clear that corruption constitutes an obstacle to the creation of the level playing field all corporations want to see materialize, and runs counter to international public order.

Therefore, ICC in 1977 issued the ICC Rules on Combating Corruption (the 'Rules'), thereby becoming the first international organization to issue rules condemning all forms of corruption and urging companies to put into place preventive measures to ban corruption from their transactions.

The voluntary ICC Rules were regularly revised to reflect best corporate practice and to mirror the provisions of key international anti-bribery instruments, such as the OECD Convention on Combating Bribery of Foreign Public Officials in International Business Transactions (1997) and the United Nations Convention against Corruption (2003).

To consolidate the progress made by the business world in its corporate practice, the ICC Rules were rewritten in 2011. The 2011 edition of the Rules contains three parts: Part I states the Rules proper, Part II deals with policies that enterprises should enact to support compliance with the Rules, and Part III lists the suggested elements of an effective corporate compliance programme. The 2011 Rules are designed to be applied by enterprises of any size, whether large, medium or small.

The International Chamber of Commerce considers that its mission does not stop at prescribing voluntary anti-corruption norms, but also includes urging companies to incorporate in their agreements, in full or by reference, anti-corruption provisions either in the form of the core ICC anti-corruption standards, listed in Part I of the 2011 Rules or by the adoption of a corporate compliance programme, as recommended by Article 10 of the 2011 Rules.

The present ICC Anti-corruption Clause will help business people and their advisors to make such essential reference, with the aim of creating trust and preventing their contractual relationships from being affected by corruptive practice.

Introductory Note on the Application and the General Purpose and Structure of the Clause

This ICC Anti-corruption Clause (the 'Clause'), is intended to apply to any contract that incorporates it either by reference or in full. While parties to a contract are encouraged to incorporate the Clause into their contract by its full name, it is anticipated that any reference in the contract to the 'Clause' or related variations shall, in the absence of evidence to the contrary, be deemed to be a reference to the ICC Anti-corruption Clause.

The general aim of the Clause is to provide parties with a contractual provision that will reassure them about the integrity of their counterparts during the pre-contractual period as well as during the term of the contract and even thereafter.

Three options are possible: either a short text with the technique of incorporation by reference of Part I of the ICC Rules on Combating Corruption 2011 (Option I) or the incorporation of the full text of the same Part I of the ICC Rules on Combating Corruption 2011 in their contract (Option II), or a reference to a corporate compliance programme, as described in Article 10 of the ICC Rules on Combating Corruption (Option III).

Where Options I and II have been chosen, if a party fails materially or on several repeated occasions to comply with the anti-corruption provisions incorporated in the contract, the non-complying party will be given the opportunity to remedy the non-compliance. Such party will also have the opportunity to invoke as a defence that it has put into place adequate anti-corruption preventive measures. In the absence of the non-complying party taking remedial action, or if remedial action is not possible and no defence is effectively invoked, the other party may suspend or terminate the contract, at its discretion.

Any entity, whether an arbitral tribunal or other dispute resolution body, rendering a decision in accordance with the dispute resolution provisions of the contract, shall have the authority to determine the contractual consequences of any alleged non-compliance with the Clause.

ICC Anti-Corruption Clause

A. OPTION I: INCORPORATION BY REFERENCE OF PART I OF| THE ICC RULES ON COMBATING CORRUPTION 2011

Paragraph 1

Each Party hereby undertakes that, at the date of the entering into force of the Contract, itself, its directors, officers or employees have not offered, promised, given, authorized, solicited or accepted any undue pecuniary or other advantage of any kind (or implied that they will or might do any such thing at any time in the future) in any way connected with the Contract and that it has taken reasonable measures to prevent subcontractors, agents or any other third parties, subject to its control or determining influence, from doing so.

Paragraph 2

The Parties agree that, at all times in connection with and throughout the course of the Contract and thereafter, they will comply with and that they will take reasonable measures to ensure that their subcontractors, agents or other third parties, subject to their control or determining influence, will comply with Part I of the ICC Rules on Combating Corruption 2011, which is hereby incorporated by reference into the Contract, as if written out in the Contract in full.

Paragraph 3

If a Party, as a result of the exercise of a contractually-provided audit right, if any, of the other Party's accounting books and financial records, or otherwise, brings evidence that the latter Party has been engaging in material or several repeated breaches of the provisions of Part I of the ICC Rules on Combating Corruption 2011, it will notify the latter Party accordingly and require such Party to take the necessary remedial action in a reasonable time and to inform it about such action. If the latter Party fails to take the necessary remedial action, or if such remedial action is not possible, it may invoke a defence by proving that by the time the evidence of breach(es) had arisen, it had put into place adequate anti-corruption preventive measures, as described in Article 10 of the ICC Rules on Combating Corruption 2011, adapted to its particular circumstances and capable of detecting corruption and of promoting a culture of integrity in its organization. If no remedial action is taken or, as the case may be, the defence is not effectively invoked, the first Party may, at its discretion, either suspend the Contract or terminate it, it being understood that all amounts contractually due at the time of suspension or termination of the Contract will remain payable, as far as permitted by applicable law.

Paragraph 4

Any entity, whether an arbitral tribunal or other dispute resolution body, rendering a decision in accordance with the dispute resolution provisions of the Contract, shall have the authority to determine the contractual consequences of any alleged non-compliance with this ICC Anti-corruption Clause.

B. OPTION II: INCORPORATION IN FULL OF PART I OF THE ICC RULES ON COMBATING CORRUPTION 2011

Paragraph 1

Each Party hereby undertakes that, at the date of the entering into force of the Contract, itself, its directors, officers or employees have not offered, promised, given, authorized, solicited or accepted any undue pecuniary or other advantage of any kind (or implied that they will or might do any such thing at any time in the future) in any way connected with the Contract and that it has taken reasonable measures to prevent subcontractors, agents or any other third parties, subject to its control or determining influence, from doing so.

Paragraph 2

The Parties agree that, at all times in connection with and throughout the course of the Contract and thereafter, they will comply with and that they will take reasonable measures to ensure that their subcontractors, agents or other third parties, subject to their control or determining influence, will comply with the following provisions:

Paragraph 2.1

Parties will prohibit the following practices at all times and in any form, in relation with a public official at the international, national or local level, a political party, party official or candidate to political office, and a director, officer or employee of a Party, whether these practices are engaged in directly or indirectly, including through third parties:

a) **Bribery** is the offering, promising, giving, authorizing or accepting of any undue pecuniary or other advantage to, by or for any of the persons listed above or for anyone else in order to obtain or retain a business or other improper advantage, e.g. in connection with public or private procurement contract awards, regulatory permits, taxation, customs, judicial and legislative proceedings.

Bribery often includes:

(i) kicking back a portion of a contract payment to government or party officials or to employees of the other contracting Party, their close relatives, friends or business partners or

(ii) using intermediaries such as agents, subcontractors, consultants or other third parties, to channel payments to government or party officials, or to employees of the other contracting Party, their relatives, friends or business partners.

b) **Extortion or Solicitation** is the demanding of a bribe, whether or not coupled with a threat if the demand is refused. Each Party will oppose any attempt of Extortion or Solicitation and is encouraged to report such attempts through available formal or informal reporting mechanisms, unless such reporting is deemed to be counter-productive under the circumstances.

c) **Trading in Influence** is the offering or Solicitation of an undue advantage in order to exert an improper, real, or supposed influence with a view of obtaining from a public official an undue advantage for the original instigator of the act or for any other person.

d) Laundering the proceeds of the Corrupt Practices mentioned above is the concealing or disguising the illicit origin, source, location, disposition, movement or ownership of property, knowing that such property is the proceeds of crime.

"Corruption" or "Corrupt Practice(s)", as used in this ICC Anti-corruption Clause, shall include Bribery, Extortion or Solicitation, Trading in Influence and Laundering the proceeds of these practices.

Paragraph 2.2

With respect to third parties, subject to the control or determining influence of a Party, including but not limited to agents, business development consultants, sales representatives, customs agents, general consultants, resellers, subcontractors, franchisees, lawyers, accountants or similar intermediaries, acting on the Party's behalf in connection with marketing or sales, the negotiation of contracts, the obtaining of licenses, permits or other authorizations, or any actions that benefit the Party or as subcontractors in the supply chain, Parties should instruct them neither to engage nor to tolerate that they engage in any act of corruption; not use them as a conduit for any corrupt practice; hire them only to the extent appropriate for the regular conduct of the Party's business; and not pay them more than an appropriate remuneration for their legitimate services.

Paragraph 3

If a Party, as a result of the exercise of a contractually-provided audit right, if any, of the other Party's accounting books and financial records, or otherwise, brings evidence that the latter Party has been engaging in material or several repeated breaches of Paragraphs 2.1 and 2.2 above, it will notify the latter Party accordingly and require such Party to take the necessary remedial action in a reasonable time and to inform it about such action. If the latter Party fails to take the necessary remedial action or if such remedial action is not possible, it may invoke a defence by proving that by the time the evidence of breach(es) had arisen, it had put into place adequate anti-corruption preventive measures, as described in Article 10 of the ICC Rules on Combating Corruption 2011, adapted to its particular circumstances and capable of detecting corruption and of promoting a culture of integrity in its organization. If no remedial action is taken or, as the case may be, the defence is not effectively invoked, the first Party may, at its discretion, either suspend or terminate the Contract, it being understood that all amounts contractually due at the time of suspension or termination of the Contract will remain payable, as far as permitted by applicable law.

Paragraph 4

Any entity, whether an arbitral tribunal or other dispute resolution body, rendering a decision in accordance with the dispute resolution provisions of the Contract, shall have the authority to determine the contractual consequences of any alleged non-compliance with this ICC Anti-corruption Clause.

C. OPTION III: REFERENCE TO A CORPORATE ANTI-CORRUPTION COMPLIANCE PROGRAMME, AS DESCRIBED IN ARTICLE 10 IN THE 2011 RULES

Paragraph 1

Each Party has put into place, at the date of the entering into force of the Contract, or undertakes to put into place soon thereafter, a corporate anti-corruption compliance programme, as described in Article 10 of the 2011 ICC Rules on Combating Corruption, adapted to its particular circumstances and capable of detecting Corruption and of promoting a culture of integrity in its organization.

Each Party will maintain and implement such programme at least throughout the lifetime of the Contract and will on a regular basis inform the other Party about the implementation of its programme through statements prepared by a qualified corporate representative, appointed by it and whose name will have been communicated to the other Party.

Paragraph 2

If a Party brings evidence that the other Party's qualified corporate representative statement contains material deficiencies, undermining the other Party's programme efficiency, it will notify the other Party accordingly and require such Party to take the necessary remedial action in a reasonable time and to inform it about such action. If the latter Party fails to take the necessary remedial action, or if such remedial action is not possible, the first Party may, at its discretion, either suspend the Contract or terminate it, it being understood that all amounts contractually due at the time of suspension or termination of the Contract will remain payable, as far as permitted by applicable law.

Paragraph 3

Any entity, whether an arbitral tribunal or other dispute resolution body, rendering a decision in accordance with the dispute resolution provisions of the Contract, shall have the authority to determine the contractual consequences of any alleged non-compliance with this ICC Anti-corruption Clause.

Commentary on the ICC Anti-corruption Clause

OPTIONS I AND II

Paragraph 1: Non-corruption undertaking covering the pre-contractual period

1. **The ICC Anti-corruption Clause aims to create trust between Parties**

   Integrity is a key factor in bringing about a business environment that gives best value for money and rewards skill and competitiveness. Best results are achieved in business transactions when predictability and trust prevail between Parties. Combating bribery and other corrupt practices is also vital for protecting shareholders, taxpayers and other entities indirectly affected by business transactions.

   While there is a need to ensure that corrupt practices do not bear fruit, there is also a need to maintain trust in the binding nature of the contractual undertakings (pacta sunt servanda), as it is a core component of successful business life. There must, therefore, be a balance between the efforts to fight corruption and the treatment of corruption as a breach of a Contract justifying its termination.

   Integrity must prevail throughout the life-cycle of a business transaction, from its negotiation to its performance and resulting remuneration. Very often a contractual transaction involves a multitude of Parties with a substantial number of personnel. Corrupt practices may not exist throughout an entire organization, and they may not be instigated by, or otherwise be attributable to, the management holding the principal responsibility for the negotiation or performance of the Contract.

   When preparing their Contract, Parties want to make sure that during the negotiations leading to the Contract and during the drafting of the Contract (the pre-contractual period), no bribe, gift or other undue advantage has been granted or promised (or that no indication in this sense has been given for the future) in relation to the Contract by a Party to a public official at the international, national or local level, a political party, party official or candidate to political office or to a director, officer or employee of the other Party, either directly or indirectly through one of the Party's subcontractors, agents or other third party, subject to its control or determining influence.

   Each Party also wants to ascertain that the other Party has put in place reasonable preventive measures to avoid that one of the other Party's subcontractors, agents, or other third parties engages in corrupt practices.

   In sum, the Clause is written with the aim of achieving a balance between the interest of Parties to avoid corruption and their need to ensure the attainment of the objectives of the Contract. The Clause builds on the doctrine of good faith, the presumption of innocence, good cooperation between Parties and the idea that many illicit practices can be remedied without bringing the contractual relationship to an end.

2. **Which Corrupt Practices are covered by Paragraph 1?**

The wording of Paragraph 1 mirrors that used in the OECD Convention on Combating Bribery of Foreign Public Officials in International Business Transactions (1997) and the United Nations Convention against Corruption (2003).

The corrupt practices covered by Paragraph 1 include: (i) 'active' as well as 'passive' corruption (also referred to at times as 'Extortion' or 'Solicitation'); (ii) Bribery as well as trading in influence; (iii) Corruption of public officials, as well as private-to-private corruption; (iv) Corruption in the national and local as well as in the international sphere; (v) Corruption with or without the use of intermediaries; (vi) Bribery with money or through any other form of undue advantage; and (vii) Bribery with or without laundered money.

3. **Is Paragraph 1 referring to even the smallest undue advantages?**

ICC recommends enterprises not to make 'facilitation payments' (i.e. unofficial, improper, small payments made to a low-level official to secure or expedite the performance of a routine or necessary action to which the payer is legally entitled), unless their employees are confronted with exigent circumstances, such as duress or when the health, security or safety of their employees are at risk.

On the issue of gifts and hospitality offered to e.g., actual or potential commercial partners, ICC recommends that enterprises establish procedures to ensure that they (i) comply with the law; (ii) are reasonable and bona fide; (iii) do not affect (or appear to affect) the recipient's independence of judgment towards the giver; (iv) are not contrary to the known provisions of the recipient's code of conduct and (v) are offered or received neither too frequently nor at an inappropriate time.

4. **Which 'reasonable preventive measures' have to be taken by the Parties with respect to their intermediaries?**

A Party is not required to prevent by all means any of its subcontractors, agents or other third parties, subject to its control or determining influence, to commit any form of corrupt practice.

Each Party shall, however, based on a periodical assessment of the risks it faces, put into place an effective corporate compliance programme, adapted to its particular circumstances; exercise, on the basis of a structured risk management approach, appropriate due diligence in the selection of subcontractors, agents or other third parties, subject to its control or determining influence; and train its directors, officers and employees accordingly.

5. **To which circumstances is the undertaking of Paragraph 1 applicable?**

Having regard to the fast evolution of the law and practice in the field of business integrity, the undertaking of Paragraph 1 should be concerned with only the very Contract itself and not other contracts concluded between the same Parties, or any other contracts.

Paragraph 2: Non-corruption undertaking covering the period after execution of the Contract (contractual and post-contractual periods)

1. **The term of the Parties' non-corruption undertaking**

Parties agree, during the period following the entering into force of the Contract and after the term of the Contract, not to commit corrupt practices in connection with the Contract.

They will have to ensure that no phase of the performance of the Contract, such as obtaining the relevant licenses or official authorizations, the passing of operational tests, or inspections of goods or sites will be obtained through illicit means. They also undertake to take reasonable measures to prevent their subcontractors, agents and other third parties to do the same during such period. The Parties' non-corruption undertaking survives the term of the Contract.

2. **Paragraph 2 contains a provision for incorporation either by reference or in full**

In order to memorialize their mutual non-corruption undertaking, Parties decide to incorporate the text of Part I of the ICC Rules on Combating Corruption 2011 in their Contract. They can choose either to make this incorporation by reference or in full. In the former case, they will opt for the text under Option I, in the latter for the text under Option II.

For the sake of convenience, the text of Part I of the ICC Rules on Combating Corruption 2011 is attached hereto as Annex I.

3. **The nature of the Parties' undertaking**

The Parties' undertaking is absolute, while their undertaking in relation to their subcontractors, agents or other third parties, subject to their control or determining influence, is limited to the taking of 'reasonable measures' in order to prevent the latter from engaging in corrupt practices.

This will include as a minimum: instructing subcontractors, agents and other third parties neither to engage nor to tolerate that they engage in any corrupt practice; not using them as a conduit for any corrupt practice; hiring them only to the extent appropriate for the regular conduct of the Party's business and not paying them more than an appropriate remuneration for their legitimate services.

Paragraph 3: Non-compliance, remedial action and sanctions

1. **Non-compliance with Part I of the ICC Rules**

If a Party becomes aware that the other Party has committed material or several repeated breaches of the provisions of Part I of the ICC Rules on Combating Corruption 2011, it will notify the other Party accordingly.

A Party invoking corruption must bring evidence that corruption is at stake. Evidence is often difficult to find, as is the disclosure of it to the other Party without losing it or causing damage for the further use of it. Therefore the requirement to bring evidence does not necessarily mean that corroborative evidence should be produced or that all evidence be disclosed to the other Party in every case. Evidence should, however, be sufficient to prove that suspicions of corruption are not invoked in a vexatious or otherwise unjustified manner.

The Clause includes no formal requirements as to how the Parties should make a notification of suspected breach under Part I of the Rules, but typically the mechanism applicable generally to contractual communications between the Parties, will apply to this notification as well. Thus, a Contract containing a requirement that any notification will be made in writing will cover notices on suspected corruption as well.

2. Possible remedial action

In order to ensure to the highest degree possible the continuity of a Contract, the allegedly non-complying Party will be allowed to remedy the situation to the extent possible. Necessary remedial action might include providing cooperation in evidentiary action in conducting an examination or calling for an external audit of the incident, issuing warnings, reorganizing work, terminating sub-contracts or contracts of employment with persons or employees involved in corruption, or correcting the detrimental economic effect on the other Party of any proven non-compliance by, for example, adjusting the amount of the price of the Contract. The nature and quantity of the remedial measures required of the Party subject to allegation will depend on the circumstances of the case in question, e.g., on the gravity of the infringement and on the conclusiveness of the evidence provided. In some situations, a remedy may consist of simply providing counter-evidence regarding non-existence of any breach. The allegedly non-complying Party will as soon as possible inform the other Party about the measures it has taken to remedy the situation.

It is recognized, however, that not every infringement of the anti-corruption provisions can be remedied, but it is expected from the allegedly non-complying Party that it will do its utmost to repair the situation to the best of its abilities.

3. Invoking the defence of adequate anti-corruption preventive measures

Where a remedy is not or cannot be taken, the Party allegedly in breach may invoke a defence by proving that it had, by the time the evidence of breach had arisen, put into place adequate anti-corruption preventive measures, as described in Article 10 of the ICC Rules on Combating Corruption 2011, adapted to its particular circumstances and capable of detecting corruption and of promoting a culture of integrity in its organization. Such adequate anti-corruption prevention measures should (i) reflect the ICC Rules on Combating Corruption 2011, (ii) be based on the results of a periodically conducted assessment of the risks faced in the Party's business environment, and (iii) be adapted to the Party's particular circumstances.

For the sake of convenience, the text of Article 10 of the ICC Rules on Combating Corruption 2011 is attached hereto as Annex II.

4. **Evidence of non-compliance**

Producing evidence of an infringement of the anti-corruption provisions, laid down in Part I of the ICC Rules on Combating Corruption 2011, will not be an easy task, as corruption very rarely occurs in the open.

One of the few means to produce such evidence will be to provide the conclusions of an audit of the accounting books and financial records of the allegedly non-complying Party. Witness statements (as a result of a whistleblowing mechanism or otherwise) may sometimes be used. Applicable criminal law should be taken into account when considering the involvement of law enforcement bodies.

5. **Audit right**

The reference in the Clause to a contractually-provided audit right does not, however, imply that an audit right can be easily obtained in all circumstances nor that such audit right will be suitable for all situations. Although some Contracts give one or more Parties the right to conduct an audit on the other Party (-ies), the reference in this Clause to an audit right does not mean that ICC advocates giving Parties an extensive audit right as a recommended business practice.

Parties will have to determine if their commercial relationship allows for an audit right, and if the circumstances surrounding the negotiation, execution and future implementation of the Contract warrant the need for such audit right.

6. **Sanctions**

If the Party allegedly infringing the provisions of Part I of the ICC Rules on Combating Corruption 2011, does not remedy the situation within a reasonable period of time or if no such remedy is possible, and no defence of adequate anti-corruption preventive measures is effectively invoked, the other Party will have the right, at its discretion, to suspend the Contract or terminate it, it being understood that the amounts contractually due at the time of suspension or termination will remain payable, as far as permitted by applicable law.

When the other Party exercises its right of suspension or termination, it bears the full burden of proof that a breach or breaches of the provisions of Part I of the ICC Rules on Combating Corruption 2011 has taken place.

Applicable law may determine whether the Party may be held accountable for a breach or breaches of the provisions of Part I of the ICC Rules on Combating Corruption 2011.

Bringing a large or long-term Contract to an end due to an infringement might be disproportionate. This should also be borne in mind when Paragraph 3 of the Clause is applied.

Paragraph 4: Dispute resolution

Parties refer all disputes related to the contractual consequences of any alleged non-compliance with the Clause to the entity provided for in the dispute resolution provisions of the Contract, such as an arbitral tribunal. However, the non-compliance may be the subject of parallel criminal proceedings which may result in criminal sanctions or civil law consequences other than contractual, in particular liability in tort.

OPTION III

Paragraph 1: Corporate compliance programmes

1. **Corporate compliance programmes, as described in Article 10 of the ICC Rules**

Many companies have put into place a corporate compliance programme with the aim of preventing their business activity from being affected by corruptive practices. Such programmes can have different forms and content and will need to be adapted to each company's particular circumstances in order to be effective. They also should make it possible to detect Corruption and should aim at promoting a culture of integrity in the organization. Article 10 of the ICC Rules on Combating Corruption 2011 provides an extensive, non-comprehensive list of measures, which may be included in such programme. Each company will select from this list the measures it deems necessary or adequate for organizing its own anti-corruption prevention system.

2. **Putting into place a corporate compliance programme**

When the Parties enter a Contract, it helps reinforce trust between them to know that their counterpart has put into place - or is going to put into place soon - a corporate compliance programme. Parties will commit to maintain their compliance programme and to implement its provisions at least during the term of the Contract, thus maintaining during that period of time an atmosphere of trust between the Parties.

3. **Designation of a qualified corporate representative**

In order to evidence the effectiveness of the programme and the continuity of its implementation, each Party will designate among its personnel a qualified corporate representative, whose name will be notified to the other Party. These qualified corporate representatives will issue, at regular intervals, statements on the continued existence and implementation of its company's programme.

Paragraph 2: Deficiencies in a qualified corporate representative's statement, remedial action and sanctions

1. **Deficiencies in a qualified corporate representative's statement**

If a Party becomes aware that the other Party's qualified corporate representative's statement contains material deficiencies, undermining the efficiency of that Party's programme, it will notify the latter Party accordingly. A statement will be considered deficient if it contains materially untrue, false or incomplete declarations.

A Party invoking a deficiency in a qualified corporate representative's statement must bring evidence that either the statements are missing or that the statement contains materially untrue, false or incomplete declarations.

Evidence is often difficult to find, as is the disclosure of it to the other Party without losing it or causing damage for the further use of it. Therefore the requirement to bring evidence does not necessarily mean that corroborative evidence should be produced or that all evidence be disclosed to the other Party in every case. Evidence should, however, be sufficient to prove that suspicions of deficiencies in a qualified corporate representative's statement are not invoked in a vexatious or otherwise unjustified manner.

The Clause includes no formal requirements as to how the Parties should make a notification of a suspected deficiency in a qualified corporate representative's statement, but typically the mechanism applicable generally to contractual communications between the Parties, will apply to this notification as well. Thus, a Contract containing a requirement that any notification will be made in writing will cover notices on suspected deficiency as well.

2. Remedial action

In order to ensure to the highest degree possible the continuity of a Contract, the Party having allegedly issued a deficient statement, will be allowed to remedy the situation to the extent possible. Necessary remedial action might include providing a new, accurate, complete and sincere statement, giving a full and fair picture of the implementation by the Party concerned of the provisions of its corporate compliance programme as well as any corrective action such Party will take to improve such implementation. The nature and quantity of the remedial measures required of the Party subject to allegation will depend on the circumstances of the case in question, e.g., on the gravity of the deficiency and on the conclusiveness of the evidence provided. In some situations, a remedy may consist of simply providing counter-evidence regarding non-existence of any deficiency. The allegedly non-complying Party will as soon as possible inform the other Party about the measures it has taken to remedy the situation.

It is recognized, however, that not every deficiency can be remedied, but it is expected from the allegedly non-complying Party that it will do its utmost to repair the situation to the best of its abilities.

3. Other Commentary

The Commentary provided hereinabove under items 4, 5 and 6 on Paragraph 3 of Options I and II is applicable mutatis mutandis to Paragraph 2 of Option III.

Paragraph 3: Dispute resolution

Parties refer all disputes related to any alleged non-compliance with the Clause to the entity provided for in the dispute resolution provisions of the Contract, such as an arbitral tribunal. However, the non-compliance may be the subject of parallel criminal proceedings which may result in criminal sanctions or civil law consequences other than contractual, in particular liability in tort.

Annex III
Key International Legal Instruments

Global instruments

United Nations Convention against Corruption (UNCAC)
http://www.unodc.org/documents/treaties/UNCAC/Publications/Convention/08-50026_E.pdf

United Nations Convention against Transnational Organized Crime (UNTOC)
http://www.unodc.org/documents/treaties/UNTOC/Publications/TOC%20Convention/TOCebook-e.pdf

OECD Convention on the Bribery of Foreign Public Officials in International Business Transactions (OECD Convention)
http://www.oecd.org/dataoecd/4/18/38028044.pdf

OECD Recommendation for Further Combating Bribery of Foreign Public Officials in International Business Transactions, including Annex II Good Practice Guidance on Internal Controls, Ethics and Compliance
http://www.oecd.org/dataoecd/11/40/44176910.pdf

Africa

African Union Convention on Preventing and Combating Corruption (AU Convention)
http://www.africaunion.org/official_documents/Treaties_%20Conventions_%20Protocols/Convention%20on%20Combating%20Corruption.pdf

Southern African Development Community Protocol against Corruption (SADC Protocol)
http://www.sadc.int/index/browse/page/122

Economic Community of West African States Protocol on the Fight against Corruption (ECOWAS Protocol)
http://www.afrimap.org/english/images/treaty/ECOWAS_Protocol_on_Corruption.pdf

Americas

Inter-American Convention against Corruption (OAS Convention)
http://www.oas.org/juridico/english/treaties/b-58.html

Asia and Pacific Region

ADB-OECD Action Plan for Asia-Pacific (Action Plan)
http://www.oecd.org/dataoecd/38/24/35021642.pdf

Europe

Council of Europe Criminal Law Convention
http://conventions.coe.int/treaty/en/Treaties/Html/173.htm

Council of Europe Civil Law Convention
http://conventions.coe.int/treaty/en/treaties/html/174.htm

Resolution of the Committee of Ministers of the Council of Europe: Agreement Establishing the Group of States against Corruption
http://conventions.coe.int/Treaty/EN/PartialAgr/Html/Greco9905.htm

Resolution of the Committee of Ministers of the Council of Europe: Twenty Guiding Principles for the Fight against Corruption
https://wcd.coe.int/wcd/ViewDoc.jsp?id=593789&

European Union Convention on the Protection of the Communities' Financial Interests and the Fight against Corruption and two related Protocols
http://europa.eu/legislation_summaries/fight_against_fraud/protecting_european_communitys_financial_interests/l33019_en.htm

European Union Convention on the Fight against Corruption involving officials of the European Communities or officials of Member States
http://europa.eu/legislation_summaries/fight_against_fraud/fight_against_corruption/l33027_en.htm

www.iccbooks.com
ICC Tools for International Business

Drafting and Negotiating International Commercial Contracts
by Prof. Fabio Bortolotti
ICC Pub. No. 743E, €125

Written by a world-renowned expert on contract law, this Guide clarifies the issues surrounding cross-border contracts and provides solutions to the problems they raise. Completely updated to take latest developments into account, this helpful tool includes advice on Incoterms® 2010, Unidroit 2010, the 2012 ICC Rules on Arbitration, Rome I, and more. It is an invaluable resource for experts and non-lawyers alike.

Fighting Corruption
by Fritz Heimann and François Vincke
e-book only, ICC Pub. No. @678E, €37,50

Fighting Corruption lays out the problems and offers practical solutions on how to attack commercial dishonesty at its source. Including subjects as diverse as money laundering, the role of agents, extortion, accounting and whistleblowing, this invaluable book is a vital reference for managers, compliance officers, lawyers and anyone concerned with stamping out corruption.

International Commercial Transactions
by Prof. Jan Ramberg
ICC Pub. No. 711E, €129

The author, a renowned expert in international trade law, explains the interrelations between common trade practice, national laws and international rules. Essential reading for anyone engaged in or preparing cross-border transactions, this volume will greatly help you to achieve your commercial objectives

International Certificate of Origin Guidelines
ICC Pub. No. 670E, €35

A Certificate of Origin is a document which identifies the origin of goods being exported. It is required by customs as one of the key bases for applying tariff rates. Presented by the ICC World Chambers Federation, the first international procedures and guidelines manual for chambers and associations in the issuance of non-preferential certificates of origin incorporates best practice from multiple national chamber organizations.

ICC Model Turnkey Contract for Major Projects
ICC Pub. No. 659E, €75

Major construction projects are an important element in international development, and it is vital that the arrangements put in place be durable, clear and equitable. This publication is a unique, balanced model contract that accommodates the desire of all parties for price and scope certainty, the need for swift and effective dispute resolution, and the need for complete and informed allocation of risks.